PRAISE FOR *STORIES OF ELDERS*

"It certainly brings the pages of the history book to life... We would do well to listen to these wise voices and try to learn from them."
— **Cynthia Canty, host of NPR | Michigan Radio's Stateside**

"Nearly a century ago, America's Greatest Generation witnessed a similar evolution of technology and social progress that changed how they lived, worked and played. Just like today, those inventions were dramatically shifting how people interacted with each other and the world."
— **Shandra Martinez, BuzzFeed Community Contributor**

"Stories are so important to remembering who we are and where we come from. The way Veronica has managed to capture and preserve these important stories about a generation that watched the world change before their eyes is stunning. We need their stories to remember where we came from and to hopefully guide us where we are going."
— **Julia Nusbaum, HerStry**

"When I'm watching TV, YouTube, or reading Facebook, I often wonder how we've arrived in a culture that is so different than the one I grew up with. In this documentary-style book, Kirin answers my question by taking us on a journey that dives into personal stories around how technology has changed the lives of everyday people. Love it!"
— **Harrison Painter, AmpifyIndy**

"In an ever-faster-moving world of technology, change is par for the course. As we travel forward, we run the risk of losing wisdom which previous generations have taken for granted. In this book, author Veronica Kirin does a marvelous job of chronicling this wisdom through stories of our elders."
— **JC Preston, Angles of Lattitude Podcast**

"*Stories of Elders* is an extraordinary book filled with emotionally powerful stories from those who have experienced things far beyond the experience of Millennials. Veronica has expertly captured the essence of her subjects, with each story being awe-inspiring in their own right!"
— Jason Schemmel, GSD Podcast

"In *Stories of Elders*, Veronica Kirin makes a compelling case for why we must use technology with intent. We must become aware of our vulnerabilities, set boundaries, and realize that technology is a tool and it's up to us to take responsibility and determine its impact."
— Laura Tucker, Free Your Inner Guru

"Through the combination of touching anecdotes and well-researched evidence, Veronica illustrates the juxtaposition of the benefits and the consequences of modern-day technologies for The Greatest Generation."
— Bri Luginbill, Compassionately You Podcast

STORIES OF ELDERS

*What the Greatest Generation Knows
About Technology that You Don't*

by VERONICA KIRIN

Stories of Elders: What the Greatest Generation
Knows about Technology that You Don't

Paperback
ISBN-10: 1-945884-60-6
ISBN-13: 978-1-945884-60-3

Hardcover
ISBN-10: 1-945884-61-4
ISBN-13: 978-1-945884-61-0

Library of Congress Control Number: 2018910085

Identity Publications
412 N. Main St Ste 100
Buffalo, WY 82834
www.identitypublications.com

Ordering Information:

Quantity sales. Special discounts are available on quantity purchases by
corporations, schools, associations, and others. For details, contact the
publisher at the address above.

To inquire about having your book produced, published, or promoted, please
email: contact@identitypublications.com

For more information about Stories of Elders, please visit
www.storiesofelders.com

Author photo credit: Bri Luginbill

For the Greatest Generation, who fought, pioneered,
and innovated for the generations to come.

CONTENTS

12,000 MILES TO INTERVIEW 100 ELDERS

THE INTERVIEW

"When they referred to them as . . . the Greatest Generation, one of the reasons is . . . most of them were farm kids, so they had to learn to repair things. So, if they grew up with the first semi-primitive tractor in their neighborhood and it stopped for some reason, they had to find out why and fix it . . . So, when they were faced with a situation, it wasn't like 'what does the manual say and what are we permitted to do' . . . you just did it. That's the kind of thing that made them great."
— Ruth Harper

We have, at this time, the unbelievable opportunity to speak with people who grew up in a 'non-technical' era. People who may have grown up with dirt floors, no running water or indoor plumbing, no heating unit, a wood burning stove for cooking, and a tub of water for a bath. These are living conditions we consider obsolete in today's America, and yet, they still exist in our collective culture, in the minds of our elders. They lived and worked without technology and have seen our society change over a century of technological development.

Millennials are the last generation that will be able to bridge this gap and reach back into living history. I felt this opportunity too great to be ignored and decided to put my own life on hold in order to record our history and demonstrate not only how technology has grown but how it has affected our society at its core. Today we have a constant barrage of scientific studies and social commentary about technology disrupting communication, relationships, jobs, and more, but the voice of those old enough to have lived both with and without tech has little been heard.

I determined to use my degree in cultural anthropology to develop a research project that would record the perspective of the Greatest Generation, Americans born before 1945. I used the following set of 15 questions in order to create a cohesive narrative. I also used Kickstarter, an online crowdfunding platform on which friends and strangers donate to projects they are interested in, to raise funds to travel 11,487 miles across America to collect stories from a variety of backgrounds.

Technology is defined in this book as any machinery or equipment developed by the application of scientific knowledge during and after World War II, including the automobile, television, radio, space travel, computers, etc.

This book is intended to be a cultural comparison and contrast between life before 'tech,' and life today. Has technology affected our lives at a critical level? Is a change in the way we use technology necessary? In my opinion, only those who have lived before it can tell.

THE INTERVIEW QUESTIONS

1. What is your full name?
2. What is your current address (so I can send you a thank you letter)?
3. When were you born?
4. Where were you born?
5. Where have you lived?
6. What was your childhood like?
7. What was your favorite pastime?
8. What has changed since then?
9. What occupations have you held?
10. How has technology affected you?
11. How do you think technology is affecting us?
12. How do you think it's affecting our youth?
13. What have we lost to technology?
14. What have we gained? -or- What are you excited about?
15. Is there anything else do you think people should know / would you like to say?

INTRODUCTION

*"The instruments and techniques of a particular technology
are the product of a prolonged process of cultural accumulation
in the past . . . Once a technology has come to include these
items . . . they become part and parcel of everyday existence,
and hence culturally necessary."*

— Peasants[1]

It was unseasonably warm the November day I packed up the
car. I was nervous about driving across America alone, but I was
committed to completing what I had started. There were too
many questions about technology unanswered, too much history being lost, and I had the investments of my many supporters
to uphold.

Even today, as I finish this writing, I find it hard to explain
how this work got started. I've been a writer my entire life. I
wrote my first short story at age eight, my first poem at age
ten, my first novel at age 12. Research came easy to me while
at university studying for a degree in anthropology. Some of my
fondest memories take place while sitting hidden in the library
stacks, bookmarking sections of books for ethnographic research
or reading something random I'd selected from the shelves. It
has only been ten years since I graduated, but I don't think today's students experience that kind of studying, anymore.

I chose to study anthropology because I have a knack for
people. I'm good at reading them and putting them at ease. I
also prefer not to subscribe to an empirical truth. Anthropology,

---

[1] Eric R. Wolf, *Peasants*, (Prentice-Hall, Inc., 1966) p. 6.

by default, approaches everything in this way to avoid bias in research. It was love at first class, and I enjoyed learning about others while dismantling my own assumptions.

Fast forward five years. I've founded a tech company that manages websites and online marketing for small businesses called GreenCup Website Services. My background in anthropology aids me in reading target markets and predicting trends for our clients. It was at this time that I started noticing specific trends in my own life as a result of my work with technology. Less in-person interactions, less letter writing, less reading. I was constantly online, and as many of us are noticing, the Internet has a funny way of replacing real interactions.

I had also noticed study after study, article after article, crowding my news feed and reporting tech's effects on family, community, and brain development. By the time this project was fully conceived, such articles were being published almost daily. We as a society were starting to wonder what all this computer technology was doing to us.

I believe that one cannot critique something unless they have lived without it for a time. An easy example is someone who grew up drinking Coca-Cola, quit drinking soda altogether, and then tried a Coke after years of abstention. To their surprise, a Coke is far more sugary than they recalled. It was their abstention that gave them a contrasting experience.

My solution to our discomfort about technology's effect on our relationships, development, and habits takes the same stance. The only people living today that lived a 'lifetime' without computer technology are the Greatest Generation. These are people born before 1945, the parents of the Baby Boomers. They are called the Greatest Generation because of their incredible work ethic which was developed by surviving two world wars and the extreme struggle of the Great Depression.

Our elders have lived through a radical evolution. Some of those who I interviewed even grew up without indoor plumbing or electricity, two things we call basic necessities today. It is through their eyes that I sought to understand just how technology has changed America.

The following chapters are organized by subject. These are the topics that came up the most for those I spoke with and reflect the questions addressed in news and research regarding technology's effect on us. I start with Communication, because it is something that everyone interviewed says has changed, and it is the most tangible for everyone living with technology today.

I then take a deep dive into some harder topics — War, Politics, and Rights. All of these have changed, but there were very specific stories told by participants that illustrated just how radically.

Transportation, Energy and Amenities, Work, and Medicine were some of the most fun topics to hear about in the interviews — how amazing airplanes still are to so many, how scary electricity really was when it debuted, and how all of this affected our work and ability to stay healthy.

All of these have affected our relationships. The ability to cook fast and eat fast, long work hours, working from home, and smartphones all have altered our relationships. And it's being felt strongly by the Greatest Generation.

Food, Money, Poverty, and Safety are some of our deeper concerns in society, and they all have altered how we build and maintain our Communities.

Generational Proximity, Family, Child Development, and finally Religion and Integrity address some of the deepest concerns we have, for there is no nobler concern than our worry for our children and how they get to know their history.

For the cohesion of the book, I chose to limit chapter content to the interviews that had the most authority on that given topic. You will take a deep dive with people like Etcyl Blair, who worked both on chemical weapons and bioengineered food for Dow, and Charlotte Lawson, who opened her heart and mind to reveal some very dark secrets in her family in hopes that younger generations may learn from them. This structure allows their contributions to be more in depth, and in that way, you can get to know the people who gave their stories to this work.

You will also notice that I use the old-fashioned double space after each sentence. This is because I often use my typewriter to start my manuscripts. Typists would use the double space because the font used on the typewriter spaced everything, even punctuation, equally. A period would have been directly in between the two sentences without the double space. I thought it would be fitting to continue to use this outdated technique for this book about technology's effects across our lives.

Should you wish to hear the words of these elders spoken in their own voices, you can find them in podcast format on the website: http://storiesofelders.com/podcast

COMMUNICATION

"In order to understand who we are, we must understand who we were."

— Unknown

Communication has concerned humankind for as long as our history remembers. As technology has developed, so have inventions of new and better methods of communication. Nearly 3,000 years ago, our first known method of writing appeared on cuneiform tablets (clay blocks the size of a hard drive).[2] This written language kept track of transactions between farmers, merchants, and customers.

When the telegraph was invented nearly three millennia later, cross-continent communication wasn't enough to satisfy our thirst to connect, and so we developed a method for sending these signals across the oceans. Though the first transatlantic telegraph wire quickly degraded in the Pacific Ocean, we kept trying to connect to Europe. In July of 1866, America successfully installed an improved wire to the United Kingdom that set a precedence for other countries to follow suit in the coming years. That was the first time it was possible for humans to communicate overseas without a ship.[3]

Written communication has had an equal effect on history. The Wild West would not be complete without stories of letters sent via the harrowing stagecoach battles of the Pony Express.

---

[2] Wikipedia, "Cuneiform Script," https://en.wikipedia.org/wiki/Cuneiform_script
[3] Wikipedia, "The Trans-atlantic Telegraph Wire," https://en.wikipedia.org/wiki/Transatlantic_telegraph_cable

Even more, Mark Twain's famous journey to Nevada during the gold rush in 1861 wouldn't have been the fodder that gave root to some of the most celebrated Americana novels without the Postal Service providing his transportation in those stagecoaches across America's last frontier.[4]

Homo sapiens is a social creature. We build family units, neighborhoods, and cities because we evolved with community equaling survival. Without community, individual humans would not be able to gather enough food, build shelters against the weather, or domesticate animals for work and transportation. Perhaps this is why we are so desperately concerned with the effect of 'new technology' on our ability to communicate with others.

Shortly before I started work on this book, there was a meme that circulated the Internet depicting gentlemen on a 1950s New York City subway commute reading newspapers. The caption stated that, whether a smartphone or a newspaper, we always had something to distract ourselves from speaking to others around us. In the words of Brother Robert Reddington (b. 1934) of the Bronx, "People are wrapped up in their iPhones. They're not talking much." It's hard to judge whether or not people really were just as distracted back then, or if we're collectively telling a story to fit our idea of how we use technology, today.

Even more so, New York City is a very different city than most American communities. One might argue that Manhattanites have always gone out of their way to avoid eye contact and any interaction with strangers. I'd like to start instead by taking a look at the stories from a different, and arguably slower-paced, community: New Orleans.

The Big Easy may be known for celebrating Mardi Gras and Carnival, but those who know it intimately know it to be a friendly and

---

[4] Andrew Hoffman, *Inventing Mark Twain*, (Phoenix Orion Books, 1997) p. 63.

tight-knit community. One where strangers helped each other through Hurricane Katrina regardless of the previously accepted divides created by race, creed, and neighborhood boundaries. It is a place I started calling a second home after spending a good deal of time there as a Hurricane Relief Aid Worker and experiencing the friendliness of everyone I met (not to mention the delicious food). Yet, in a city where strangers customarily greet each other when passing on the street, and car horns are used to say 'hello' instead of express annoyance, the effects of tech on human connections are being felt.

Dagmar Booth (b. 1945) is a native of New Orleans and is both mother and grandmother. She spends a good deal of time with her grandchildren and has noticed concerning changes in their education compared to hers and that of her daughters. We met to talk about it with her husband at his favorite restaurant, McDonald's. There, she confided her concern about something that has been a hot topic of late — the removal of cursive writing from school curriculums.

> It's sad to the point where the schools are not teaching cursive writing anymore. When my grandson came down last year, we went to the D-Day Museum. He couldn't read the letters the soldiers wrote to their mothers. I had to read the letters to him. He was 12 . . . What does that tell you about the future of our written past? 'Cause our kids in the future won't be able to read it unless it's printed.

A thousand miles and a year of interviews apart, my elder cousin Pauline Attisani (b. 1934) of Long Island, New York, echoed Dagmar's concern.

> Young people aren't taught to write in script. So, I guess you have to use an email or print. With all the texting, nobody's going to be able to spell anymore.

> And it may get to the point where . . . you're not go-
> ing to understand what they're trying to tell you.
> We've lost a lot of human contact with this technology
> and I don't think it's for the better . . . It's nice to be
> called . . . or to receive an invitation. It's so much
> nicer . . . you're in touch with humanity.

She expands on this to say that those who do not have a computer, or who did not grow up with technology and don't default to its use, are put at a disadvantage. They lose out on some
critical communication. "In order to join a women's golf group,
you have to email," she says, continuing the idea that if you
don't have a computer you have no way to receive invitations,
schedule updates, and more.

Urcell Schulterbrandt (b. 1938), a former teacher in Compton, California, agrees with this sentiment. "We've lost personal
communication. That one-to-one . . . Can we gain it back? Is this
Pandora? I don't know, but I hope not. Because once it's out you
can't put it back in."

I use Facebook to schedule most of my events. I default
to it because of the quantity of people that I'm trying to stay in
touch with. When one of my friends steps away from the social
media platform, I find it difficult to keep track of them and to
remember to invite them to events, something I am ashamed of.
Facebook has trained me to only remember the people I see in
my News Feed on a regular basis.

Like my friends who choose to stay off Facebook, Jim Hayes
Jr. (b. 1932) has intentionally kept technology out of his life and
echoes the disconnect Pauline and Urcell have observed in trying
to stay in contact with others.

> Well, I was always one of those people who felt like I
> was not going to let technology control my life. And
> so, I didn't keep up with a whole lot of the trends and
> stuff like that. One part of me says you don't have to

let technology control your life, but somewhere along the way you're going to have to control it.

So, how's that affecting my life? Well, it's affected it, but I'm still not going to let it control me. I miss out on a lot of stuff, 'cause people want to email me and text and all that kind of stuff. I'm not into text, and I figure if it's important enough, people are going to call me on the telephone and tell me.

So, people try to make me feel useless. That's not the right word, but that's what it amounts to. In fact, you can't communicate with them, with all the methods of communicating, but I don't let it bother me.

STAYING IN TOUCH

"I have my family in Japan. [Now] I can pick up the phone, and dial it, and talk to them."

— Yoko Mossner

Is it fair for me to express only the challenges technology adds to communication? I admit I find myself frustrated at times. I forget to personally connect with friends because digital messages seem like enough — until I find myself feeling very lonely. I miss the intimacy of phone calls and letter writing, yet I get antsy for the next thing when I do make time to slow down.

This is a one-sided outlook on technology, isn't it? How many of you sit and read this and think, 'Without tech like social media and smartphones I couldn't maintain the long-distance relationships I have'? You're right. I myself maintain hundreds of national and international relationships because of Facebook and Skype. In fact, I wouldn't have such good contact with my family in the Old Country without it! It is through Facebook that we first reunited.

Grace Stinton (b. 1922) of Midland, Michigan, brings this point home with a sobering story.

> You can keep in touch with people so much better. I can remember one time at my grandmother's house, we would gather for a game of bridge in the afternoon, and of course, two or three of the daughters-in-law lived nearby. One day [during World War II], we had a letter in the mail from mother's uncle, who was from New York, and it was actually a card with a black strip across it, to tell her that her uncle had died, which had been maybe several days beforehand, because it took the letter several days to get from New York to Tiverton [Rhode Island]. Nowadays, you're in constant touch with people.
>
> My uncle was in the Service . . . This was when I was in high school or college, and he was in France . . . And we had an announcement . . . that he was going to be able to talk to us one Sunday afternoon. We all gathered around the phone, waiting for that call, and I was so happy that they let me have just a few seconds on the phone to talk to my uncle who was in France! Just couldn't believe you were talking to someone that far away. And, of course, now we Skype the kids. And it's amazing. I have great-grandkids in Arkansas, now, and with Skyping you see them, and it's just great. There's been such a great advancement in communication.

I visited Harriet Berg (b. 1924) of Detroit, Michigan during Autumn. Ironically, we met at the Wayne State Farmers Market, where slow food reigns and every other person that walked by knew her by name. It was, in a way, a demonstration of how neighbors used to interact by running into each other on market days (a topic we'll dive into in future chapters).

Harriet affirms the fact that technology has allowed us to stay in communication with our loved ones despite a more global economy and greater distance between family members.

> [Technology] has definitely changed [everything]. For instance, I can Skype or FaceTime with my grandchildren who are in California! I maybe get to see them once a year, but this way I know what they look like and how they behave to a certain extent. And that is wonderful! But making the connection and having it fade when you're in the middle of saying something very important, you know, if something goes wrong or your battery runs out and you have to plug in [is hard]. You can't just go to sleep, you have to plug in or turn off, you know, so that's an added pressure. The computer, as everyone knows who uses it, it's a blessing and it's a detriment.

Marge Darger (b. 1934) of Midland, Michigan, also uses Skype to stay in touch with her loved ones. Bringing this point home, she told me the story of her husband's death. The entire family was able to be with him through technology despite being hundreds of miles apart.

> My kiddos are in Minneapolis, Chicago, Colorado, they're away from me, except for my son Tom . . . But all my grandkids and kiddos are across the country . . . I chuckle at times and think we are a virtual family. For instance, my daughter-in-law is French, and she's over in France for a month, so I can talk to her and email . . . It is just wonderful to be able to do that . . .
>
> When my husband was dying, the kiddos in Colorado couldn't get to . . . Midland. So, Dick is on his deathbed, and this is the day before he dies, and

my son Michael has this smartphone and he, and Alex, my grandson out in the Denver Area, get this Skype going and they are singing, and we're singing together to my husband who is dying in the bed . . . That is a very favorite, a very wonderful memory for me, 'cause they couldn't be here, and yet, there they were, I mean, virtually, and it . . . gave me great peace and serenity to know that.

ISSUES DISRUPTING TECHNOLOGICAL ADAPTATION

So, what is happening with communication? And where does our discomfort with technology stem from? Based on the interviews I conducted, I have discovered two major issues: 1) Intergenerational Miscommunication and 2) Personal Discomfort.

What do I mean by Intergenerational Miscommunication? Consider the wave of acronyms that took us by storm with the advent of AOL Instant Messenger and again with texting. It may not be it's as simple as new words with a new generation, however. After all, the hippies repurposed words like 'awesome,' 'cool,' and even the victory sign (now known as the peace sign) to the confusion of their parents and elders. Despite that confusion, these changes took place without the all-encompassing discomfort we are experiencing today as a society.

We now have a generation of parents who are raising children into a wholly different culture than that in which they themselves were raised. Imagine raising your child in the Amazon jungle, not having grown up there yourself, nor totally having integrated into the culture. The tools, language, customs, and more, would all be different, and your parenting go-tos (based on your own childhood) would be useless.

Not only are there significant differences between the childhoods of these generations, but those differences change seemingly minute-to-minute. The physical tools of technology change year to year. The software on those devices are constantly evolving, sometimes day to day. This creates an even larger challenge for parents who are trying to keep up and keep their children safe.

I grew up in a society only slightly altered from that of my parents' generation. Most homes had television, and eventually desktop computers. These were easily regulated and could not totally permeate one's interactions. Mobile devices like laptops and cell phones did not yet exist or were not yet adopted into daily life. As a girl, I still had to memorize phone numbers, use pay phones, look words up in the dictionary, and even wash the chalk from classroom chalkboards off my hands. Our vehicles didn't talk to us. I learned cursive and multiplication tables, and even took shorthand in addition to typing in high school. My parents could understand, relate to, and react in a mostly informed manner to the things I was experiencing, and make educated guesses on the newer technologies affecting my adolescence.

Contrast that to our current generation of children. Scientists aren't sure how screen time at young ages will affect brain development. Cyberbullying is a reality for most grade-school-aged students. New video games come out multiple times a month. 90% of two-year-olds know how to use smartphones and tablets, and many adolescents own one.[5] It is much harder for parents to discipline and regulate behavior, and that much harder to communicate on a level of mutual understanding. If teenagers historically feel that they are far different and incomprehensible to their parents, how much more is the sentiment validated when it is now mostly true? In the words of Renee Scott (b. 1938) of Portland, Oregon, "Same old same old. They don't look you in the face when they talk to you."

---

[5] University of Iowa, "How do Toddlers Use Tablets," https://now.uiowa.edu/2015/06/how-do-toddlers-use-tablets

All this is furthered by a lack of intergenerational support. The nuclear family has also changed to a large extent over the past century. Even before the 1990s boom of computers, better transportation made it easier for generations to disburse across hundreds of miles. Grandparents aren't always close to home and can't provide the close support to their younger generations like they would if they were. Add the generational and cultural divide our youth are experiencing, and parents are finding themselves without the traditional support group they might turn to for child-rearing guidance. The tips and tricks a mother may have provided her daughter as she starts her own family may have little relevance today.

Dave Chicoring (b. 1937) of Barraboo, Wisconsin, described the rapid pace of technology versus the slow pace of society beautifully while we sat at a picnic table outside at Devil's Lake State Park. We were nestled in the mountains and looking out at the lake. I find interesting which elders chose to remove us to quiet or 'slow' places to speak with me.

> In terms of technology, I've always worried about technology because I see technologically we speed up. We're ever accelerating. However, it comes back to [the fact that] societies change at a much slower pace. I see that societal change is generational, and you can look at any problem, like racial relationships in the United States, or various government programs, it takes a long time to reach an equilibrium. In other words, societal changes are generational, in my mind. Whether we can get along with Catholics, or get along with, in the future, Muslims, and so forth. And that might be many, many generations!

Unfortunately, we don't have generations of time to adapt to this new technology. Sometimes it feels like we have only moments to catch up before the next thing comes out. My smartphone is already old hat, and I've had it for less than a year. The operating system has updated five times since I purchased it, which could change many functions. New apps are released to the App Store every day in the thousands.[6] How, as someone who didn't grow up with a smartphone, might a parent adapt fast enough to regulate their child's online reach? And how might a grandparent advise their child's parenting when a problem arises with technology that was released only a month ago?

We just reviewed the first issue affecting communication, which is Intergenerational Discomfort with the changes we're experiencing. The second issue is much more broad, but just as important. Edwin Gould (b. 1936), the man who worked on America's first spy satellite during the Cold War, alluded to it beautifully when he said, "My father helped electrify New Hampshire. I flew spy satellites. That's quite a quantum leap in just two generations!" The issue is Personal Discomfort with technological changes, both culturally and individually.

Personal Discomfort seems to play a large role in how technology is accepted and used today, and not just by our elders. For example, would you be comfortable with a FitBit® activity tracking implant in your arm? What about every vehicle on the road being autonomous? Generally, we are amused by new tech, but when it comes to personal use, we each have a threshold of comfort.

Imagine, for a moment, that we are forty years in the future. Our children are all 'driving' autonomous vehicles. They were too young to ever experience manual vehicles. Even their first car had parking assist and adaptive cruise control. As this generation looks back at the past 100 years, they are astonished that we ever attempted to manually control a complicated machine

---

[6] 42 Matters, "App Market Stats," https://42matters.com/stats

like a car, all while fussing with the radio, gauging traffic, keeping tabs on vehicles nearby, maybe even talking on the phone or (heaven forbid) texting.

We like to write off 'non-adapting' as something only our elders do, but everyone has a line they feel uncomfortable crossing. Even if autonomous vehicles and smart implants don't bother you, perhaps a robotic OBGYN or prostate exam might.

The Internet creates a false sense that the world is moving at breakneck speeds. In fact, only the Internet, a collective thought vehicle, can move that fast. It has the power of millions of humans acting together in one place that propel it forward. If that's not understood, however, it can seem too large a barrier to entry. Several of the elders I interviewed lament that they aren't smart enough to get into technology, or even fear it. Ray Green (b. 1930) owned an employment agency in Detroit and used all kinds of tech in his office, including fax, teletype, typewriters, word processors, and computers. Yet, he still feels he can't deal with it.

> I was always afraid of technology. I'm not good at that. I just feared, not because it was something new, but because it was technical. And I can't ever do anything technical . . . In those days computers were only for the highly educated people with special courses and degrees . . . I mean, my degree was from a long time ago. So, I was scared.

The idea that one must be highly educated or knowledgeable to break into technology is an old one, and one I disagree with. Today, all one needs is a device connected to the Internet, but from the outside, it may seem more complicated than that. An elder may remember a time when it really did take a large amount of training to understand how to use a machine or other technological advancement. I think this is the story we allow our elders to maintain, rather than patiently show them how or why to use today's tech or adapt marketing to their language and identity as a generation.

More and more, Facebook and other social media platforms are dominating our lives. It is nearly impossible to pass a day without some sort of interaction with them, including texting. As of February 2018, Wikipedia listed 209 active social media networks.[7] That number is constantly growing, with visual platforms dominating the growth in the social media world.

In turn, a new language is evolving specific to these interactions. We saw such acronyms like LOL, A/S/L, and ROTFL (or the more crude ROTFLMAO) with the advent of chat rooms and AOL Instant Messenger in the early 2000s. What we did not foresee, however, is how those acronyms would integrate into our in-person conversation. Words like "status," "profile," and even "friend" have grown and changed in meaning over the past 15 years. Even "liking" something has a dual meaning.

In some ways, it could be argued that this language is leaving our elders behind. Only 34% of seniors (those aged 65 and older) had adopted social media use by the end of 2016, according to the Pew Research Center.[8] So, when a younger counterpart begins speaking in social media slang, seniors may be left out of the conversation.

In fact, several of the elders interviewed for this book suggested that the heavy use of social media to market today's businesses was a significant tell in their decision to retire. One elder described going through the adoption of word processors, computers, printers, and other technology in the workplace, and the fatigue she met when social media was added. Enough was

---

[7] Wikipedia, "List of social networking websites," https://en.wikipedia.org/wiki/List_of_social_networking_websites

[8] Pew Research Center, "Technology Use Among Seniors," http://www.pewinternet.org/2017/05/17/technology-use-among-seniors/

enough — it was time to call it a good career and leave it at that. Unfortunately, that means we lost a lot of legacy knowledge that could still be passed on to younger business professionals.

Some elders simply don't want technology in their lives — again, I think this is more a failure in marketing than anything else. As Ray Green continues,

> Why do I want to put my stuff on Facebook so the whole world knows about it? So, here's the difference between me and the younger generation, because that's what they do all the time. They put something on there and it goes viral. Well, I don't want any of my stuff to go viral. I value my privacy.

Here, again, is what I perceive as a lack of transparency in marketing to seniors. Facebook provides excellent security and privacy options. Even my own mother was afraid that, in recently setting up her account, the entire world would see her pictures and posts. Not true, but the company has failed to communicate effectively the strength of their privacy features to anyone outside their target age group, and news syndicates that publish social media posts don't mention that they only have access to public posts.

Elders that have taken advantage of Facebook or other social media have discovered friends around the world, a widening viewpoint, and travel opportunities. Dave Chicoring is living a kind of life that I wouldn't venture to, myself. I keep social media close to my chest, only allowing people I know into my profile. Dave has widened his circle, and, as a result, has a wide international network of people he's never actually met.

> I've got friends all over the world, and they're different ages, and different cultures. What have I gained? I have gained an insight into the world that is vastly different because I actually have friends, I guess you

could call it friends, from all over the world, and we can talk on a daily basis.

Technology has definitely facilitated globalization. We're able to communicate with and get closer to people that otherwise would have not stayed so close. We can work closely with colleagues we never meet. My best friend lives two states away. I rarely see her, but the phone and social media allow us to stay immersed in each other's lives.

Unfortunately, this also means that one can lose friends. Fifty years ago, one's closest friends probably would have lived in the same neighborhood. If one of them hadn't been seen in a while, it was easy to walk over and knock on the door to ask if they were okay. I can still do that to a large extent in my city today. I can even drive across the State and find someone if I know where their home is. But that's the catch.

Last year I lost a friend. Not lost as in they passed away but lost as in I can't get in touch with her. She was one of my best friends. We met working disaster relief after Hurricane Katrina, and we'd bonded and stayed in touch over the years. I'd since visited her at her home in Asheville, North Carolina. She was even helping to coordinate elders in her region for this project.

Now, I can't find her. She moved around a lot, so I don't have a current address. She didn't like social media, so there's no Facebook profile for me to look to. She rarely kept an active phone which means her phone number often changed. We would communicate via phone most of our friendship, and by mail otherwise. I'm at a loss for what to do, and our mutual friends have no idea where she might be, either.

This is a strange situation, but it is not unique to me. Our elders are experiencing something very similar as they move into retirement communities and nursing homes. Family and friends don't always know to update address books or even which friends have moved. Often, our elders learn of a friend's status only after an obituary is published, sometimes years from their last communication.

In many ways, communication was far more difficult before the telephone was popularized 70 years ago. Perhaps it was easier to 'lose' people without the social profiles we keep online. We were much more likely to keep a permanent address during that time period, however, making one easier to find if needed.

So, what else can I do but wait and hope to hear from my friend? Almost two years later, I can only hope she happens to read this book and reaches out.

The stories I have gathered here are not to be written off because they come from those advanced in age and so presumed to be 'out of touch.' In fact, they are the only ones alive who can remember life before tech — some even lived without electricity, running water, or a family vehicle. One gentleman you'll meet later in this book rode a tamed wild bronco to school every day. I turned to them for this reason, and their stories have not only been invaluable, but a wonderful experience for yours truly.

Communication came up repeatedly during interviews, but many other subjects did, too. These will be explored in the following chapters. Some were things I'd never considered. I could have spent years on this project, and may, yet. But the book needed writing, and so I halted interviewing to get it done. If you have a friend or relative who was born before 1945, I suggest you use my interview questions and take a moment to learn about a life and about your own history in a manner not possible any other way.

"I think you personally, and the job that you're doing is important, because you will gain from the past, and I've always said what you put out there is what you will get back in the future. I think it will make you think what progress is [in] every area of life, and how it's going to affect you as a person."
— Renee Scott

WAR

"This is the President of the United States speaking. Through the marvels of scientific advance, my voice is coming to you from a satellite circling in outer space. My message is a simple one: Through this unique means I convey to you and all mankind America's wish for peace on Earth and goodwill toward men everywhere."

— President Eisenhower, 1958, speaking over our first satellite communications system[9]

Two of the most interesting people I interviewed were completely unexpected. In fact, when I left Michigan on the first of November 2015, I didn't even know I would meet Edwin Gould. Only a few days beforehand had I received an email regarding him via the Kickstarter page I'd created to fund the research. It read like this:

> My uncle, [Edwin] Ned Gould, is a retired Air Force Colonel and engineer born in 1936 who lives in Fountain Valley, California. I recently learned that he was involved with spy satellite programs, that have now been declassified, during the Cold War era. I think it would be fascinating to hear about the technology used in the development of these satellites and how that technology has changed, as well as the impact, if

---

[9] Dwight D. Eisenhower, "Message Recorded for Transmission Via Atlas Satellite," December 19, 1958.

any, it has had on our country's security and the use of satellites for other things.

At the bottom of the email was his phone number.

Of course, I knew I had to meet him. Someone who built spy satellites was at the forefront of technological development, to say the least. Little did I know that he hadn't just built them, he'd engineered much of the technology. Not only this, but some of his work is still classified to this day. During the interview, he literally said, "Then I went to Germany, but I can't tell you what I did there." What a trip!

I met Edwin at his home in a posh area outside Los Angeles directly after conducting an interview in Compton with Urcell Schulterbrandt. The contrast between the neighborhoods was obvious. Front yards were kept differently, homes were larger, the stores and amenities outside the subdivision were newer.

Edwin and Esther (b. 1937) welcomed me into their home when I arrived. It never ceased to amaze me how welcoming those I interviewed were to a perfect stranger driving across the country. The air conditioning felt really good, but soon I was cold (in usual fashion). Most of the interior was white, except for the exposed wood trim and furniture.

I didn't expect Esther to be there. In fact, I didn't know about her at all. It is common that participants are widowed when I meet them, so I make no assumptions about the make-up of a household. The goal of the project is to gather a large quantity of diverse interviews, so I gently encouraged Esther to consider being interviewed after Edwin. Reluctant at first at the surprise (and perhaps feeling her story wouldn't measure up to Edwin's), she consented after Edwin told me his story.

It quickly became obvious that Edwin loved his work. His attitude was that of a child who got to play with toys all day. He paraded models out to demonstrate his work — those that had been declassified and he could discuss. He is responsible for engineering the cameras in the spy satellites. Imagine going to work and dealing with the problem of not just how to make a camera work in space, but how to get the film back to Earth after the pictures are taken. There were no such thing as digital photographs when Edwin was doing this work.

I worked on the very first spy satellite this country ever built called 'CORONA.' You can Google that if you want — you'll learn all about area . . . photography. You think it's tricky to take a picture of something accurately that's a hundred yards or more away? The satellite's at a hundred miles. To take a picture of something a hundred miles away and figure out what you're going to see and make a good photo . . . and clouds kind of get in the way, too. Clouds are very uninteresting to look at. And so, there was a lot to be done about whether you turn the camera on, how do you build this thing, how do you fly it. [It was] 13 failures before we had success.

We brought back the first bucket of film . . . I'll tell you how we did that. You'll find that interesting. We flew the first satellite, took pictures with a rotating camera that comes down and turns on, when it gets over here it turns off and goes to the other side, so it takes a continuous set of film strips laid down. We would take that film, put it in a small sub-satellite we called The Bucket, eject that from the satellite, spin it to stabilize it — 'cause spinning something creates gyroscopic stabilization — we would spin it, fire a rocket, bring it down, and catch it in midair with an airplane by snagging the parachute and reel it in and take it back to our processing facility in Rochester New York at Eastman Kodak, develop the film very secretly, and so forth. We recovered the first film, I think it was six days after Gary Powers was shot down in the U2 and we stopped all flights over the Soviet Union.

The problem that made all of this worthwhile was the Russians. We knew they had missiles. We had no idea how many, and no idea where they were, so this was a photographic thing to photograph the entire Soviet Union and find the missiles. It had about 13- to 20-foot resolution, so you could see a house but not a car. From a hundred miles. We had another project going at the same time that was like looking through a straw, and it could take things down to a three-feet resolution, so you could see cars and other stuff, railroad cars, things of military interest.

So, the bright eyes in Washington [DC] — that [higher resolution satellite] was called Gambit — they wanted something with the coverage of Corona and the resolution of Gambit. Extremely difficult, and I worked on the first one of those called Hexagon. If you want to have an interesting read, go ahead and Google Hexagon Spy Satellite, and you will learn about the biggest satellite we ever built in this country. It sized the Space Shuttle; secretly, that's what determined the size of the Space Shuttle . . . roughly the size of a railroad car. It was 33,000 lbs. of weight, had 108,000 feet of film on it, with four Buckets. It was originally set off for 30 days at a time, but we lengthen that out to almost a year . . . because you wanted pictures of everything that was clear. Now you want pictures of places like South China, and it's never clear in South China, particularly at noon when the sun's right to take a good picture, so you're waiting four days to get a good picture of anything that's interesting, and so forth. We also took those in Buckets, and they're about this big — she [my wife] has seen them. We declassified it a few years back here, about five or six years back, and we had a big get together of all of us guys who worked on this at the museum outside of Washington DC, the

Air and Space Museum. So, she got to see a Bucket . . . Actually, got to see an entire Hexagon. We had parts enough left over that we put one together in a tent outside, [and] we couldn't get it inside the building, even though they have a complete SR-71 in there, we couldn't get it inside the building. It's now at Wright Patterson Air Force Base if you ever want to go see it. At the Air Museum. The Hexagon Vehicle is there.

It had two simultaneous cameras. Now to give you an idea of what it could do, it went around the Earth every 90 minutes, [and] in one pass it could photograph all of California and count every car in it if it was clear. If they weren't behind clouds . . . It was that good even out at an angle. It had the coverage at a hundred miles, so you could see California side-to-side. So, you could see the whole state and every car in it. Very useful in a battle scenario if you want to know where the enemy's got his tanks, 'cause you can see them all at once, and all his encampments, and all his trucks, and a lot of his troops. So, I worked on that . . . then I went overseas and operated spy satellites or secret satellites out of Germany and Europe and England which I really can't tell you about those yet. Then I came back here and worked on more secret satellites that I also can't talk about very much . . . it would still be useful for people to know some of this stuff.

Edwin was arguably on the front lines of technological advancement and in aiding our country through the Cold War. Indeed, war is often one of our most technologically advancing periods. It's believed that at the dawn of man, weapons themselves were adapted from hunting tools, creating more effective hunting after a battle or war was fought. The book I studied for my capstone course in anthropology, called "How War Began," describes just how innovative a time war can be.

Weapons use by early man probably occurred for defensive reasons: to defend the group when attacked by felids, canids, or other predators, for example. If a predator was nearly within arm's reach, early humans grasped a stick to serve as a club, fending off the attacker with blows. If the predator was at a greater distance, early humans grasped and threw stones or other objects, hurling them in the direction of the predator . . .

Homo Habilis made a variety of chopping tools, tools designed to cut flesh from bones and to break up bones . . . Confrontations between bands may have been similar to chimpanzee encounters, where lone individuals were ambushed, and groups of males made threat displays to each other. If stones and clubs were used in the ambush or in the group challenges, my minimal definition of war applies — there was armed combat between independent groups. The basic pattern was ambushes and lines. Thus, war could have begun with Homo Habilis . . .

The lengthy discussion of hunting . . . suggests four possible reasons why hunting and warfare are related: Hunters have weapons that are likely to be suitable for use in warfare; hunting itself involves searching for and killing prey; if seeking prey involves the coordinated activities of hunters, a quasi-military organization has been created; and hunters, particularly hunters of large herd animals, may range over a vast region and come in contact with other peoples who also range over a part of the territory and do not wish to share it.[10]

---

[10] Keith F. Otterbein, *How War Began* (Texas A&M University anthropology series, 2004), 47, 60, 85

WEAPONS OF MASS DESTRUCTION

Unfortunately, with the development of weapons and their defenses comes additional danger. Many of the elders I interviewed spoke about their fear of such weapons and our potential for global destruction today. None were so adamant about this possibility as Sister Ardeth Plattie, OP (b. 1936). I'd been referred to her many months before my trip began while interviewing in Midland, Michigan. Like Edwin, I didn't actually get in touch with her until I was already on the road.

I was particularly excited to interview Sister Ardeth because she is a Dominican Nun, and diversity is important to truly understanding tech's effect on all of us. I knew I had to meet her, however, because she has dedicated every aspect of her life to peace — so much so that she spent three years in a Federal Prison for protesting nuclear weapons.

Sister Ardeth lives on the grounds of the oldest Catholic cemetery in Baltimore, Maryland, in a home called Jonah House. There she cares for the grounds and uses available land to grow fruits and vegetables to help supply a local food kitchen. Though I arrived only six months after the end of the Baltimore riots which protested the police brutality that had resulted in the death of Freddie Gray, there didn't seem to be much evidence of its occurrence. The city felt settled and quiet.

I met Sister Ardeth at Jonas House, in an area of Baltimore that would have been considerably affected by the riots. The grounds were beautiful and clearly well-kept. She showed me the vegetable garden and told me of her experience of raising goats and chickens in addition to the produce she grows today.

I admired her candor as we began her interview at her kitchen table. She was very open and upfront with me about her past. Little did I know that the peacekeeping work she had participated in which resulted in her incarceration was in my home state, nearly in my home city.

I've seen the weapons of war escalate in power and destruction, and there's no such thing, anymore, as just war. I mean, once nuclear weapons came into being, and once bombing from the skies happened, I watched all that. That has all become, you know, a technology that, for me, is evil . . .

When I was first missioned I was an educator in junior high, and then I began the next year to teach in high school. So, I taught for eight years. I've been a principal of a high school at a school for dropouts and expellees for 11 years. In the midst of that I was a City Councilwoman, an elected official, in the City of Saginaw [Michigan] for 12 years. I was mayor pro tem for the city for the last two years of that stint.

[During] political life I became very involved in the fact that nuclear weapons came into Michigan. I worked for 12 years organizing all of Michigan to reject the nuclear weapons. We had 680 cruise missiles deployed on B-52's, both in Oscoda and the Upper Peninsula. That's the reason I moved to those places. We were right in the heart of it. And so, [I worked at] peacemaking and Justice-making in Saginaw. However, as a City Councilwoman I also established a home for peace and justice, advocacy for justice. We worked on multi-issues, trying to stop the Midland Nuclear Power Plant and working to clean up the rivers, working on the poverty issues of the area, along with the other work I was doing as City Councilwoman.

Now, I would say that my full-time ministry is the work for justice and peace. The key focus issue that I have taken to is to abolish nuclear weapons and to ban War as a matter of policy and as a matter of practice. And so, the last 30-40 years of my life I've been working on those issues, and I do it full-time now, although I moved to Jonah House and I find myself-care taking

for the cemetery and going back to the Earth and trying to work on the issues of climate change and focus
issues of poverty in this area, also.

Sydney Rushing (b. 1930), whom you'll officially meet in the
chapter about Work, reminds us that all technology is simply a
tool. It's up to the user to decide what to do with it.

> It's very good, but it can be used in a very destructive
> way. It can destroy all of mankind . . . It can make you a
> better society, or it can destroy your society. It depends
> on how man will use this knowledge, this new knowl-
> edge, and skills that he's gained.

Sister Ardeth repeated many times to me, "Is this for destruction, or for good?" She felt strongly that by analyzing each action
or technology with that saying, we might not destroy humanity
with technological development. I agree.

Judith Blair (b. 1944) of Ithaca, New York, made me laugh
when she told me her solution to managing weapons of mass
destruction — keep technology away from men.

> I kind of feel like we should have kept technology away
> from the men. [*laughs*] Because if they could build a
> bigger weapon, a better weapon, drones so they don't
> even have to be there, oh boy! You know? 'We love this
> technology because we can impose our will and kill
> people.' I don't think women would have, that would
> have been their first thought, if they were the ones
> controlling technology.

There seems to be a fervor for new tech today. We're amazed by
it, enthralled with it. Unfortunately, that means we may adopt
a new system or product without considering its consequence.
'Cool' isn't an adequate reason for accepting a new technology,

especially when it may disrupt our community, health, or — as Sister Ardeth is concerned — safety. How might we begin paying attention to the true potential, positive and negative, of tech?

As Donald Wensel (b. 1927) of Detroit reflects, "I don't think those kids realize the changes that have occurred even in their lifetime. I don't think they really appreciate what has been done to advance their lifestyle." This means they also may not realize the effects it has and is going to have as it develops. Are we frogs in a warming pot, growing closer to boiling but not noticing because, for some, technology has always been a fact of life? If so, can Sister Ardeth's mantra give us a much-needed temperature gauge?

WAR AFAR

"I was six years old in 1917 when the boys came back from the war. Before the end of the war, my mother bought me a pair of knitting needles . . . and taught me how to knit, and she told me that we had to knit socks for the boys in the war. I remember I had that red yarn for a long, long time. I never did get a sock knitted. But I remember the day the boys . . . returned from World War I. There were very few of them because St. Cooley was a small town, but I still have this memory of these eight or ten men marching down our one and only street. They had just arrived. And Mother was trying to inform us about what war was, and it was a terrible, terrible thing that we don't want to ever do again... She knew what she was saying. But we still have it, don't we? Every single day."
— Emma Lommasson (b. 1911)

War today doesn't happen like it used to. World War II was still present in the United States, though the fighting never occurred on our soil, due to rationing of goods and the absence of most of our men. Delores Duncan (b. 1933) of Illinois was fortunate that

30

her father was a salesman and had connections most families didn't during this time.

> I loved to roller skate [and ice skate] . . . During the war, my dad worked where he had customers who traveled a lot. So, during the war, when you couldn't find ice skates or bicycles, he would ask his customers, 'Do you know anybody who has a pair of ice skates or a bicycle?' My brother and I both had a bicycle 'cause he knew people who would go back and forth to Florida . . . He bought our ice skates the same way.
>
> We would go to [my grandparent's] house about every other week, but during the war we had to take the elevated [train] and the subway to get there because . . . we couldn't get gas. You had to have a stamp (ration ticket) . . . My other grandparents lived just south of Kankakee, we didn't get to go there very often. But my dad had a customer who had a small cab company, and sometimes he would have extra gas at the end of the month, and he would give my dad a tank of gas and we would go visit my grandfather and grandmother in their small town.

Recall my visit to Harriet Berg at the Wayne State Farmers' Market in Detroit. She brought up war and technology and the evolution during her lifetime of how we treat war in America.

> We don't know what war is here in the United States. We have no idea. It's always 'over there,' and it has been, except for the Civil War. We never ever had war on our own soil . . .
>
> I don't know why every mother isn't fighting for peace! There was an organization . . . during World War II, Another Mother for Peace, and it had a feminine symbol for peace in it. If mothers don't do it, I don't know who is.

And you realize the formidable forces that are against us, formidable. It's very hard to be for peace. And, of course, there are all the patriots that say the patriotic thing is to [go to war] — no, no, no, no, no! The patriotic thing is to say, 'We are not going to kill people,' 'We are not going to let our sons die for our country.' You live for your country, you don't die for your country! . . . Put that kind of energy that we put into war into making peace.

[World War II] was very different than any war since, because we were a part of it. At home we had rationing, rationing of meat, sugar, and gas. We felt the effects of that. We didn't fight, but we felt deprivation . . . I saved aluminum foil from cigarette packages and from gum. Rip it apart from the paper and you make a big ball and then you take it into the war office. And we saved rubber bands — different things like that. So, you were involved in the war, and you were constantly sending things overseas — letters, knitted goods. So, people felt they were a part of it. They haven't done that since then. They've kept it as quiet as possible, but still the killing goes on.

Now, of course, we're finding out, as the guys come back without limbs, and shell shock, we're finding out, 'Oh yeah, I didn't know there was a war that was happening!' So, I don't approve of that . . .

Yoko Mossner of Saginaw, Michigan, was born in Tokyo in 1933. She was ten years old when Tokyo was evacuated during the bombings. She told me what rationing and the effects of World War II looked like from the other side.

Pretty soon I noticed things are getting very tight. You cannot buy anything in the store. Many stores they don't have anything to sell. Food was getting scarce, so it was all rationed. We did not have any sweets or, you know, anything like that. And so, everything was very tight. I think we were losing the war, but at that time, we were not told. All my friends' father or brother, they're all taken and drafted into the army. Every couple of days the neighbors get together, and we send off somebody else's father or husband or brother to the war.

Then we were told to mass evacuate . . . We were [evacuated] for about 14 months . . . While we were [away] we were kept very secluded. We could not hear anything. While we were in Tokyo I was keeping up because you could hear the news . . . While we were away from Tokyo I didn't know what was going on.

Then I heard about the atomic bombs. Japan was bombed after we left . . . some of my friend's families were burned, and the houses and everything was burned. Then I heard our caretaker and the teacher were talking about some terrible bomb was dropped and then they said, 'We have to surrender,' and I thought 'Japan is surrendering? That's never happened before.' But we did. So, after two months, I went to Tokyo... There was nothing left there, and it was so dark at night.

I met Chris Smith (b. 1927) at his home in spring. He was third-generation owner of Chris Craft, a boat building company that made its first boat in 1874, before engines were invented. His grandfather was the first to put a car engine on a boat, which led them to building racing boats, including the Miss Detroit boats that won the Gold Cup races on Lake Huron.

They eventually broke away from building only racing boats. Chris doesn't remember the Great Depression, and only just remembers rationing during World War II, but he does recall his father building the landing boats used in Normandy.

Dad, of course, being a defensive plant, Chris Craft built government boats all during the war. I can show you a picture of them down in the basement. So, he got a card for gasoline, you know? Some people didn't. I remember a ration, I think it was $5 worth of gasoline, and another $5, and my wife and I were set for the evening. We could go to a movie and get gas go to a different town. [*laughs*] That part of it I remember.

[My dad] built 12,000 36-foot landing barges [originally designed by] Higgins . . . [They went] all over. The islands in the Pacific . . . I was talking to a group of elderly people . . . I was talking about the war years and the landing barges, and one guy in the back of the office stood up and said, 'I'm glad I was in a Chris Craft boat because my friends were in Higgins boats and they didn't make it.'

Chris later showed me the photos of the different styles of the landing barges. He explained how they modified the design they received from Higgins, moving the propellers lower so the soldiers could sit lower in the boat to protect them. The driver stood at the back of the boat, and they redesigned the position to also be lower and more protected. This explained the gentleman's comments about his safety during landing in Normandy.

As Harriet Berg stated, we don't go overseas in the numbers we used to. Man-to-man combat is no longer the norm. She proceeded to describe how war has changed for America with the advent of the drone.

And now — I can't believe it! — Look what's happening. All these refugees that people are refusing to take in. The English, after World War I, the way they divided up the Middle East, are the roots of the wars that are going on now. We are involved over there, whether we know it or not.

The drones . . . I know a kid, my girlfriend's son, all he wanted from the age of ten was to join the Air Force and fly a big Air Force plane. And he did, he got into the Air Force, and he became an instructor. She kept waiting for him to be sent overseas, he was dying to be sent. They sent him to Florida and put him in a room, and he operates a drone. Do you know they don't let them do that longer than two months because they go crazy? They go crazy killing people. They know they are killing people, but they don't see it, and so they show them the photos afterwards. There's something schizophrenic about it. They're just pulling a lever, that's all. And, of course, we've radicalized a lot of young people that were, what do we call it, collateral damage? Their mothers and sisters were killed by a drone bomb. 'America is inhumane, [so] I'm going to go out and fight the Americans.'

Harriet and Betty Segal (b. 1931) of Illinois are both extremely well-read women and former educators. I don't know if that's why their opinion on drones aligns so closely, but I couldn't help but notice the parallel in Betty's interview when I visited her months later.

We have drones which could be very useful, but we've used them to kill people, hastily . . . I was looking at this thing about the brain on TV the other night, the thing about the puzzle about the train is coming and you could [choose to] run the train on the side track and kill one person or let it go on and kill four people, and the fact that most people will make it kill the one person. But then if you had to push somebody in front of the train to stop the train to kill one person, they won't do it, because it's personal. Drones have taken us a step that you don't see. We have people sitting in a bunker in mid-America killing people in the Mid-East that they don't see very well, that they don't know, and they make assumptions that this person is an enemy, and they kill people.

Bettilew Turk Gaskell (b. 1925), whom you'll officially meet in the next chapter, told me a story from World War II that wouldn't have happened with today's technology. Not just because we send less soldiers into the field, but also because we have technology like surveillance cameras to help keep watch over prisoners of war. And yet, something in it echoes of Abu Ghraib, in which American soldiers tortured and abused prisoners of war.[11] Even though we can watch over POW's better, we might not actually be doing so.

[My husband] guarded [Robert] Ley, the German [Nazi politician who committed suicide while awaiting trial at Nuremburg].[12] During the day and into the evening, he would have different things to check on. And at night he was checking on the eyeglasses, 'cause they could break them and cut their wrists and commit suicide. And he spoke to a lot of the big top German officers, befriended them, [because] he would just talk to them.

But Ley would not come to the door to talk to him or give him the glasses [that night]. He said he was in the bathroom. When he got through taking up the other ones he went back to ask him to come to the

---

[11] Wikipedia, "Abu Ghraib torture and prisoner abuse," http://en.wikipedia. org/wiki/Abu_Ghraib_torture_and_prisoner_abuse, (April 14, 2018).

[12] Wikipedia, "Robert Ley," https://en.wikipedia.org/wiki/Robert_Ley, (July 17, 2017).

door . . . [Ley] didn't answer him, so [my husband] went and asked the guard to come and open the door, and they found him behind the wall, there, where he had tied sheets together and hanged himself from the plumbing apparatus in the wall. It was in the national newspaper.[13] I have a copy . . . [My husband] thought he was going to get in trouble because he didn't insist on those glasses the first time, but [Ley] didn't use the glasses, he used the sheets that he tied together to hang himself.

Warfare has changed dramatically as technology has evolved. We no longer line up in battalions and await the General's order from horseback, swords drawn, bayonets ready, cannons afire.

With technology, our weapons have evolved to greater precision and higher consequence. I had the amazing fortune of meeting Etcyl Blair (b. 1922) through a friend. He was at the forefront of developing some of these kinds of weapons for the United States government during World War II.

I . . . went into bacteriological warfare. I did not know what this was when I went into it at the time, but I had taken science, see, all this time, basically chemistry. Before the Invasion [of Europe in June 1944] . . . I was at Ft. Custer. I had not had basic training — when you're in the Air Force you don't get basic training 'cause you end up being a Cadette. You're never on the ground, you're in the sky, flying. So, I had to take basic training with the military police on Ft. Custer.

We were all put on a troop train when things got bad in Europe and headed for the East Coast. Before

---

[13] Detroit Free Press, "No. 4 Nazi Hangs Himself," October 26, 1945, http://www.rarenewspapers.com/view/630250.

we arrived on the East Coast, the train stopped and two of us were taken off the train and put in a car that you couldn't see out of. Very strange. This would have been about 1944 — end of '43, beginning of '44. And we drove all night long, and we ended up in a strange situation where everything looked like military, like aircraft, like big drones where you'd park the airplanes into the hangars, except it wasn't. It was a secret chemical warfare area in Frederick, Maryland, halfway between Washington DC and Baltimore. There I spent the last two years. I worked on anthrax and botulism, which, in the case of chemical warfare, would be what would be used. It was never used.

Though the specific weapons that Etcyl developed were never used, the chemical weapon Agent Orange was. I spoke with a former soldier, Gus Katsoris (b. 1947), who was, in fact, sprayed with Agent Orange while he was stationed in Korea. Today, he has three different types of cancer and has been written about in medical journals. He described what it was like to be sent over there, and his medical situation, today.

I thought it stunk over there. I thought . . . to see poverty, at that level, it just struck me . . . They weren't beyond a mud hut and raw grass for roofs. And if they could find a sheet of linoleum to lay down for a floor, they were doing good . . .

They didn't [tell me it was Agent Orange] . . . They were saying I had COPD, and then I got pneumonia . . . I got my yearly physical . . . and somehow a lady physician from Poland is telling me to get into a hospital and get checked . . . she talked me into doing it. Next thing I know she's making appointments for me to get in there . . . So, they set up an examination, and the next thing is they come back and say, 'you've

got cancer,' and two kinds, they figured, that was before. I'm dying, and I've got two to three months left.
[That was] two years ago.

I asked Gus if he knew they were spraying Agent Orange when
he was there.

Not at all . . . That part's a mystery to me. I used to
say, 'Huccome it's so devastated here?' Like, the ter-
rain, there, the greenery, nothing . . . It's dead. Something's not right. And I never knew of it. Like, they
talked about it in Vietnam, but I never put it together
with Korea. I think they must have kept us stupid, or
fairly stupid . . .
What is the reason why we sacrifice Christian
lives for these wars, for others to benefit? I mean, what
good did it do me? It took my health, my life. I stop to
think of that, and it's like, I don't know, I'm trying to
put it together.

Though some of the technology we develop during war remains
dormant, like the chemical work of Etcyl Blair, others have been
turned into daily use tools. I met Hal Royer (b. 1926) at his
home just North of Denver, Colorado. He grew up on farms and
had amazing stories to tell about the Great Depression. He also
loves to fish and reflected during our interview how his fishing
radar might have been used during World War II had it been as
developed as it is, today.

My fish finder on my boat — if we'd had that during
[World War II] with the Nazi submarines, we would
have found them and blown them up!

Unfortunately, technology can also be a vehicle for further warfare. Today, beheadings by so-called terrorists are put on the

Internet to generate more fear. On the flip side, revolutions have been started by using the Internet. Technology plays a massive role in both warfare and peacekeeping.

Dave Chicoring, whom we met in the last chapter, is a former immunologist and endocrinologist. He studied relationships all his life, though they were focused on the internal structures of the human body. He described the relationship technology has as a vehicle for societal change in depth while we sat looking out over Devil's Lake during his interview.

> So, what does technology have to do with this? I think technology is just a factor in the rig of change of society. And humans have been magnificent in that we have been able to live in places like this, in places like Greenland, in places like the Amazon, in places like the desert. I see several of the major religions of the world — and what are religions, they are rules, they are mythologies, and they are rules to live by that have been worked out over a long time, and sometimes they work, sort of — but I see three of the major ones, Abrahamic religions, came out of the deserts. That's the way I see it. Desert people, and many of them were on the edge of survival. What would happen? They would go out on raids, or they would have people living in settled places, but there were always raiders coming in. And you can go to various things, biblical or whatever, and there were people ranging in. And they were predatory. Predatory rules of existence don't necessarily work for cities and civilized societies, unless we want to continue being predatory tribes going around stealing women and children and food and land, or whatever. But how long have we been doing this? Well, humankind has probably never ceased, so Darwinism continues to express itself not necessarily in who is biggest and strongest or smartest but in the social realm . . .

Countries can be upset, now, by a few videos, and we see it on a daily basis. And it's very strong, the amount of information that we can have. I think it upset most of the countries of North Africa. They overthrew their governments, and it was very much enabled by the Internet . . . The Al-Qaeda is very good, and ISIS is very good, at Internet. Will we ever get the genie back in the bottle? No. It'll never happen. Will Internet always be as good and free? Will it be enraptured by the political and economic forces? Yes, probably, because the potential's there, if it's possible it's probable. Given enough time and enough chances, it's probable. Right now, it seems to be free and free willing and open, but I think probably that will change. I don't know for good or bad, but probably, because there are many forces that want not to see that.

Technology as a force of good or of war can go either way, now, and it's up to us to temper our reactions and put them in perspective. If our leaders can do that, I think technology in the form of the Internet will remain for the good.

Like myself, Wanda Moore (b. 1925), a former stewardess (as they were called in her time) and radio operator for the airlines, sees technology in the same light as so many of these elders.

I get concerned about the nuclear . . . and the weapons, that they now have knowledge, and that concerns me. If our technology is used in the right way, I think it's fantastic. But I think often times it can cause a lot of damage, too . . .

The question is, how do we systemize technology and the Internet so that we continue to lead the world in not just its development, but in its use as an empowering tool rather than a tool of destruction? I return to Dave Chicoring, once more, to discuss this possibility from the eyes of a scientist and theorist.

> People continue to like violence and warfare. They might not like it, but it happens. Stuff happens, and I think that is where we are evolving, now. Not so much on the physical basis, but our institutions have always evolved. You might say the [Native Americans] were always fighting . . . [and then] they were at a level of sustainability, or barely on the edge of sustainability for their lifestyle. And probably they were weary of other tribes coming in. Some of the tribes were sedentary and built houses and developed societies that would work. Some were very tribal, very predatory, might be cannibalistic, certainly would steal the women and children to gain an advantage. And I think many places in the world were that way. That people were . . . at the edge of sustainability in an economic sense.
>
> Probably people were starving for a good bit of our history. We can tend to eat too much, now, and get to the edge of our weight, but I think that comes from a legacy of living on the edge. And you think of humanity even spread as far as the polar areas, and you say, 'My God, how did those people, with nothing, survive?' Well, they had to devise a lifestyle, an ethics, they had to devise a way that it would work. And how would it improve itself? By living. By reproducing. And you would say is it moral? Well, maybe that isn't a good question.
>
> We have all kinds of societies all over the world, and we want to jam them together quickly. They came from different areas, they survived in many diverse ways, and to think we can get through this neatly, I think we're hurrying too much. I don't think it's going

to work out. I see a major problem. Say in Europe, we had Iraq and Iran. We had Iraqi people going into a deluge, a very liberal, democratic country, like Norway and Denmark. But at the same time, those people, based on a system they devised of religions and laws, want to go in and kill somebody that has insulted this idea they have. This God or prophet. So, they go into Denmark and spray the place with guns.

So, can you take all these people, with these ideas, and put them into modern democracy? What's going to happen? Stuff will happen. All kinds of stuff. And I don't think there's any guarantee that it will work. You take all these systems that have evolved, and I think we continue to evolve, religions evolve, where did this come from, it came from that, pretty much it's a big circle. Does it make any sense? It doesn't have to. People will kill for it and do kill for it.

A regular consequence of war, which we will explore further in the chapter on Rights, is fear of a group of people. Today, our fears are of people from majority Muslim countries, as well as people from Central and South American countries who may be here illegally and involved in drug trafficking. Typically, however, people are simply coming to America for refuge and a chance at a better life.

This was the case for my second cousin, Lampros Kakitsis (b. 1941). Not only did he arrive in America as a refugee, he came illegally. Today, being illegal in the United States is considered a grave offense, often garnering mistreatment from authorities when discovered. In the 1950s, however, it was safe for my cousin to turn himself in. Rather than be deported, he was given instructions about what to do next. (Note: *The grammatical mistakes he made due to English being his second language remain in his statement.*)

I left the island and got employed by Greek shipyard. The ship [went] from Italy, and then to America. After quite a few trips, I decided to stay out and live in America. There was trouble among themselves in Greece, and I didn't go back, I stayed here [in] Norfolk, Virginia. Then I came to Pittsburgh, and, naturally, I couldn't speak English.

There was no trouble, but first time, I came in illegally, like anybody else. Then I went to Immigration and told them I'd like to stay in America . . . two, three years [later], and they told me I have to leave the US and go another country and have someone sponsor me to come back legally to this country. And I did that. I went to Dominican Republic, and I stay there for few months, and I couldn't speak their language, but rapidly I learned the language, and now I speak very good Spanish, and I go to work in some places, there, in order to make a living and to make the money to come back to America, because I didn't have nobody to sponsor me. But lately, I make my own, and, naturally, after I marry my wife, as you know, I became American citizen. Now, I am American citizen, and legally entering into the United States.

Lampros eventually became a serial entrepreneur, opening several successful bars and restaurants in and around Pittsburgh. When I interviewed him, he shared some of his latest venture with me, Greek food for lunch-time vending machines all over Pittsburgh. The rice pudding, in particular, was phenomenal.

Dave Chicoring spoke on the topic of war and discrimination as well. He told me he met some German POWs, and as his family got to know them, he realized that they were people, just like him, caught in a war they hadn't themselves declared.

And I can still hear the declaration of war to Japan [on the radio]. It was a serious thing. And we knew it was going to affect us. In fact, that farm, grandpa's farm, later on, in the war, there were German prisoners of war that lived in Lake Odessa, which is southeast of Grand Rapids [Michigan] . . . we'd go down in the truck and get 20 or 30 of them, and they'd work in the onion fields. They did beautiful work, and they had one guard . . . and grandma would say, 'These are just guys, these are just boys, they don't need to sit out there.' And so, she made a thresher's meal, what you might call a thresher's meal. Lots and lots of good things. They sat down and had a meal with the family before they went . . . Grandma actually got into trouble. Daisy was the type of person who never had an enemy in the world. She was a good person, through and through. After the war the Germans would send a Christmas card, a gift, to grandma, that sort of thing. But she got into trouble, I don't know how far it went, for consorting with the enemy. But I think in the final analysis humanity prevailed.

POLITICS

"We don't have enthusiasm for the future, or hope. Because we are too affluent, and we have everything. It comes so easy, so I think we probably lost the spirit and desire to do something to better yourself, or better your country."
— Yoko Mossner

There were some subjects that I expected would come up over and over during interviews. Technology's effect on relationships, child development, and communication I'm sure has crossed your mind — they've certainly graced the media more than once. There were others, however, that I was not prepared for. The most notable of these is politics, and it goes to show that I am the product of my era when something so obvious was unnoticed by someone who was actually looking.

The first time it came up was in an early interview in Birmingham, Alabama. Actually, it was a surprise interview — totally unscheduled and the result of happenstance. I was visiting my partner on an out-of-state work assignment as an opportunity to conduct more interviews and was taking some time alone in a local cafe. The woman at the table across from me complimented my earrings and we got to talking. She introduced herself as Barbara, a fellow entrepreneur and boutique owner. I told her I was visiting Birmingham for only two days (perhaps my northern accent gave me away) and, when asked why, told her of the research I was conducting in the area. Being an entrepreneur teaches one to evangelize a bit, as you never know what may come of it. In this perfect example, her response to hearing I was interviewing elders was, "You should interview my grandma and great-aunt!" When she heard that I was in town for only one more day, she immediately called and left a message with her grandmother. She told me they're very busy women, and had an event to attend that afternoon, so to cross my fingers that they might make time.

Barbara soon had to leave the cafe to pick up her sons from school, but she left with my phone number and promised to call. One never knows how sincere strangers are, but not long after we parted, I received that call. Could I be ready in a half hour to be picked up to go to the retirement community where her grandmother and great-aunt live? I sprang into action, packing my things and speed-walking back to the hotel to retrieve my recording equipment. Soon, Barbara was waiting in the hotel turn-around with her two sons, and off I went in a car with a complete stranger.

Bettilew Turk Gaskell and her sister by marriage, Ann House Veren (b. 1931), met me in a sitting room off the lobby of their community. They were dressed for a luau, the traditional Hawaiian dance featuring grass skirts and floral lei necklaces, and Ann made it clear that they didn't have much time before they needed to be at the party. I don't like being late to events, either, so I did the best I could to gather good information without monopolizing their time.

It was Ann that first brought up politics.

Politics, too, [has changed]. Voting, and having the ability to see [politicians] with Television and the interviews and things. When I was growing up you just voted, and that was it. Might hear them on the radio, but not much.

If you are concerned about the country, you should be concerned about the voting. Very much so. Because that's what's makes us what we are. And we haven't been doing so well for a while. And I hope something will change. Hopefully.

Penny Gardner, whom you'll officially meet in the next chapter, is a lifelong activist. She paid close attention to social media's impact on the 2016 election.

> Many times, like Twitter did in this campaign, they got a lot of media around [the election]. It doesn't matter if it's good or bad. Just talking about it is worth it. Do you know what I'm saying? The Twitter stuff shows the power of that platform and how it is assumed that stuff on it is true . . . but I guess it's the same thing as newspapers or radios . . . and that's technology, too.

Edwin Gould, whom we met last chapter as he told stories about engineering the first spy satellites, reflected similarly on tech's effect on politics.

> It has certainly changed politics. The communication, the TV I mean . . . Have you been to the Holocaust Museum in DC? [*I nod.*] Ok, you know the first place you get off at the top of the elevator, if you pay attention — and particularly because I lived in Germany — you have to wonder how in the world did they ever get those good people to support the things they were doing. And I'm not just talking about the holocaust, of killing Jews, I'm also talking about 'go attack Poland.' How did they ever convince them to go and do that?
>
> That first aisle does a really good job of showing how media was used to do that, and to shape the minds of good people to do evil things. I think our society is greatly affected by whatever agenda the media decides. They can sway things tremendously with how they spin things and how they decide to do [it] and get away with departing from the truth quite a bit . . . So, I think technology has changed our politics a lot.

I'm not sure if there ever was a time that the media wasn't spinning the news, but the elders I interviewed seem to think it has increased. Certainly, being able to regularly see and hear political officials makes a massive difference in the building of trust with their constituents. The 'if you don't look like me, I don't trust you' vein of thought is of greater consequence today than ever before because we have nearly unlimited access to photographs and videos of our politicians.

Patriotism has changed as well. When I met the Gale's in Grand Rapids, Michigan, they first asked me a lot about my own background. As an anthropologist, I've been taught to be a fly on the wall, observing but not influencing. I was uncomfortable, at first, as they asked me about myself, but their point was fair — if I ask about them, why can't they ask about me?

Both Douglas (b. 1927) and Thelma (b. 1930) Gale lament that patriotism has seemingly decreased over their lifetime. They reflected on community turnout for parades, the energy that their community had during and after World War II, and how a lack of patriotism may be affecting our youth. Thelma opened the topic.

> I think that people back in the Depression . . . of course everybody grumbled during the Depression, they were very upset with the government, and I can remember when Roosevelt came in and everybody said, 'Oh, he's going to turn things around.' And he did. There were a lot of things that he did do right, and there were a lot of things that he did do wrong. As a child, I remember my parents were Republicans, proudly, and so they didn't like what Roosevelt was doing most of the time. [*laughs*]
>
> The people back when we were young were very patriotic. I don't see that patriotism, now. People loved the USA because they came out of the Depression, things turned around, and they have been wonderful

ever since. If you can get out of bed in the morning and go to work, no matter how small a job, but make a living. We have wonderful blessings in this country. The patriotism that I saw back when I was a child, and then during World War II, we would have an opening prayer in the morning before school, and the pastors would come in once a week from seven or eight different churches in town and they would have a message. All of it was patriotism for our country. They would say 'God bless America' with all their hearts.

Then we pledged allegiance to the flag, we did that every day, and we meant it. I did, and most of the kids did, too. There was no goofing off or making fun of it at all. Everyone was very patriotic . . .

Somewhere somebody decided that you shouldn't have to pledge allegiance to anything or anybody, and that's the attitude nowadays. I'll do it my way, not your way.

Thelma's husband, Douglas, thinks that it's because of technology that children aren't growing up with as much patriotism that we once had.

[I was in my jewelry store] when Kennedy got shot. I remember somebody brought us the story that Kennedy had just been shot, and we had never had a President shot in our lifetime. And nobody came into our store . . . for the rest of the day. The whole town, the whole country, was in total shock.

Patriotism in this country . . . [isn't the same] with young people like it was when I was growing up. [We did] anything you can think of to help the war [effort] . . . You couldn't get kids to do that today. You couldn't get them to lay down their computer long enough.

I feel for what Douglas is saying. I too have observed young people who seem to have their phones glued to their hands. As an anthropologist, I think there's more to the decline in patriotism than just being distracted, but the distraction of the phone, television, and other devices beeping and hollering for our attention definitely affects motivation. It also provides more information than we've ever had before, some good, some bad, which may have affected the younger generation's view of the country.

I suppose that implies that our media didn't provide as much give and take, good and bad, before social media and the Internet. It is much easier to know more about someone today without ever having met them. All one must do is Google search their name, and everything they have ever done publicly, and sometimes privately, comes up. If someone is running for office in my district, I have access to their entire history. Before the Internet, books and newspapers reigned, and it was much harder and took much longer to do this kind of research. And so, it was left to the media. Perhaps that is why the media was trusted more before television and the Internet. Journalists had access to documents and spent months researching a story. In many ways they still do, but the chatter of social media dilutes their effect.

RIGHTS

RACISM

My interview with Ann House Veren and her sister-in-law Bettilew Turk Gaskell took place in Birmingham, Alabama, the center of some of the most important civil rights events in the 1950s and 60s, so I expected race to come up at some point during the interviews. Unfortunately, oral history can at times be murky, whether because of the storyteller's own accepted beliefs or a specific wish to obscure the truth.

I didn't get much in response from Bettilew when asked about the riots. This wasn't surprising — it's likely not a subject discussed with outsiders. Though we are both white and female, I'm a northerner. Please do not read an accusation of racism here. For someone who lived through the era, it was an extremely complex time period affecting more than just what the news covered. For someone living in Birmingham, this was everyday life, and things were changing fast. At times, one may not have entirely understood what was happening or its ramifications. It's easy for us to look back, now, and pass judgment, but when a person is in the middle of an upheaval, all possibilities are still available, and one just tries to be the best she can.

This assumption on my part is supported by the story Bettilew told me of her maid, Ethel. Ethel worked for the family for over 20 years, until the children were grown and the family need for her had faded. By the time Ethel's story came up, Bettilew's daughter, Gail, had arrived at the assisted living center and was sitting with us, listening. She nodded along, affirming her mother's words.

> One day I had a phone call and this young lady said, 'Ms. Gaskell, my mother is Ethel, and we are in

Detroit.' And she said, 'For quite a while she has not really known what is going on, but once in a while she will say the number "TR14230." I just decided to call it and it finally dawned on me that it was your number.' And I said, 'Well, how is Ethel?' And she said, 'Well, she's blind and . . . she's alright, we're taking care of her. But I just wanted to say hello.' And I said, 'Well, may I talk to her?' And she said, 'Well, no, ma'am, not today. She don't hear well.'

But Ethel was quite a card. She was so funny. [She called the children] "Miss Gail" and "Mister Billy," I was "Miss Gaskell," and she'd ask me to come in and see if the room was clean like I wanted it. Always trying to please. And every hat and every pocketbook I [gifted] her you would have thought came right out of Sak's, she was so excited to have a new hat to wear to church.

I paused to ask when Ethel's daughter had made that phone call, and she supposed it was the late 1970s or early 80s.

I always wondered when she died. One day she was out sweeping the yard and Billy had his Cowboy outfit out there, and had his guns and things, and said, 'Ethel, I'm going to shoot you!' and she said, 'Lawd Mister Billy, don't shoot me!' 'Yes, and when I do shoot you, you should fall down.' And she [told me], 'I knew if I fell down on that ground I would never get up.' [*laughs*]

[One time they] were walking around the block and this dog came out and barked and, 'Miss Debbie climbed up me faster than I thought anybody could climb!' 'Cause that dog was after her.

At this point Gail jumps in, "She respected us, and the respect is no longer there between blacks or whites. There was always that respect, and it was mutual respect." Bettilew continued,

If she wanted me to check something she would [say], 'Scuse me Miss Gaskell, I don't mean no harm, but would you come and check the kitchen floor and see if it's like you like it?'

I had to make her go home. She worked eight hours, all day long, 50 cents an hour. She felt like she was [part of the family]. The time she told me finally she had to only work two days a week and I said, 'Well, Ethel that's fine with me.' I just kept her 'cause I hated to not. And the children were coming in and out, the grandchildren, so it was quite a help for me to have her when she could come, but finally she had to quit working. Well, they moved out of Birmingham to Detroit. [She was] about seven years older than I am.

I had to tell her about how to handle all the new fabrics that came out, 'cause she would bang that iron [on them] and I said, 'Ethel, let the iron do the work. You'll kill your shoulder banging it. Just let the iron go.' . . . She was old enough to remember the kind [of iron] that went on the fire, so she didn't understand [the new irons] could get the job done no matter what.

The story about Ethel was their way of showing me the way things were. Ethel received a fair wage and was treated kindly, like family. But the South had its own caste system. They didn't invent it, and Birmingham wasn't the only place in the United States that it prevailed. Fifty years later, in the suburbs of Detroit, my parents would forbid their teenaged daughter from dating a black boy, to my express shock. Old cultural habits die hard, and often, their perpetuators don't realize they persist.

I met Mary Muscatello (b. 1929) at her home in New York state. She was joined by her husband and daughter for her interview. Sadly, though I attempted to interview her husband, a recent head injury made it impossible for him to provide a cohesive narrative about his time as an FBI Agent and attorney, and his interview was unusable.

They had lived through integration in Arkansas. She saw it happen in real time, but just like I propose regarding those who lived it in Birmingham, she didn't realize its impact until years later when she was no longer in the same culture.

> Living in Little Rock, Arkansas . . . [there were] changes like where the blacks were getting to go into the high school for the first time, so we were feeling the vibes of that, but we were supporters of that. After seeing [the movie] 'The Help,' [I realized] we lived it, and didn't fully realize the impact that it had until we came back home [to New York].

The Internet has often been called the great leveler. As we explored in the chapter on War, it provides access to information without prejudice, allowing the masses access to what is happening for people across borders, boundaries, and races. Word travels like fire across platforms like Facebook and Reddit when police brutality occurs against minority communities, with mass shootings, or hate crimes. Users of social media are able to spring into action to aid those in need, to fundraise, protest, or call politicians. Users who expose their hateful believes are often called out by others, boycotted, or blocked. It is a driving force for change.

The day after the 2017 election, a campaign to make others feel safe began via social media through the use of safety pins. Worn on the lapel, they were meant to be a symbol of an ally to minority groups. Rapidly, the symbol was co-opted by hate groups or used to identify allies in attacks. Again, social media spread the word within days that the symbol was no longer a safe one. Perspectives of people from a myriad of backgrounds continue to be shared across the Internet in order to truly understand the needs of someone who looks or feels different than oneself.

A few days after Bettilew shared her fondness of Ethel in Birmingham, I sat across from Shirley Tate (b. 1938), her sister, Charlotte, and brother-in-law, Tom in Louisiana. Shirley spoke of "the help" in the same way that Bettilew did, but read closely. Her sister, Charlotte, will expand on Shirley's words below, casting them in a new light.

> [My grandparents] lived on a large farm that I can really remember well. All their children worked on the farm, as well as black people in the fields . . . On daddy's and momma's farm . . . we had colored people to help us as well. Daddy went, once a year, when the crops started coming in, to Pascagoula, Mississippi, and he picked up a family of people to come and help us. It was the same family every year . . . Some dropped off and more came on as their children got older. The Pierre family. They helped in the fields and they also helped in the house with the washing and the ironing and with momma's children. We had six in our family . . . The colored people were really, really good. They loved all of us, and we loved them, and daddy took them, every Saturday . . . to Ponchatoula to go to the show and buy things that they needed and everything. They were also allowed to have their own garden as well as eat out of our garden . . . and there was plenty for them to eat out of the field and out of the gardens. They were a big help to momma. They stayed through until there wasn't anything else to do, and they would have stayed longer if daddy could have afforded to feed them, but they kept their garden and as long as they had something to eat they stayed. They loved it out there. They loved it on the farm.

After Shirley spoke, we took a break. Then her sister Charlotte Lawson (b. 1946) took over. Charlotte's description of where they grew up conjured images of the dusty roads in the segregated town of Atticus Finch.[14] Soon it was clear that her reasons for giving her history and thoughts to this book were about more than preserving pre-tech history. By the end of her interview, we were all in tears.

> I was born in Lizard Creek, Louisiana, at home. I was delivered by my daddy's brother. He delivered me, at home. Whoever happened to be there did the job.
>
> Our life in Ponchatoula was wonderful. Every store along here were drug stores, shoe stores, clothing stores, movie theatre, a variety store . . . You can't shop here, anymore. There was a grocery store in town, [only] one, and everybody went to that one . . .
>
> You were safe. We lived six blocks from the middle of town, and when I needed to go to town I hopped on my bicycle and rode back and forth. In the summer time, there was a library here, and I would fill my basket with books, take them home, and the next week I'd come back and get me another bunch. There was a swimming pool here, and I'd go swimming once or twice a week. But when integration came along, the black kids came and [we] were mixed. They closed the pool. They didn't just close it, they filled it up with dirt so nobody could use it.

Charlotte went deeper and deeper into the details of her story. She, like me, was unable to understand the racial bias of her parents. But unlike mine, her father was a true and active racist.

> [The] things that I was thinking about since I talked to you [on the phone to confirm this interview] are number one, like Shirley said, black people were called

---

[14] Harper Lee, *To Kill A Mockingbird*, (Warner Books: New York, 1960).

colored people. We did not eat in restaurants with them. I knew when, what you call the movies we called the picture show, and they were upstairs, and I never knew how they got up there. But I think there was something out back and they went in there . . . and we never saw them, and they never saw us.

Now there's a little restaurant on the corner over here that I used to eat lunch at when I was working. What you would call a pharmacy we would call drug stores and I would come and eat there. There were no colored people where we ate. They ate in the back, in the kitchen. We never saw them, they never saw us.

After we moved to Ponchatoula, and daddy built a grocery store, most of our business was colored, and once a month when their check would come in, they would come in and pay their bill. And then for the next month they would charge whatever they needed to eat and so forth. Now, we found out who we could charge to and who we couldn't, and they learned. I would say 90% of our business was colored.

The colored people lived in quarters, and that comes from the days of slavery. Their living area was called colored quarters. Well, in Ponchatoula, we had three different quarters, and they each had their own name. I don't remember the name of any of the quarters . . . but they had their own church, their own little grocery store, like ours.

One day I was playing in the canal across the street from the house and across the street was where the colored quarter started. A little girl and I were crawfishing with a piece of a meat on a string, and my daddy saw me, and he went over there, and he grabbed me up by my arm and drug me to the house and said, 'What are you doing!? Don't you know that little white girls don't play with little Niggers!' And he said, 'Don't you ever let me catch you doing that again!' My daddy was a racist, of the worst kind.

One day my brother got into a fight with one of the colored boys, and they fought down a block, and my daddy was running along the road while they were fighting. The colored people came across the street and the white people who were there came. They wanted to see this fight. And my daddy hollered at my brother, 'You better beat his black ass or I'll beat yours!' And I was shocked. Totally shocked and upset. I did not understand that kind of thinking.

Typically, those that I interviewed will tell a story like this as a glancing blow example of life as they knew it. But Charlotte went on, alluding to the activities of the KKK and other such organizations.

There were ugly things that were done that were kept from us. And if we asked a question and got an answer, even if we knew it was not right, we did not ask again. And you were to believe what you were told.

Now my sister has many, many family secrets. I've gotten most out of her, but there are still some she hasn't told. Most those things happened in my mother's generation. I found out, for instance, I have a half-brother . . . We had sexual abuse. We had rape . . .

We had a crazy person, but you didn't call them that. You just referred to them as just 'being a little slow.' And we loved them. Every big southern family had at least one crazy person in it. And we just brought 'em out, set 'em up in the front room in front of God and everybody, and we loved 'em. Now, one of my cousins was mentally retarded, but we did not call him that. He was 'a little slow.' And there were a lot of other things that we dealt with that we kept our mouths shut about. It wasn't told. It wasn't supposed to be told . . .

I found out a lot of things by being quiet and just listening. I hid when a man came to talk to my daddy and offered him $10,000 to get on the stand and [say] this [car] wreck they were in, that they weren't playing chicken. But they were playing chicken and the boy lost his arm. And I was listening to this conversation in the alley, and daddy ran him off. He said, 'You can keep your $10,000. My boy isn't going to get on the stand and lie.' He was the only one [who saw it], so they didn't win their case . . .

I was abused, sexually, as a child. But I got over it, and I didn't tell my daddy who did it, because he would have killed him. I told my momma about it after I was married . . . and she said, 'Well, honey, you did the right thing. 'Cause if you had told your daddy, he would have killed him.'

One of my uncles physically abused and beat and beat and beat one of my aunts. And two of her brothers went to see him, and said, 'You beat her one more time and we're going hunting, all of us, back in those woods, and you're not coming out.' And he believed it, and he didn't beat her anymore. That's the kind of thing that happened in my mother's generation . . .

I could see ghosts and demons dancing in Charlotte's head as she recalled these moments. It was clear she had been holding much of this for a very long time. As she spoke, I couldn't be sure if her husband, Tom (b. 1943), knew much of the skeletons she was summoning, though he echoed her feeling about racism.

I think this country needs to band together. We need to forget about black and white and purple and green. We have people of many different colors and races in this country and we need to all live together and work together and help each other and we need to all band together and fight this terror that is coming our way. It's just now started, I think it's going to get much worse before it's all over with.

I wish I could say the racism, gender bias, and abuse she experienced happens less, today, that we're better than our predecessors, but I know from my own experience and the personal stories of my friends that we haven't gotten there, yet.

I live in a community dense with migrant workers. Immigration and migration has been an intense topic in this country for many years. Owen Aukeman (b. 1932) lives in Holland, Michigan, right in the middle of that population, and feels the tension between families that are part legal and part illegal.

I think they say there's 12 million Mexicans... I think it's closer to 30 or 40 million that are here. They have to do something about that, and I think that's going to fall in the Millennials hands, but I don't think anyone wants to deal with it, but somebody has to deal with it. These are people who have children here that are citizens. You can't break those families up. You can't send two of them back and keep the rest of the family here. You can't do it.

GENDER & FEMINISM

Charlotte wasn't the only woman who shared gender bias and oppression with me. Many of the women I interviewed experienced gender bias in the workplace. I, too, have experienced such bias. A year ago, I experienced extreme sexual harassment from a colleague. Social media provided a safe outlet for me to discuss what had happened. I learned so much about my friends' experiences and received tools for handling the situation I found myself in.

Feminism has grown, changed, and shifted over more than a century. It began in 1848 with Susan B. Anthony, Elizabeth Cady Stanton, and other suffragettes fighting for women's rights in the workplace and home but settling 50 years later for the right to vote as a first step into freedom.[15] The Summer of Love in 1967 brought feminism back to the forefront alongside protests against the Vietnam War and the now famous book *The Feminine Mystique* by Betty Friedan. Today, feminism means dismantling a system that oppresses all genders.

When I interviewed Wanda Moore, the former stewardess of Kansas City, I audibly moaned when she told me she was forced to retire when she got married.

> You could not be married and fly in those days, and so
> I had to resign [when I got married].

A week before I met Wanda I was in Detroit, Michigan. A friend of a friend coordinated interviews through a network called Village Crossroads, which provides services to elders in the community, so I didn't know much about the people I was going to interview before I met them. Little did I know that my first day would be spent with an amazing woman named Sonee Lapadot (b. 1936) who blazed trails for women through the Detroit automotive industry, never taking 'no' for an answer.

I interviewed Sonee at her home, a gorgeous ranch of several acres that she had renovated herself, in Bloomfield Hills, Michigan. She gave me a tour, showing me the old orchard that was once active on the property, the deer trails, and horses her neighbor keeps. To me, it looked like paradise.

---

[15] Alan Graebner, *After Eve: The New Feminism*, (Augsburg Publishing House, 1972), p. 35-38.

She started her story in her vigorous manner by telling me about her parents, who were incredibly supportive of what were classified as her tomboy tendencies.

> I had a great growing up. My parents spent six months trying to find me a [college]. My mother didn't understand me because she was raised when you were supposed to be in little velvet bows and rose buds and helpless and my mother was as helpless as an iron rod up her back — and my dad . . . was very traditional. They supported where my head was and where I wanted to go, [though it was] completely foreign to both of them . . .

She continued that her career was deeply affected simply due to her gender.

> I needed a job after my son was born, 'cause if I didn't work we didn't eat, and I went to interview for a secretarial job because that's all we [women] were supposed to do — secretary, nursing, teacher.
> When I was looking for a school, my parents spent six months looking for an engineering school that would take [a woman]. It was legal to say 'We don't take women' [in the 1950s] and they all said it. That was 1954. The last school that we stopped at was the University of Pittsburgh and the guy there in charge of admissions was a classmate of my dad's in college. My mother had a dance studio for 47 years, and I had started sewing costumes at about six. She designed them, cut them, the mothers pinned them, and I sewed them. So, I was at an interview with a shirtwaist dress I had tailored. And he said, 'Why don't you go into fashion?' And we all looked at him like, 'what marble have you lost' and he said, 'No, it's engineering in fabric, and it's

something you're allowed to do, and one of the finest schools in the nation is 90 miles south of you at the University of Cincinnati.' Ok, and I said, 'Well, let me go down for a senior weekend and I can see if that will work.' And I came back and said, 'I can do that.' The first two years of industrial design, commercial design, architecture design, engineering, fashion design, are all the same. Drafting, all of that kind of technical stuff.

So, when I went to interview for this secretarial job when my son was nine days old, they said, 'Oh, we wish you had come earlier, we hired somebody not nearly as qualified as you are.' And, being hungry, and I'm looking for a secretarial job, and so I said, 'Do you have anything else? 'Cause I need to go to work.' And he said, 'Well, we just moved the engineering staff about 25 miles down the road, and what we need there is a secretary two hours a day and a draftsman six.' And I said, 'Would two years of orthographic projection at a college level be enough training?' [He exclaimed,] 'What are you doing with that?' Well, I got the job! I worked there for three and a half years and when I left I was doing preliminary road design and I had [my own] secretary.

Went to Akron . . . I had 17 interviews, I had a letter of recommendation from my boss and from the now Head of Department of Highways because he had moved up in the world, and I never got past the reception desk. 'We don't hire women.' This is now 1960, somewhere around there, ok? Ok, so I ended up back as an administrative assistant, and they finally bought out Ohio Salt, and I was back on the job market, looking for a secretarial administrative job again. I had to take typing and a shorthand test, and by this time I had been doing some very interesting work. I got hired because of the funny background that I was now packing to be secretary to the VP of sales, but my job was to create the sales sheets, so they could be used as an input blank for the numerically controlled machinery.

That company eventually went defunct, and I went back on the job market, and I took typing and shorthand tests again, and now I've had training in programming and systems because I'm writing my own, and I'm a single mother, and I need a job with benefits. So, I looked at Goodyear, and General Tire, and General Motors. And I had to take a typing and a shorthand test to get an interview at any of them. What I wanted was a job in programming or systems, or both.

I finally got to GM, I got past all of that with GM, and they said, 'I think you ought to talk to the Head of HR.' Well, he made me wait 15 minutes, and he came in and I'll never forget that man. Templed his fingers, rolled back in his chair, and said, 'Mrs. Lapendette, why do you reject your job as a mother?' I damn near wanted to cross the desk at him! I said, 'I'll tell you what, if I don't work, my kids live in a tent and we don't eat. I think I'm doing my job.' All he needed was a push-back. He said, 'Well, the . . . Head of Programming and Systems is a youngster, a GMI graduate. He's younger than you, let's see if he'll talk to you.' I got the job. I talked my way into more damn jobs than I had a background for. Today you can't do that, because if you don't have one of the things on the computer on the list you get rejected no matter how qualified you might be.

The odd thing to me isn't that she was called a 'bad mother' for trying to get a job in the early 1960s, but that one of my best female friends, amazing mother, and fellow entrepreneur was told the exact same thing about her career choice in 2016. It's easy to write off what Sonee experienced in the 1950s as a product of the era and feel as if we've come a long way. Yet, as my friend can attest, such thinking has not faded into oblivion, and is not separate from that of 50 years ago.

Feminism as a movement has done a lot for women. So has technology. Ruth Blair (b. 1924) of East Grand Rapids, Michigan, pointed out that the washing machine, a technology we generally take for granted today, liberated a woman's time to focus on career or anything else she wanted, including spending more time with her children.

> One of the things that freed women so that they could have more time to do other things was the automatic washer and dryer. Because I can remember standing there and then running [laundry] through a ringer and having to take it out to a clothesline and clothespins. And you had to iron everything, so, you know, having wash and wear has made a big difference in the freedom of women being able to do other things.
>
> I was a person who made my own clothes at that point. And I made the drapes for the house. So, today, most everything's already made. Those are kinds of things that [has made a difference] in the mobility that women have.

Dagmar Booth describes in even more detail how amenities like the washing machine and dishwasher changed her motherhood for the better.

> A little while later we got our first dishwasher . . . I thought, 'Oh my God, we have arrived' . . . [It] was even better, 'cause with the baby bottles all you had to do was put them in the dishwasher. You didn't have to sit there and boil all the baby bottles. Which was something else. When [our first daughter] was born, you had to wash the baby clothes separate. You had to

boil the bottles . . . [Our second daughter you didn't have to do all that as long as you lived in the city], but you still had cloth diapers. When [our last] daughter came along, oh that was out the window . . . you didn't have to boil the bottles because now you had liners. You just put the formula in the liners and pop it in the microwave oven for 20 seconds for ice cold formula . . . you didn't have to do all that stuff anymore . . . And then [came] disposable diapers.

In a few chapters, we will discuss amenities further, but for now, let's dive into a community that is still fighting for the freedom to choose their own life.

LGBTQ+ (LESBIAN, GAY, BISEXUAL, TRANSGENDER, QUEER) RIGHTS

The LGBTQ+ community is still fighting for basic rights and recognition, mirroring the struggles of the women's movement and civil rights. None of these movements seem to resolve, but they do make progress, little by little. The LGBTQ+ community has fortunately made huge strides toward acceptance over the past decade. The media has played a supporting role, casting characters in movies and television that both show LGBTQ+ people in authority roles and living ordinary lives. Social media has elevated the struggle for acceptance and rights, offering a voice to those who might find themselves in isolation. This is the blessing of chat rooms and online communities.

Many in the Greatest Generation weren't allowed to come out like those in my generation. They walked the conventional path, ignoring their true selves and not allowing anyone else to know. Penny Gardner's story is just that.

I met Penny (b. 1941) a year after I had completed the main research for this book. A friend connected us, and I felt compelled to drive the 50 miles through an icy January in Michigan to reach her. Diversity is critical to the project, and I hadn't yet interviewed an elder who identified as LGBTQ+. A former professor at Michigan State University, Penny had seen it all and surprised me several times during the interview.

Her career started in Washington, D.C. in the very female specific role as a Gaslight Girl. She was then picked up to work as a Playboy Bunny in Baltimore. She was twice married to men, both of whom she thinks of fondly, and has three children. Slowly, she found herself, first through her work in writing and advocacy, and then within herself. When she was 53, she left her second husband and came out as a lesbian.

> I came [to MSU] at the age of 53 to get my graduate degree, and to be a lesbian. I left a family of a husband of 28 years and my kids who, I love this part, although kids are expected to leave, to, you know, move from the house, they were angry. Even though there were a lot of women in my life as President of NOW [the National Organization for Women] and stuff like that, being lesbian wasn't new to [my children], but it wasn't okay for their mom, and it was apparently not ok for their mom to leave home . . . They were in their 20s or 30s. I mean, it wasn't like they were little kids. But they felt like I had taken their home away from them.

Marge Darger acknowledges the changes we've seen in the LGBTQ+ community, especially for trans people, and how these rights came off the cusp of the 'sexual revolution.'

> Of course, the sexual revolution. Right now, we are seeing the, I don't know if we would call it a revolution, but it's very interesting. Right now, we're looking at transgenders and gays and they're coming up and getting their rights.

Others in the Greatest Generation were set against the LGBTQ+ movement until someone close to them came out. Charlie Rusher (b. 1931) was one such man. A widower, I met Charlie at his home one evening in Kansas City, Missouri. He had a lot to say about a lot of things, and you'll get to know him well throughout this book. However, what he told me of his shift in understanding of what it means to be gay was powerful.

> My other grandson . . . I found out he was gay. Back in my time people who were gay were made fun of, and your parents even made you shy away from them . . .
>
> He was in high school and had gone with some girls and everything. He called [my daughter and son-in-law] and asked them, 'Can we meet just the three of us? I've got something really important [to tell you].' And they thought, 'Oh my God he's got her pregnant.' . . . So, he told them that he's gay. It was a shock to us, but it changed my mind 180 degrees. I was not going to give my grandkid up because he's gay. It's completely and totally changed my outlook on the whole thing.

It was heartwarming to hear Charlie talk about his grandson in this way. There are so many, both friends and colleagues, that I have met whose parents refuse to associate with them after their coming out. To hear a grandparent, one step further removed in generation, realize that knowing his grandson was far more important than the label he had been taught to avoid, was beautiful.

Virginia Sears (b. 1915), a former teacher and one of the oldest women I interviewed, aged 100 at the time, also agrees that attitudes toward the LGBTQ+ community have changed over her lifetime, though she doesn't have direct contact with an out family member or friend. She reflects the same attitude that Charlie had when he was young — that perhaps you had an idea that someone was gay or lesbian, but you didn't know for sure and you stayed away from them.

One thing, gay people have come out, now. When we were little, we had a girl that we called a little bit odd, and we wouldn't walk on the side of the street where she was. We thought we shouldn't do that. Walk with her. Walk where she walked. It was kind of funny, but that's the way the kids felt.

You didn't hear about gay people, either. Now they've come out, it's probably better for the world . . . That's one thing that I know has changed so much. In fact, even marriage, which they can marry, now. I always thought they could live together, that's fine, but I guess there's some advantages to them getting married . . . Children, too, I think, [is] quite different than it used to be. Adoptions are different.

RIGHTS

Virginia's comments bring this chapter full circle, back to racism. She is half Japanese American, and both her and her brother Virgil, whom you'll meet in a moment, experienced racism during World War II. Americans often forget that racism means more than just whites against blacks. Yet, there are, in our history, concentration camps for the Japanese Americans who had entrusted our country with their safety.

When I got out of college . . . I couldn't get a job because of my name being Oriental. 'Cause my father was Japanese. They wouldn't hire me, they were afraid. We were having a war, you know, in 1938 . . . Finally, I joined the Detroit Teacher's Agency . . . it was some kind of agency that would get you a job. You had to pay them a certain percentage of your salary for your first year . . . I was working at a bakery in Kalamazoo, and they called me and said, 'You'd better get over to

Grand Haven because there's a job there.' This was in September. School had started. I found a bus that would go to Grand Haven from Kalamazoo and took that. I went out and bought a decent dress, so I would look decent. And so, he interviewed me, and the super-intendent said, 'Well, there's seven people for this job, so I'll let you know.' And I thought oh, there goes the job, they won't hire me because of my name. But the night before I went to this interview I was waiting on two gentlemen in the restaurant, and they happened to be two professors that I'd had, and they were psychol-ogy professors. I was so excited, I told them I had an interview for Grand Haven, and they were excited, too, for me, and they said, 'We'll wire the superintendent there immediately, and we'll recommend you.' And I said, 'Oh, that's beyond thought!' I didn't think any-one would do that for me. And they did, and I'm sure that's why I got the job . . . Nowadays they would send an email. See the difference? Technology!

Mary Lou Aukeman (b. 1933) grew up in California and remem-bers seeing the Japanese internment camps as a young girl.

In the early 40s, all the Japanese were taken and had to live [at a camp] . . . The internment camp that I would see was on the fairgrounds in Stockton. You'd go past there and there were big fences and you'd see people walking around in there and living in there. It's amaz-ing that that could happen.

Virgil Westdale (b. 1918), Virginia's brother, also experienced racism and prejudice during the same period in the Air Force. In fact, he was removed from the Air Force, despite having some of the highest marks in his class, because of his Japanese heritage. I really felt his disappointment when he told me how he lost his flying license because it was something he had wanted to do since childhood.

So, I went into the advanced program. The second day I walked into the terminal, and the lady said, 'Virgil, someone is here to see you.' And I said, 'Oh, who's that?' And she said, 'An inspector.' I said, 'An inspector? What does he want?' And she said she didn't know. I wondered about that, and I asked, 'Well, where is he?' And she said, 'Over at the top waiting for you.' I thought that was kind of strange. She said, 'He didn't want to talk to you with the other instructors around.' That worried me a bit. I knew he couldn't wash me out of the program because I was a top flier.

So, as I was walking out, she whispered under her breath something about a license. And I said to myself, a license? Oh man. And I started thinking about what they were doing with the West Coast [Japanese] people. They were moving them, you know? So, I walked over to the tower and climbed the tower steps, and Mr. Humphrey was there. He was the inspector. I'll never forget that name. He opened the door and he said, 'Well, it's good of you to come over, Virgil.' [We] shook hands, and he said, 'I have to ask for your license.' Well, I waited for an explanation, and he didn't give one. He didn't say another word. Of course, my dad always taught us to obey the authorities, and don't ask questions, and so on. So, I reached in my pocket, pulled my license out of my billfold, and gave it to him. And I worried about what he was going to do with that, but he said, 'I'm sorry.' So, I walked down without my license. Walked across the field. I felt about that high [gestures close to the ground]. And I knew I would have to tell all my friends that I was out of flying, probably because of my nationality, but I didn't tell them that.

I didn't know for sure why they pulled it, but I had a good idea. So, then I left. The instructors just couldn't believe it. At the time they felt I was probably the best flier they had ever graduated from acrobatic flying.

They kept my license for five months. That's a long time to be without a license and not flying. You can't fly without a license — it's not like driving a car. You get in a car and away you go. You have to show your license every time you jump in a plane.

During the meantime, then, I did a lot of thinking. I thought, 'Why did they take my license? Probably because of my nationality.' That's hard to believe, now, you know. That would never, ever, happen again. But it did, then. Although they never told me, they never, ever told me that. Isn't that strange?

I went to court and they translated my name. Not changed it but translated it to Westdale from Nishimura. [Virginia] changed hers, too, I think. Nishi means west, and mura means village. Well, you can't say Westvillage for a name . . . so someone in the family long before . . . the war, someone mentioned 'how about hill and dale?' . . . instead of village, so we thought that would be a pretty good translation to English. They were always asking us, 'Well, how do you spell that?' and then 'What kind of name is that?' We got tired of that, eventually. That was back before the war.

Alright, so, I translated my name to Westdale, and I can't tell you the exact date, but it had to be 1942, and then I went to Romulus field right here in Detroit, joined the Air Corps, held up my hand, Virgil Westdale — they never questioned anything. Now, if I had looked more Japanese, they may have asked all kinds of questions, but they didn't. Not me. In five months, I got my license back. Did they tell me why they had kept it? No, not one word. Not one word.

They gave it back and I continued flying. Went through the whole program for a year and a half. I was so good at the instrument flying and so on they asked me to be an instrument flier.

Virgil would eventually be ordered to go to Mississippi to join the 442nd Combat Team. To this day, they are the most decorated regiment in the history of the United States — and they were all Japanese Americans.[16] At the time, Virgil didn't know how it would turn out. No one would tell him why he was moved away from flying, but he could see that the entire regiment was comprised of Japanese Americans.

It was a regiment of Japanese Americans . . . So, I walked into the company office, the First Sergeant Officer, and he looked up at me. He was Japanese, but American. He said, 'What can I do for you?' I said, 'I'm supposed to report here.' He thought I was in the wrong outfit because I didn't look Asian at all! In fact, in his book, he mentioned that I looked Caucasian to him.

To me it seems a private joke on the government that a regiment they formed based on discrimination ended up being the best they've ever had. Virgil was a party to liberating Dachau Concentration Camp, though they were told to wait for another regiment so the Japanese Americans wouldn't get historical credit. He told me of seeing men in pajamas eating a dead horse on the ground, not totally understanding what he was seeing at the time. He had many stories like that — so many that he wrote a book about his time in the war called *Blue Skies and Thunder*. He is yet another elder responsible for bringing tears to my eyes during our time together.

---

[16] Wikipedia, "442nd Infantry Regiment (United States)," https://en.wikipedia.org/wiki/442nd_Infantry_Regiment_(United_States).

TRANSPORTATION

"When I look back at the cars we had in those days. What a dif-ference. You talk about technology . . . When you would drive in the mountains there were certain places you could stop and [there was] a cement trough that you could stop to get water. The front of the car always had a little place to put water in, and sometimes all of a sudden, the thing would almost explode with steam coming out, so then we would stop and find a place to get water and pour it in and go on our way, again. That's quite different from what it is, now."
— Mary Lou Aukeman

Fifty years ago, this book wouldn't have been possible. Cultural-ly, a woman couldn't have traveled the United States alone and been welcomed into so many strangers' homes as an authority researcher. Technologically, I never would have reached them in the first place. The phone and computer allowed me to make the connections, but it was our advances in transportation that allowed me to visit 40 states over six weeks. While I had to use two different rental cars because the oil light came on halfway through the journey, I had no breakdowns, flat tires, or any other problems. The vehicles performed perfectly, and what's more, they were luxurious in comparison to what our elders knew, as shown in several of the following interviews. I could Bluetooth (wirelessly connect) my music and map from my iPhone into the car stereo, sleep in the comfortable back seat between in-terviews if needed and saved money with amazing gas mileage. Even something we take for granted, the key fob, still has some of our elders fascinated.

I tend to think like our elders in regard to transportation. Airplanes continue to strike awe in me every time I come in contact with them, even though I grew up with them as a normal part of my life. I fly several times a year and spend spare time at the airfield to watch take-offs and landings, neither of which has reduced my impression of their magnificence.

Some months ago, while traveling through Chicago, I arrived early at O'Hare International Airport for my flight to Europe. Rather than enter the airport, I found a grassy area to sit in just outside the airport where the ascending planes passed overhead. One after another renewed the grin on my face, all fantastic demonstrations of engineering and human creativity. One in particular made me exclaim out loud that day. It was a large international plane, so big that its ascension path was shallower and slower than the others. From my vantage point, it looked close enough to touch, as if it had barely cleared the building between myself and the runway.

How can we not be in awe? Only 75 years ago, these machines were used only for very specific purposes. The general public had no business being on an airplane. Consider how complicated these machines are, how large, and how many things must go right in order for them to fly. Add to that how completely unable we humans are to accomplish this feat unaided and you start to get the feeling our elders had when they first experienced planes.

Airplanes are an incredible part of the evolution of transportation, one that took centuries of development to achieve. Just as with all other technology, it is important to start at the beginning of transportation's development: our own two feet. For nearly our entire 2.8 million year[17] existence on this earth, humans have been migrating and traveling simply by foot. Today, the Hawazina Bedouins of Sudan still travel this way, migrating across an average of 300 kilometers a year.[18]

---

[17] Wikipedia, "Human Evolution," https://en.wikipedia.org/wiki/Human_evolution

[18] Muhammad Suwaed, *Historical Dictionary of the Bedouins* (Rowman & Littlefield, 2015) p. 91.

Domesticated horses have been a part of our history for a comparative blink of an eye. Evidence of horses being used by humans first appears in 3500 BCE in Europe.[19] For the first time in human history, we were able to move large quantities of goods or heavy objects. In 1200 BCE, the chariot appeared in Asia.[20] It was first adopted as a status symbol by leaders, but soon evolved into a major battle advantage for soldiers, ubiquitous to war for 600 years, only giving way to the more mobile mounted soldiers. It took hundreds of years more for the saddle and stirrup to come on the scene. The stirrup was originally developed in China around 200 AD and aided warriors in staying on their horses during battle.[21] The stirrup remains important to riders, today.

Fade-in to Bob Johnson (b. 1937). He is a family and couple's therapist, still practicing in Salt Lake City, Utah, at the time of our interview. We met in his office, full of driftwood art that a friend had given him. Bob was sharp and kind, a pleasure to listen to.

When he was a young man growing up in Ontario, Oregon, he had a pony that he used for shooting and riding, harkening to a lifestyle rarely seen today (and what may seem the stuff of storybooks to those of younger generations). That's not the most interesting part of the story, though. This horse, named Smokey, wasn't a horse born and bred on a farm. Smokey had been purchased by Bob's father at a wild stallion auction — and broken (tamed) by the family. If you have ever seen the Disney movie "Spirit," you have an idea, albeit biased, of this horse's origin.

> I had a horse. I had a horse I could shoot a shotgun off of, which is amazing. Dad bought this pony, in fact, at

---

[19] Wikipedia, "Domestication of the Horse," https://en.wikipedia.org/wiki/Domestication_of_the_horse

[20] Keith F. Otterbein, *How War Began* (Texas A&M Press, 2004) p. 166-172.

[21] Wikipedia, "Stirrup," https://en.wikipedia.org/wiki/Stirrup, 2018

a wild horse roundup for ten dollars. And he broke it, and it was my horse. Every spring dad would get on the pony and it would buck him off, and you'd have to settle it down before I could ride it again, but that was Smokey. That was my horse.

I want to show you a picture of Smokey. Can I? [*proceeds to show me a black and white photo of him with Smokey.*] That's me on my horse. That's Bobby on his horse, Smokey. It was a nice little quarter horse. And he wasn't a large horse. It was a little bit hard riding because he was a wild animal that we bought, that they were doing a roundup of wild horses, but he was my horse it was just fun to have that as part of my life.

So, that was my life. The first car I had I paid $70 for, and it was an old Oldsmobile, a black two-door Oldsmobile. And then I remember buying a '42 Ford, but that was cool because the sound was so cool. That cost me $150 dollars. So, you know, it was a different world.

Bob spoke highly of Smokey, saying that, once broken, he was a very trusty steed. I, on the other hand, had to remember to shut my gaping mouth at this point in the interview. Even though I knew better than to be surprised by the stories I heard, I still was. Smokey would have been captured 70 years ago. That's not so long ago, not by a long shot. Still, I didn't think wild horse roundups happened after the Roaring Twenties. I have been trained to imagine the 20s full of Model T's and women dancing at clubs in Manhattan, and then the Dust Bowl of the 30s with lines for credit at the grocery store. Smokey's time was during the 1940s: fighter jets and bombs, not Cowboys and Indians. Somehow, pop culture has trained us to think of wild horses belonging to Mark Twain's era — the 1800s — a bygone era not belonging to those still living today.

Bob wasn't the only person I interviewed whose main mode of transportation was horseback. Hal Royer of Kansas also rode a horse to school. In fact, he had a photograph of the family horse, too.

> That pony that you saw [a picture of] a moment ago I rode to a little country school . . . I tell my grandsons and my great-grandsons, 'You know I rode a horse to school.' And they roll their eyes and say, 'And it was uphill and in the snow both ways!' Well, it wasn't snow. That was back in the really drought years, when Kansas was blowing away. I recall, probably the second grade, 1934, a big dust storm rolled in and we didn't have lights in school. So, we had to dismiss school. I think there were three other kids [who] rode horses. I had about a two-mile trip home, that's about all I had . . . The kids that lived further away from the school [the teacher] took in her car and took them home. The kids that could walk home, they left to walk home. But she didn't worry about us kids on horseback, because horses know the way home.

Horses were where human dreams of transportation began. Before we tamed and bred the horse for carrying goods and ourselves, we had to walk. Horses expanded our horizons. Though they were not the most energy efficient mode of transport (we had to feed them and care for them), they grew on their own, requiring no assembly on our part aside from breeding.

Yet, humans are always dreaming of broader horizons. As shipping engines developed, so did our ideas about ground transportation. How might we redevelop that engine to motorize our horse-drawn buggies? Imagine the leap of creativity it took to see the everyday transport of buggies and carts, but moving on their own. It's the same leap that changed shipping from wind and oar powered to steam and coal powered engines.

ENGINES

"In high school, we took a school trip from Tokyo to Osaka ..
. it took all night to get there by train . . . Now, a bullet train
[gets you] there in three hours."
— Yoko Mossner

Ruth Wilson was the daughter of missionaries and grew up in Congo. For her, transportation often involved the steam engine of a train. During her interview she told me that the cross-continent trains would sometimes stop for no apparent reason. I can imagine younger generations being upset at such delay. I imagine everyone pulling out their smartphones and impatiently browsing the Internet, ignoring their seat-neighbors. Ruth describes a very different reaction to these delays.

> In my day, everything was rail . . . And the line was from Cape to Cairo, it was a direct line . . . At one time, you had borders, and everybody had to have a passport to cross over, I remember. We would go through the Belgian Congo, so you had to have the French stuff, you know, but otherwise it was very slow. Any railroad was very slow. And it used to stop for no reason. And everyone would pile off to see if it had run out of water or if there was an animal crossing the line. We would all get off to see. And if it didn't move on for another two hours, so what? There were no deadlines.

The horseless buggy was just becoming mainstream during the childhoods of those I interviewed. As with Bob and Hal, not every family had one in the early 1900s. Yet, some elders did have the luxury of a family car and being driven to school instead of walking or riding horseback. Virginia Sears was driven to school every day, but her story was heartbreaking to me. Cars weren't reliable in the way they are today. The cold affected them greatly, as did heat and anything else the machine felt like being bothered about that day.

> We finally had one of those touring cars, a Ford Touring car. I can't remember the year. I wish I'd remember the year, but I don't remember the year that we got it. But it had side curtains, and you didn't have any glass in it. It just had side curtains you'd roll up in the summer, you know? You'd roll 'em up. In winter, you put them down. It didn't have very good heaters, so it was pretty cold.
>
> When I went to high school, the car wouldn't start. That old car. And we had to drive four miles to high school — we didn't have any busses. And so, we'd drive, and that car wouldn't start. You'd have to get a jack out and jack up that back wheel and crank it. Crank the car. And then you'd get it going and every day I was late to high school and the principal would say, 'Same excuse, Virginia?' and I'd say yes, so he didn't do anything to me. And we'd try to get there on time and it was always late. And I hated driving up in front of that high school 'cause all the kids could look out and see ya coming in late. I hated that. But that's what happened.

Walking, our oldest mode of transportation, was the surest way to get anywhere. To today's students, a five-mile walk to school one way may seem outrageous, especially when municipalities provide school busses. In Onalee Cable's day, there wasn't even a bridge the bus could use to get to the school. Onalee (b. 1930) is Native American. She grew up on Mackinac Island in the "Indian Village" (officially Harrisonville), a cluster of inland homes formed as the Ojibwa Natives were pushed by the whites from the attractive coastline, now the touristic quaint boardwalk. The school she attended was on the mainland, five miles away across Lake Huron.

> [School on the island] only went through the tenth grade. And I did that, I completed that. Then we had to go St. Ignace, on the boat, to go to school . . . As a poor student, I would take a boat from the island to St. Ignace to go to school in St. Ignace, Michigan. And the school board paid for that. When it got so bad that the boats wouldn't run, we would cross the ice with a sled or [skates] and go to school over there. When the weather got too bad, we couldn't go . . .
>
> When Christmas was over . . . we would take those trees down on the water's edge. The old timers on Mackinac, men who were familiar with the ice — 'cause we were right in the middle of Lake Huron — they would check the ice to make sure it would be safe to cross the ice to go to St. Ignace. There were no boats, and flying was expensive. So, people would put their Christmas trees out on the beach. When the men would start checking the ice to see if it was safe to go all the way over they'd use these Christmas trees to mark the trail to St. Ignace. When we walked over there, it was a four-and-a-half-mile walk. So, when we would walk over there, if we had to pee, you'd go behind those Christmas trees! [*laughs*]

Today's technology can digitally measure the thickness of the ice. Onalee supposes she would trust the meter but refers back to her neighbor who would walk his horses across the ice to the mainland. "If it was safe for horses, it was safe for us."

Onalee's transportation evolved over her lifetime. On Mackinac, there were no cars allowed, and she was accustomed to riding her bicycle everywhere. When she moved to Detroit and began working as a phone operator for Bell Telephone Company, she continued to ride her bicycle to work. She laughed as she told me about her husband's first car — and how she wouldn't ride in it.

> He bought this car 'cause his family owned the Lakeview Hotel [on the island], and in those years they would get a little dividend every year. So, he bought this old Hudson. So, we're driving around Rocky Mountain North Carolina. Before we moved there, he had this car in St. Ignace, and I had grown up in Mackinac with no cars. When he first got this car, I wouldn't ride in it. I said no! He was going to go down that one hill and I said, 'No!' 'Cause I had never been in a car . . .
>
> My brother came home. He had his car, and we go downtown St. Ignace in that car, and he pulls into [a] snowbank, and I said, 'Oh my God! It's the first car accident I have ever been in!' He says, 'You're not in a car accident, you're in a snowbank.' [It was] some kind of living.

Betty Segal, whom we first met in the discussion about drones being used as weapons, remembers one of her father's first cars. She recalled what qualified the car as "out of date" or "high-tech" and laughed about it during our interview.

> Father owned a Ford, briefly. His cars came and went, depending on his finances. But at one point we owned an old Ford that was [already] old at the time. I had a cousin that laughed at it, because even then it was out of date. A year before he died, we bought a car that had a plugin cigarette lighter, which I was fascinated by. It was high-tech. But a lot of the time the cars that we owned had to be cranked by hand in front, which was always a problem. There were no heaters — going on a trip in the winter time was an adventure . . .

I bought a very fancy leather seat Honda, which is a very sedate sedan, but new. New. And partly I bought it because I love the technology of the door clicker. I had rented door clickers and I love them. You can have the door unlocked when you get there. And it has all kinds of fancy gadgets. And lots of safety features, which I always like. I was early adopting seatbelts. When I married my husband, he had a car that didn't have seatbelts, and I insisted on having them installed, 'cause you could buy them and have them installed . . . I like the technology of safety.

Ruth Harper (b. 1942), a former teacher in Grand Rapids, Michigan, is a wealth of information with a steel trap mind. Today, she runs a book store with her sisters called the American Opinion. She grew up as cars did and saw how things changed. She described the development of cars in a manner that weaves a story.

Heaters in cars. They didn't start out with heaters, and they certainly didn't start out with air conditioning. They didn't start out with safety glass. Getting in a car accident was much more dangerous going 35 miles an hour with a car where the glass would shatter if you happened to hit something and would go through that glass, and then we had these long, knifelike pieces of glass . . .

Henry Ford was very distressed when he would hear about somebody going through one of his windshields and getting [their] jugular cut. So, he went to his engineers and one by one he's saying, 'You tell me why we can't make glass that doesn't shatter.' And they'd say, 'Well, yeah, glass by its nature...' and so on. He went through all the same gobbledygook . . .

He went out on the factory floor and started talking to people and one of them said, 'That's a really interesting question. I don't know. It doesn't make sense that it couldn't be made more flexible or something.' And Ford said, 'I'll give you an office, phone, books, raise your pay. You find that for me, and I'll make you rich.' And so, the guy went at it — of course, he had to have a lot of glass and a hammer — and he'd be breaking it and noticing things, and there were these patterns and stuff. And then he thought if it's kind of like grain on wood, just supposing that we took these two pieces and we did this with this to them, and by gluing them together you get some lines going this way and lines going this way, and you get little squares instead of shards.

I learned about that in the '37 Ford . . . A pebble would hit the glass and days, weeks, months later, the glass would have turned a milky blue, and that's a natural question. 'Pa, why is that?' . . . And you'd get the whole story. He might do it by backing up a little [by saying], 'That's the glue from between the layers of glass . . . They haven't figured out how to get a glue that won't get opaque when it gets wet.'

So, cars last longer, go faster, all that. Now they're putting numerical limits on the roads, but I think they're getting wiser about that. Because a few years ago Michigan did a whole lot of speed checking, they had those counters across the road, and you remember the result [was] they raised a lot of speed limits because they said they were going that fast anyway and they weren't having accidents, so let's do it. But there's the other camp that wants to make things harder and slower and more difficult and more expensive all the time, [and] they go along and put these extra burms in the road.

FLYING

"I remember very well the first airplane I ever saw was an old Ford Trimotor. Would you have any idea what that was? Old propeller-driven plane. And it had one motor in the front, and a couple out on the wings. Really high-tech stuff! [laughs]"
— Hal Royer

Many stories I was told were about transportation to school, likely because they were the earliest memories of those I interviewed that could be compared to today's transportation. As transportation has evolved, so has travel and its affordability. Ann Atkin (b. 1934), a former teacher living in Kansas City, Missouri, reminds us of this when she admits she never thought civilians would use planes for travel.

> Planes were just starting to make intercontinental flights [when I was a child]. Lindbergh made his flight across the ocean in '27, so it had only been eight years that we had been able to do anything like that [when I was born]. I remember out at our airport in Springfield, [Missouri], the Fancy Fliers would come through and give shows, and we would go out and look and 'ooh' and 'ahh' at biplanes and wing walkers and all of that. But we didn't fly. I never thought we would. Nobody ever dreamed that we would be hopping on planes without any thought and flying to Australia . . . The mass population did not foresee anything like what we have.

Indeed, Lillian Carrara (b. 1937) of Long Island, New York (whom you will learn more about in the chapter on Generational Proximity), thinks that travel has become far more available to the general public, and certainly easier to take advantage of, than when she was young.

> I've been able to travel all over the world, which [is] thanks to technology. Airlines were not always that available to people when I was growing up.

Ruth Harper reminded me that when planes were new, children would run outside just to see them flying by because they were so novel. That was entertainment. Again, many never imagined they would actually travel on them as a normal means of transportation.

> There were very few airplanes, so there was no jet or jet stream or contrail or whatever. When we heard an airplane, us kids would run out to look at it. And sometimes, because it was wartime so there was a little more activity, sometimes we'd see planes in formation. So, they'd be flying in a design, or whatever. That was our excitement, that kind of thing.

Enter Dot Hornsby (b. 1934), a hobby pilot and flight teacher. I met with her at Barstow Airport in Midland, Michigan. She told me that, as a youth, she wanted to see the world.

> Where I grew up people just kind of stayed put, which my parents did . . . Even in high school, I wanted to go around the world, which I got to do.

The generation before hers would have found it nearly impossible to imagine such experiences without also considering abandoning their home and never returning. It was only the rich that could afford summers in Paris and the two-week voyage across the Atlantic to get there.

Dot grew up as flight travel did. After World War II ended, flight travel increased in popularity. It became possible, and much more affordable, to cross the Atlantic by airplane. By the time Dot came of age, flying to Europe was a tangible aspiration.

Dot's high school sweetheart and husband was an Air Force pilot, whose career made some of Dot's earliest world travel even more possible.

He was in the military, ROTC [Reserve Officers' Training Corps]. In those days you mostly served your country after college or after high school. So, it was a program called ROTC in college . . . After Cincinnati, we were in San Antonio, Texas, and Wichita Falls, Texas, and that was because of his Air Force. And then the assignment was Nouasseur Air Force Base in Casablanca, Morocco, which is no longer there. So, that's how we got to Morocco. We were there about two years. He got an early out because things sort of became no military conflict in the area at the time. So, we came back . . .

He had played professional ball before he went into the military, but he didn't get to play in Morocco, that was the bad thing. We were hoping for Germany where he could play baseball for a few years, but Morocco was just isolated. We did learn to play golf 'cause there was nothing else much to do . . . We did try baseball when we came back [to Geneva, New York], but at that point he was 24 or 25 which, nowadays, is old for a baseball player, plus he had no bonus, so he had nothing to invest in.

So, back to Cincinnati where he got his master's. I taught school, and then what brought us to Midland [Michigan] was that he joined Dow Chemical . . . He was sent out to sales offices in Charlotte, and then Chicago, and then back to Midland, and then Hong Kong . . .

Dow would do job trades within the US. For a year you would go to someone else's house. You'd trade, actually. So, ours was the first international [job trade]. I still remember when he came home, we were living in the city we're in now, and the kids were in the family room, and he brought me in the living room, and he knows I love traveling, 'cause even in high school my goal was to go 'round the world, which I got to do. There's just something in me that I love those foreign places . . . So, he took me in the living room, and I can still picture it. He said, 'How would you like to go to Hong Kong for a year?' 'What!?' [*smiles*] Now the only bad thing was I'd have to quit my job teaching. They wouldn't give me a leave of absence.

An interesting job trade that we got to Hong Kong . . . I'd get up one day a week and volunteered at the local school. I didn't teach English, but just to have an English-speaking voice because they all had to learn English. So, it was a wonderful year. [Except for] that day [of teaching], I'd get up in the morning and get on the double-decker bus, take ferries to all the islands. I could go on and on. We had a chance to stay over there, but our boys . . . we wanted the American education.

On our way home, I took the older boy, and my goal was to visit all those countries that you usually don't get to . . . A sixth-grade kid going around the world with his mom, what does he want to do that for? So, I said I'll let you pick two places that you want to go. He wanted to climb the Eiffel Tower, which he got to do, I don't think I did all the way up, I forget what it was. And he wanted to see Lenin's body, you know, in Moscow. So, we did accommodate that, but most of our stops were the Far East . . . And then my husband came back 'cause he was working for Dow and brought the other two boys back. So, that's how we got around the world.

When we lived in Hong Kong, that's when you couldn't get into China. I would go to the border, and you could look across, and there was a train that would take you, but you had to get off there . . . I remember going to the border and seeing those Chinese, and thinking I'm going to get back there someday. So, that was when Nixon . . . was doing Ping Pong Diplomacy. But Americans couldn't get into China . . . So, I went back [to China] by myself in '88 or '89 and spent three weeks by myself . . .

Not many women my age [got to do that]. Most women my age did the work . . . But I had such a supportive husband that said, 'you do what you want,' which in those days was not the standard. Most of the husbands, the corporate husbands, the wives were doing their stuff. And he said, 'Do whatever you want to do.'

Tragically, Dot lost her husband in 1992 after a year of battling cancer. After a term of depression, Dot chose to become a pilot, herself. This was not just because her husband had flown. Her father had also spoken in awe of planes when she was a child. It was also a way for her to continue teaching and adventuring.

It was my grief therapy. That was therapy. Since then I've helped kids, I founded this Midland Aviation Camp, it was perfect . . . Family influences you . . . My father would be driving in the car, in those days it was a crank down window and I put my hand out, and you know how your hand goes up if you stick it up? He'd say, 'That's why airplanes fly.' But he never really went into anything more.

> We would go down to the local airport. It used to be Lunken in Cincinnati. Now it's a big airport. We'd watch planes. Not a big, big memory of that, but that had to be what probably influenced me, you know, when I was in such grief to think what would be good.

In the mid-1990s, the small planes that Dot was flying and using to instruct weren't equipped with the latest technology. Dot became well-versed using steam gauges and paper flight plans. Since then, GPS and other technology has totally changed the profession. She's had a front-row seat to the changes to aeronautics over the past 30 years. Certainly, things have become easier with automation, but Dot worries about her student's ability to read a map in an emergency.

> When I learned to fly there was no GPS . . . Even when I would travel and would get out of an elevator in a strange city, [I had to consider] would I be able to find [my way] back to the hotel? What a comfort, now! And with the flying my fear was that I wouldn't be able to find Midland . . . I've got autopilot, now . . . I think about the days when I would fly to Florida . . . without GPS, [with only] paper charts, so when I would go to Florida . . . I would have like seven paper charts and you had to unfold them, and one would [overlap the other]. If you get off course, you wouldn't know it. You'd say, 'Does that lake look like that lake?' Now there's no paper charts. You get a subscription on here — everything is on the iPad. So, we've got that. I've got another GPS with a moving map. I've got a Garmin, so three or four redundant backups. I couldn't get lost ever again.
>
> I still fly by . . . steam gauges. You look at the cockpit, the round little [gauges]. Nowadays there are two pieces of glass in front of you. I'm too old to learn it.

It's called the glass cockpit and all the instruments are on there. So, that's what the younger kids are learning on. It'll probably be like cursive. They won't be able to go back and fly by what we call steam gauges.

Dot is not the first and will not be the last to raise the question of what would happen if the electricity or other amenities went out. The worry our elders hold is that without knowing the old ways we may someday find ourselves at a dead end, unable to get food, find our way, or contact loved ones. The last time the power went out like that in my life was 2003.[22] The entire Northeastern United States and Canada had a power blackout, ironically due to a software issue at First Energy in Ohio. It was historically the second-largest blackout at the time. I spent much of it with my best friend at her family's home just down the street from my house. We watched a movie on the laptop until the battery ran out. Then we made our own fun. What does that say about us, that even in a blackout we turned to technology for entertainment?

THE FINAL FRONTIER

I had the good fortune of interviewing both Dagmar Booth and her husband, John Wilkes Booth, in New Orleans, Louisiana. Though I requested they not influence each other's interviews as much as possible, they still, at times, tag teamed their stories. I enjoyed the dynamic, watching how they have formed a strong team after years of marriage, finishing each other's thoughts and adding strength to them.

---

[22] Wikipedia, "NorthEast Blackout of 2003," https://en.wikipedia.org/wiki/Northeast_blackout_of_2003

John (b. 1945) worked on the Saturn V as the pneumatic and cryogenic technician for Boeing, and, in fact, showed me the full-sized model still on display outside of New Orleans, Louisiana. Dagmar broached the subject during the interview.

> When we first got married we got to see the moonwalk. We got married in May, and I think it was July [when] we were sitting in the living room watching on the little black and white TV trying to watch the moonwalk. 'Cause John worked on the Saturn V.

"That was a rocket and a half," followed John.

> Oh yeah. It had to go 25,000 miles an hour in order to get out of Earth's gravitational pull. And that rocket put two men on the moon. It brought an automobile over there . . . the moon rover, you know. I worked on that son of a gun . . .
>
> Space helped us out a lot. Look what we got outta space. CorningWare, that's one thing.

"That's true, I love my CorningWare," replied Dagmar.

> You know where we got CorningWare, right? The space tiles. The tiles on the shuttle and all. Teflon. Microwave ovens came out of that radio technology. And that was an accident I think in a lab where a guy had . . . a candy bar in his back pocket [which] melted. And this was back in the early 50s. We didn't get the microwave oven until the 70s. So, that's how long it took to develop the technology to bring it into the house.

John resumes his story about working on the Saturn V, always the card.

We fooled around over there a lot. With the cryogenics over there, you had nitrogen that was boiling at 240-some-odd degrees, and you fooled around with liquid helium, that was about 270 degrees minus, you know? And that's what we did.

Now, when you leak tested something that was going on the Saturn V, you had to go ahead and use liquid nitrogen, because the molecules in liquid hydrogen are smaller than the other compound over there in liquid. If you put liquid hydrogen to a specimen and it didn't leak, and you could hook it to anything and it wouldn't leak. But if you tested with liquid nitrogen, it didn't leak, then you'd put liquid hydrogen on it and it'd be whistlin' Dixie!

They used to go ahead and take my lunch and put it in that liquid nitrogen and freeze it. They could go ahead and pound [my banana] with a hammer. Oh yeah. You drop a banana in there and pull it out man you throw it on the cement and it'd pop a million pieces.

"Like glass," finished Dagmar.

Lillian Carrara thinks back to when we first started the Space Race, and how her mother reacted to landing on the moon versus her own reaction. It seems a good example of the different intergenerational reactions to technology that I discussed in the introduction and begs the question: Is there a point at which we stop learning (or wanting to learn) which, in turn, creates a social barrier as technology and the world evolves?

And, of course, the technology of going to the moon and everything. My mother used to say, 'Ah, that's not good. We don't need to go to the moon.' But I never felt that way. I felt that there may be something good that comes out of traveling to the moon and I'm thoroughly interested. I don't know. I don't study astronomy, but I'm thoroughly engrossed in it. My niece, who's a physician's assistant in Ohio, when she comes here we go out on our upper deck and we lay out there and watch the stars and watch the shooting stars and we're very interested . . . I think good things have come out of the astronauts traveling to the moon. I think they researched and [have] done all kinds of medical technology and food. I do feel that something good has happened there.

ENERGY & AMENITIES

"In those days we used candles or little paraffin lamps. We had no phone system whatsoever. I remember when the radio came in. We were living in Africa when I was young. My father used to bring the battery in from the car and plug it in at six o'clock at night, because that's when the news was on. They never had anything on during the day. You'd be half-killed if you talked during that . . . BBC time. And that was the only way that we kept up with [World War II]. There were times during the war you couldn't get mail from overseas. We were just cut off completely."

— Ruth Wilson

For some of those I interviewed, technological development in our amenities could be simple and still be amazing. Recall Betty Segal and her love for the simple key fob on her car. I take that for granted, but her eyes lit up when she told me about her amusement with it. She also told me of another technological advancement that many in my generation do not appreciate.

There's another technology that I like. I've been thinking for years that I want to write a letter to some kind of professional organization . . . What I want to do is write a letter to thank all the industrial designers, and little designers, who do things that make life so much more easy. The example that I would like to use in the letter is detergent bottles. Laundry detergent bottles. It used to be that they had lids — you poured the stuff into the cap, you pour it into the washer, you put the cap back on. What was left in the cap ran down the sides. It got sticky. If you kept it on your washer, it got on your washer you had to wipe it up. Somebody invented a laundry detergent cap that, when you put it on, drained back into the bottle. That is such a simple thing, but it makes life easier and there are technical designers out there who do that every day, and I just want to write a thank you letter to them.

I grew up in the time when you didn't have detergent, you had lye soap . . . made in the pot. And my mother didn't have a washing machine, she washed the clothes on the scrub board, and had big, big laundry tubs that sat on benches out under a tree. [Then] she got a washing machine that had just the rollers that you could roll it out and then you would put it in the sink and rinse it out.

It's unimaginable to younger generations to do laundry like that. We take washing machines and pre-starched clothes for granted, but many argue that the washing machine was a major leap for women and feminism alike.

When I sat down in front of Etcyl Blair, whom you met in the chapter on War, I didn't expect him to tell me that he'd worked on chemical weapons. While that was the most surprising, he still found other ways to catch me off guard. Where he grew up in Northern Oklahoma, the oil companies used to give away natural gas. For free. Though I've done my best to be generationally knowledgeable, in this moment I was the product of my era. I grew up with oil wars in the Middle East. I am used to price fluctuations for gasoline. I remember it cost 88¢ a gallon when I was a child and watched astonished as it shot to over $4 a gallon in 2012. Natural gas has always been a part of the conversation on natural resources during my lifetime, especially since fracking grew in popularity. But in front of me was Etcyl describing his childhood in Oil Country.

The nights would be full of light because they burned all the gas when you drill for oil. In those days they didn't collect the gas. Today we are collecting the gas. And so, they would flare that stuff off at night. The house that I grew up in didn't have electricity. It had gas lights. Everything was run by gas, which was worthless at that time.

It's easy to take the amenities we enjoy today for granted, especially if we are born into them. We have prioritized them so highly that there is financial support available from government and private organizations alike to those who cannot afford them. Even cell phones are provided to those who qualify for welfare. It seems the stuff of Laura Ingalls Wilder to consider life without electricity, gas, or running water. But today there are still living thousands of The Greatest Generation who grew up without a car, phone, electricity, or running water. In the North, heat came from wood or coal when it was needed, and even then, sometimes it was an expense not afforded by the family.

Ruth Harper, the former teacher born in Grand Rapids, Michigan, has only lived in two houses her entire life, both old enough to have been heated by coal. She explains that her father had to sometimes choose the type of heat the family would afford during winter.

There was a radiator in the bathroom, radiator in the kitchen, radiator in the dining room, and the living room, and the bedrooms were supposed to be cooler anyway, right? [laughs] So, it worked fine. Every so often the coal man would come, because that's what you burned, mainly. He had all kinds of chutes on his truck, and we had one basement window that was bigger so that you could open that, and he'd send the coal down the trough. And when we had sufficient money we bought anthracite, the hard coal, and then it wasn't dusty and stuff. But if times were really tough we'd have to get a softer coal, and then there was a lot more coal soot and dust and stuff and . . . Pa wasn't happy when he had to do that.

One woman that grew up without electricity, running water, or an indoor commode was Onalee Cable. Onalee's childhood home on Mackinac Island had no electricity or running water. When water was needed, she or one of her siblings would go to her grandparents' home up the hill, which had a water hand pump. The toilet at their house was an outhouse that her father built. The stove in which her mother would bake several pies a day to sell was heated with wood.

> We were a poor family. Poor. I remember the house we lived in. It was called the Moses Home. I don't know if it was a house that had been repossessed by the city but [we had] squatter's rights. My dad got in there, a big old building, not much roofing. Bedrooms, we slept four or five together. No water. We had to go up the hill from our house to my grandma and grandpa's house and get a tub of water then pull it back down to our house. That was for drinking, bathing, cooking, laundry, the whole works. We didn't have water in our house until, I think I was six [or] seven years old. Other than that, we had to go get our water.
>
> Then we moved from that old house up to the yellow house. We thought we were in the rich area. No bathroom, outside toilet, but my dad had one put in. No tub though, for a while, just the toilet . . . There were seven of us kids, so it was not always easy.
>
> [My mom] had that old wood burning stove . . . it would be 80° outside, and she would have that old stove all heated up making pies [to sell].

Onalee wasn't the only person I interviewed who grew up with a communal drinking source. Hal Royer's grade school in Kansas just had a bucket and ladle that everyone used.

> The kids in school, we all drank out of a big bucket. Had a dipper, and a big wooden bucket we would bring in from the well. How we lived through that I have no idea. [*laughs*] 'Cause we surely passed, anybody who had germs, we surely passed it on.

Many of the elders grew up with outdoor plumbing or out houses instead of toilets. Douglas Gale and his wife, Thelma, also lived with an outhouse at their home in Michigan and reminded me that it was a very cold way to take care of business in winter.

> We rented a cottage on Muskegon River, and you talk about cold. We had an outside toilet, and it was cold in that outside toilet in the winter. That was one of the coldest winters in a long time.

ELECTRICITY

Indoor plumbing became mainstream in short order, and slowly, electricity did, too. Electricity affected indoor plumbing in a way we take for granted today — hot water. A friend once asked me what amenity I wouldn't give up if the apocalypse happened. I said hot showers and baths. Juanita Laush (b. 1923), whom you'll truly meet in the chapter on Medicine, describes life as hot water became available without boiling the water over a fire.

> I think primarily [what has changed is] electricity in the house, and hot and cold water in the house. The first time I visited my in-laws near Pittsburgh, they had a pump outside and an outhouse. My New Mexico

family had the same thing. They didn't have water in the house — it was a pump outside. I think that electricity probably changed so much of [life].

For some, the arrival of electricity was nerve-wracking, even scary. Downton Abbey,[23] a show set in early 20th century Britain, features several episodes of electricity being introduced to the protagonists' home. The cook, Mrs. Patmore, was unnerved by its abilities and was ardently against its arrival in her kitchen. She argues with her assistant, "Why would we need it?"

"It's a mixer. It beats eggs and whips cream and all sorts," replies the assistant.

"You and I can do that."

"I'd rather not to thank you very much."

"You don't understand," Mrs. Patmore complains, "Before too long, her ladyship could run the kitchen with a woman from the village, what with these toasters and mixers and such like. We'd be out of a job!"

Mrs. Patmore's character was representing the very real reaction that many had as electricity and electrified machines became mainstream. I return to Hal Royer, who was in the middle of it all as he grew up in Kansas.

We had electricity when we lived on the farm area. That had been granted to my grandfather — great-grandfather — for this electric railroad. They gave him electricity. And that was totally new to the whole neighborhood. We had some friends that wouldn't come to the house because of the electricity. They were afraid it would sneak out of the circuits and get them. Really, I'm serious! They couldn't come to the house . . .

---

[23] http://www.worldcat.org/title/downton-abbey-season-4/oclc/862013173?page=citation

> When we moved away from there, we didn't have electricity, per se. We had wind power. So, when Pearl Harbor [happened], we didn't have any wind for a few days, so our radio didn't work, so we didn't know that Pearl Harbor had happened until the following Monday morning at high school . . .
>
> Wind power's not new. It wasn't very reliable then. I hope it's more reliable now.

That our earliest power lines would spark during the dust storms which defined the Great Depression didn't help the confidence people had in electricity. Hal grew up in the Dust Bowl. As he stated in the previous chapter, dust storms would interact with power lines and create sparks. I had just seen the movie Interstellar at the time of his interview, and his description of life in the Dust Bowl reminded me of the situation in the movie. Of course, the movie used stories from the Dust Bowl for its own purposes, but I didn't realize just how exact it was until speaking with Hal.

> I remember riding home [on horseback] in this godawful dust. I went by the power lines of this little electric train . . . and the dust created sparks from that. It just scared the horses to death. Boy, it was like little bits of lightning coming off of those high-tension lines . . . but we got on home alright.
>
> Those days are just unimaginable today. Mom hung wet towels and so forth in the windows, kind of filter out the dust, and it didn't work very well. Better than dust. Even to this day, I find myself rinsing a glass to make sure the dust is out of there.

Grace Stinton of Midland, Michigan, reminded me that radio was an utter novelty, an invention that came with electricity, which was at first unreliable.

> I think my mother and dad had the first radio in town. People came to our house to listen to the radio.

We had electricity, but we also had oil lamps because you never knew when the electricity would go out. And we all had little Sterno burners for cooking because the electricity was there, but it just wasn't reliable at that point . . . If you had a storm, you just knew that the electricity was going out. And you were prepared with your oil lamp and your little Sterno cooker.

As Hal and Grace described, the radio not only enabled homes to receive to-the-minute news, the radio also became a source of entertainment. Families would sit around the radio at scheduled intervals to listen to their favorite shows. Do today's children even know what it means to wait until a certain day or time to catch a show?

Ruth Harper illustrates the radio schedule in detail.

We had no television. There was a radio in the house and there were stories on the radio in the evening, and so we would listen to those. You know, like Monday, Wednesday, Friday was the Lone Ranger, and Tuesday, Thursday, and Saturday was the Cisco Kid at the same time as the Lone Ranger, so you could get one or the other.

Dave Chicoring continues this topic during his interview by Devil's Lake in Wisconsin.

My grandfather's house was just getting electrified, and they had their own electric generator previous to that. They had a windmill to pump the water up to a tank. Elevated, so they had water pressure. We had a radio, and I can still remember grandpa turning on the radio and we could hear President Roosevelt saying, 'These are the days we'll try men's souls.'

Electricity allowed for many, many innovations besides the radio. It wasn't until recently that I realized my family still owns the icebox that my great-grandparents used in their home. I always assumed they used an icebox, just like the rest of those in their era, but seeing it, touching it, and bringing it home with me as an heirloom as we prepared the family homestead to sell made their history so much more tangible.

Thelma Gale remembers what life was like in her family's household while they used an icebox. It's a reminder of two things. The first is the transportation of the day. The second is that salesmen were common and wouldn't necessarily come to the door.

> I can remember when we got our first refrigerator. We had had an icebox. The iceman came in horse and buggy, would go by the house and he would call, 'Ice man Ice man!'

Where I stay in New Orleans, there is a man known as Mr. Okra who still sells his vegetables in the quarter in the same manner. He drives through the streets yelling, "I've got okra! I've got cucumbers!" Whatever he has that day, he yells. It's a rare practice today, but it was common in the age of our grandparents and earlier.

HOUSEHOLD AMENITIES

With electricity came another innovation, one that Dagmar Booth mentioned in the last chapter: the microwave. This is another technology that many of us take for granted today. Dagmar describes the marvel of having one in her home for the first time and how it utterly changed everyday life.

> There was a place on Elysian Fields called Stone Lumber. John had to go over there one day to get something,

and they were giving demonstrations on the micro-wave . . . The guy put a potato in there and it came out three minutes later and you could stick a fork through it. A hot dog, I think, was 40 seconds or 30 seconds. I was like . . . what!? So, one day, John was at work . . . They had the Litman Microwave oven [on sale for] about $158 bucks. So, I called them . . . I said, you know, you've got an ad in the paper for such-and-such, and he goes yes ma'am we do, and he asked do you want that one or the one with the defrost feature? I said well how much is the one with the defrost fea-ture? And he said, and I said can you deliver that to-day? And he said yes ma'am. I said how much do I owe you, wrote out the check. The guy delivered it in two hours. Just long enough to [take] everything off the kitchen counter, put it in the corner, and it was big.

[John] came home from work and he goes what the heck is this? And it's like it's the microwave oven we saw at Stone Lumber. And that night I could actu-ally take a plate of food, take everything out the pots, fix his plate, and put it in the refrigerator. He came home at 11:30 at night in those days, and all I had to do was put the plate into the microwave oven to heat it up with wax paper on top. I didn't have to have a little pan for the potatoes, a little pan for the meat, a little pan for the vegetables [from] supper and it would sit on the stove until he came home, put it on the stove, go take a shower, it's heating up, he'd take a shower and sit down to a hot meal. You didn't have to do that anymore . . . So, that was fantastic.

Just as Betty Segal alluded at the beginning of this chapter, one of the biggest time-saving innovations was the laundry machine. Yes, there are some machines that qualified as laundry machines before electricity (my great-grandmother used the hand crank machine and tubs that Betty described), but they weren't as time-saving as the electric machines.

I met Adrienne Bard (b. 1935) in New York, and she described something not so obvious about the innovation of the washing machine — the change in our standards. Just as we have created funding for anyone who needs these amenities, though we used to be satisfied to live without them, our idea of what is acceptable in the home has also changed. This is an idea we'll explore more in the chapter on Poverty.

> [I was visiting a friend] and someone from social services or some other agency was there that day to see her about something, and [the agent was a] young gal. And she said, 'Well, I'm going to have to go back to my office and see about that.' She said this in regard to the wringer washer. She said, 'I don't know if that's legal or not.' [*laughs*] That one took the cake. I don't know if she'd ever seen one . . .
>
> Still, so many things these days . . . are push button, and even though [we have these] conveniences, a lot of people still burn wood in the winter time. But still, people that have oil furnaces or burn propane, the heat just comes on and off, so long as you get your tank filled. But your heat just comes on and off. You don't have to carry the wood in, you don't have to take the ashes out . . . there's so many different conveniences now.

At first, these conveniences were expensive. They took machining and welding to create, usually by talented tradesmen. Today's technology allows us to injection mold many of our products, and the advent of plastics has made this process even faster and cheaper. This means more access to these amenities, but, as many of the people I interviewed pointed out, things don't hold up the same way they used to. Ruth Harper laughs as she describes that these things used to last and last.

> In my time there were toasters, but they lasted forever. [*laughs*] No dishwashers, initially. We didn't have a refrigerator, but all my friends did . . . and when we got a refrigerator, it opened up great luxuries because we could make ice cream . . . things changed in that way. No microwaves, no plastic wrap, in fact very little plastic. Plastic was coming in after the war.

Though plastics have made mass production possible, and our products cheaper (monetarily and in quality), they also have another consequence — plastic is derived of oil, a limited supply resource. Without oil, plastic is a challenge. We have made advances using cellulose (corn) to make cups and compostable silverware, but I still recall being outdoors at a music festival and watching my cellulose cup melt in the sun. Dave Chicoring reminds us, however, that there is only so much that can go around, especially with such oil-based products. If we continue to grow without innovating and diversifying, we will eventually run into a wall — a very catastrophic wall.

> We have a finite world with a finite supply of fossil energy, whether it be oil or coal, a finite amount, but we have increasing population and much increasing demand. The one line is going down, the other line is going up, and that can't happen. We cannot accelerate our ways of dealing with the environment. We have to instill generational timelines on this. Otherwise, it will crash. And I think an optimist will say, 'Yes but humans are smart. They will adjust to it,' and I think there are certain things that cannot be adjusted for, whether it be — I don't like the term Global Warming, I think a scientific term would

be Global Heating, because warming sounds good — but Global Heating. If you drive around Iceland, you can see cascades of water coming off the ice cap. The ice cap is almost not an ice cap anymore. It makes beautiful waterfalls, but that's a very transient thing. It'll happen, and soon there won't be ice left on the top of Iceland, and there won't be waterfalls anymore.

So, I'm upset. I think things are coming unraveled quite a bit in terms of the environment. They're burning vast areas of Indonesia. The smoke is overwhelming Southern Asia, the amount of carbon dioxide going into the air. And it's based on economics, and economics isn't moral, necessarily. In economics, if something makes somebody a buck, they'll do it. We cut all the forests here. We cut the forest. We did so many things. It's like being short-sighted. Can you drive fast when you're short-sighted? If you look only one foot . . . down the road? You're in big trouble. And really our economics hasn't evolved very well.

Dave makes very good points about the evolution of technology, growth in population, and energy requirements. This is the moment when I wonder if we will truly listen to our elders — this is the opportunity. Dave has all the authority in the world to speak on the topic. He is educated, an endocrinologist who studied immunology and worked with chimpanzees in a lab, and he has seen more of life than most of us alive today. We were taught at an early age to listen to our elders. These are his words, not mine. Will you consider them?

Hal Royer's family owned a gas station after they lost the farm during the Great Depression. He describes a gentleman who would come to get gasoline every day and was very careful about his fill. I know many young people who also are as frugal and detailed about their purchases, today.

We didn't have a telephone until 1940. This farm, Depression Era, folks lost the farm in 1935. [*Me: Your family did?*] Yes. So, we moved to a small acreage with a little cabin camp. Motel today, a little cabin camp with a filling station with a few 7-11 type, bread and so-forth, in the back of the store. Wasn't very successful. Gasoline sold for ten cents a gallon. We had an old guy that was quite a character . . . He would stop by the filling station there every evening, get two gallons of gas and two cigars. So, he'd spend a quarter for two gallons of gas and two-for-a-nickel cigars. [*laughs*] Every evening. We'd pump the gas into an open area, the old pumps anyhow. Boy he would watch to make sure he got his full measure — two gallons for ten cents a gallon! So, that was different.

The gas pumps that Hal is describing had a large glass reservoir at the top of the pump that held the gasoline. The customer was watching the gasoline exit that glass reservoir to make sure he got every last drop he'd paid for. It was at that station that his family got their first telephone.

TELEPHONES & PARTY LINES

Phones were a big change for those in the Greatest Generation. Most of those I interviewed didn't have a telephone in the home while growing up. Today's youth find it hard to imagine life without a smartphone, let alone a landline, and some may not know what a landline is. One study predicts that, in a few more generations, the concept of a telephone pole will no longer exist in our day-to-day culture. The dial tone one once heard when starting a phone call has already faded from our collective memory, as is picking up a phone to hear an operator ask for your directive. To those in the Greatest Generation, it was the existence of the telephone that was an anomaly.

Despite their hardship, Onalee's family on Mackinac Island was one of the first to have a telephone line installed in their home. This is because her father became an air raid warden during World War II. When he would receive the warning call at night, it was his duty to communicate with the other homes in the village to turn out lights and blow out candles so enemy planes couldn't target the village. This was called a blackout. This, too, is an experience today's youth do not know. I was taught about the duck-and-cover days when I was in school — we even watched one of the instructional videos that showed students how to get under their desks and cover their heads when the air raid sirens went off, but I, too, have never known that fear. Bombs dropping on American soil is not a real and present threat. The panic from the airplanes flying into the Twin Towers and Pentagon on 9/11 is as close as my generation got.

These early telephone lines that were installed in the homes of the Greatest Generation were party lines, or shared telephone lines. One line, one phone number, but that rang to multiple houses.

A game many young people play on the swings is called "party line." I recall in my early school years we used to yell "get off my party line!" when our swings would match movement for a few paces. But in my youth, I never encountered a true telephone party line and didn't know what it was I was referring to until I conducted these interviews. In fact, my young mind had rationalized that the phrase was created because our tandem swinging formed a line, and more than one swinger made it a party. Dagmar Booth describes life with a party line.

Telephone-wise, I remember when we had parties. You picked up the phone and listened. If someone was talking, you had to put the phone down. And the day we got the phone . . . without the party line was like 'Guess what, we can pick up the phone and use it. We don't have a party line to consider!' And you don't have to . . . listen for the click for someone eavesdropping your conversation.

And with the cell phones, who's eavesdropping? God knows who's eavesdropping. The government or whoever. But in those days that was a big deal. Eavesdropping. You'd hear the click. My aunt would say, 'Uh, excuse me, who's this?' And then you'd hear a click, and she would say, 'Please hang up.' You would learn to hear when they would actually hang up and when they wouldn't.

Now when we [got a] cordless phone, we thought, 'Oh my God, a cordless phone!' A phone you can walk up and down the house and you can dust mop and talk, put clothes in the washing machine. That was fantastic! And look what we've got, now . . . [Cell phones] are attached to us.

Some of the stories I heard during these interviews made me laugh. On a party line, several homes shared one phone line, each with a different ring sequence so they knew when the call was for them. However, every generation has its nosey parkers. Party line telephones just made eavesdropping easier. Bob Johnson describes why it was predominantly women who were the eavesdroppers.

What I do remember, in that little house we lived in, is we were on a party line, and there were six families on that line. The only way you knew if [the call] was [for] you or not was by how many times the phone rang. And so, of course — now, this is a sexist statement — all the women knew what was going on in everyone else's household 'cause they all listened to the phone. [*laughs*] It obviously wasn't just the women, except they were the ones in the household when the phone rang [during the day].

I can remember, as young boy, listening to the phone to see how many times it rang to see if it was a call for us or not. That was long before computers, or — in fact, I was a sophomore in high school the first time I saw a television. And that's amazing. I can remember watching a Yankees ball game that was coming across. You couldn't hear the sound. It was just black and white, and you could see the picture, and it was so exciting. It was a new world, and that was our technology.

TELEVISION

Just as Bob says, television was an incredible advance that was fascinating to the Greatest Generation. They were very excited to have the chance to see the scheduled programs or sports games. When the first television came to Dagmar's neighborhood, they would wait with anticipation to be invited to the neighbor's house to experience it.

My family didn't get a TV until I was ten years old . . . the people down the street . . . were the first person in the area to get a TV. So, on a Saturday morning, maybe [they] would call you up and say, 'Hey Dagmar, would you like to come watch TV?' Which we would get up early just to wait for that invitation, because you got to see things like Fury, Sky King . . . and I can't remember the other ones. But that was a treat for us.

Grace Stinton echoed Dagmar's excitement about the advancement of television as she told me about the first time she saw one and what she watched.

Television was absolutely amazing. In fact, I can remember the first time I saw television. It was at my grandmother's house. She had a television and we went over and listened to it and watched it. And the first thing I saw was a very big fat lady singing. And all I could think of was, 'This would have been so much nicer on radio, when I could have been imagining the whole thing.'

But yes, I can still remember that first television and I can remember listening to the radio. *The Hound of the Baskervilles* on radio was much better than watching it on TV, because your imagination did so much with the story. You could just sit there, and your imagination could do a lot more than they could do portraying it on television.

However, television is wonderful. For kids, they have such marvelous programs. My grandkids really learned so much from the programs they have on TV. They learned a lot that they shouldn't know, too, but [*laughs*] some of the commercials aren't that great for them, but they do have the wonderful programs.

This kind of excitement about something new still happens today, when a friend or acquaintance gets the newest smartphone before everyone or receives a game they backed on Kickstarter as a donor reward before the general public. Our innate curiosity takes over and we want to see it, know how it works, and be part of the new wave of innovation.

These innovations in technology affect every aspect of our lives. In the next chapter, we will find out just how far technology has gone in changing how we work, and even what work means.

WORK

"When it comes to the world economy, we have globalization. For those that can profit by it, that's good. And all the jobs that have gone overseas, I'm not happy about that, but that means that some people that didn't have jobs have jobs, now."
— Harriet Berg

How many times have you heard someone say 'technology is stealing our jobs'? I hear it on the news, online, and even from the lips of family members. Holidays are often a little uncomfortable, but my family's Thanksgiving dinner argument over whether or not self-checkout at the grocery store was good or bad for jobs was particularly memorable. To summarize my uncle's thoughts: self-checkout took jobs and made the checkout process slower. It is a net-negative innovation.

I wonder if it's short-sighted to say self-checkout is critically affecting the job market. I'm sure the blacksmith who closed shop because there weren't enough horses to shoe after the automobile became prevalent was upset in a similar manner as my uncle.

I met Sydney Rushing in his Mississippi office one April afternoon. He is equally concerned with low-tech jobs, or trade jobs, no longer being available. He worries that there won't be anywhere for someone who isn't tech-savvy to work.

> Unless they can acquire these technological skills, they're just not going to be able to function well in this new society. There's just not going to be anything they can do, first of all, if they can't fill out the application for the job [on the computer]. If you do get the job, you've got to be technologically savvy to maintain

that job. At the bottom line, unless you can use that technology, you're going to be a lost cause. There's very little that you can do. Perhaps you may be able to get the low-skill jobs and that's all there's going to be. A low-paying job, and that's all there's going to be available. There's not going to be many of the low-skill jobs. [Even] operating the equipment to cover a run out there, it's the new technology of doing that. Everything you do, this is a highly technological society. And it's becoming even more so every day. They're coming up with something new every day. You go to a cash register. They used to have the old cash registers, now they have the cash registers that talk to you . . . It's not going to come. It's here. And it's here right now.

Sonee Lapadot echoes the fear that technology will not only leave some behind, but it is moving us so far away from how things used to be done that we won't be able to function without it.

God knows we've gained the ability to think faster, do faster, get things accomplished faster, test things faster, develop things faster, you know, all of that stuff that the computer allows us to do that we used to grind with a calculator and a pencil. The learning curve has just shot through the ceiling! But you don't want to give up the other, and that's the only thing I worry about.

It is true that some lose their jobs 'too late in life' to make a career shift. We are also losing some of the technical know-how that belongs to labor jobs, as is Sonee's concern. In fact, we no longer have the ability to send a space shuttle to the moon using the methodology we did in the 1960s. The people who invented the welding techniques to create the structure of the shuttle didn't document their knowledge, and most have already passed away.[24]

Still, ageism is a real concern for the Greatest Generation and Baby Boomers. Ageism is a bias a younger person holds that their elders simply can't grasp new tech or concepts and their ideas aren't relevant. This generally isn't true, as several of the elders I interviewed embrace new technology, but it is so common to think this way in our society that it isn't questioned.

Unfortunately, this means that employers often feel that it is easier to force an older employee to retire than to retrain them on new tech. This is not borne out by the numbers. It is a far higher cost to hire and train someone new than it is to retrain an existing employee, and precious legacy knowledge is often lost when a long-time employee is let go.[25] With a new, younger employee, other training issues may arise. Pauline Attisani describes what may happen when a generation grows up using smartphones to manage independent online identities.

> Even though they are polarizing people by having them use all this technology, they want people to work as a team when they have a professional job. So, if they're not trained as young people to work as a team, it's very difficult now that you're a professional and they expect you to contribute to a team.

The fear of job loss and workplace shifts due to technology continues as it has for more than a century. The invention of the

---

[24] Forbes, "How We Lost The Ability To Travel To The Moon," https://www.forbes.com/sites/quora/2015/12/11/how-we-lost-the-ability-to-travel-to-the-moon/#56d723231f48

[25] FosterEDU, "The Cost of Hiring the Perfect Candidate vs. Training an Existing Employee," https://fosteredu.pennfoster.edu/the-cost-of-hiring-the-perfect-candidate-vs.-training-an-existing-employee

sewing machine in 1829, the first machine to eventually enter the home, caused the same reaction that my uncle is having about self-checkout today. Tailors in the city of Rhone, France, burned down the inventors' factory, fearing the machine would make their jobs obsolete.[26]

They weren't the first to protest machinery and it's effect on the job market. From 1811-1816, England saw a movement of textile workers burning down factories that housed new textile machines in order to save their jobs. The movement leaders were called Luddites.[27] Today this term stands for anyone who fears new technology.

Every major invention has been received with backlash. Even today, self-driving cars offer us the convenience of automated grocery pick up, diminished traffic jams, and road trip naps while threatening the careers of truck and taxi drivers. Still, the economy always evolves and there are 'enough' jobs.

Ray Dirks (b. 1932) has seen the effects of technology on farming firsthand. Born and raised in Longmont, Colorado, he was a farmer all his life, eventually inheriting the family homestead. He feels that technology raised efficiency, yes, but has also eliminated some farm jobs.

> It takes a lot of people out of the workforce, this technology. This big combine that goes out and combines many, many acres . . . Nowadays you can farm a tremendous amount of land without many people. It's ridiculous what they can do.

His remarks circle back to the point my uncle was making. Technology does reduce the need for a large workforce to accomplish

---

[26] Wikipedia, "Barthelemy Thimonnier," https://en.wikipedia.org/wiki/Barth%C3%A9lemy_Thimonnier.

[27] Wikipedia, "Luddites," https://en.wikipedia.org/wiki/Luddite&s

large tasks. It also makes our work safer, and more efficient, and opens up new opportunities. As I observe the story arch of our economy and workforce, it seems that the job market is an ever-shifting tide. Jobs are lost every day, whether because a business goes bankrupt or because they were made obsolete by technology. Jobs are also created every day by entrepreneurs and new technology that requires a new kind of management. Is my uncle's argument valid, or is it just another example of our discomfort with change?

WORK SAFETY

My grandmother was considered a 'Rosie the Riveter' during World War II. Sadly, she hardly talked about it. I only know she worked in the shipyard while the men were away at war. World War II required so much manpower overseas that many jobs were left unattended. Some of these were non-critical, but machining and shipping were necessary to the war effort,[28] and so women stepped into roles unconventional for the era. I had the good luck to interview a woman whose summer job in the 1940s was a 'Rosie' job.

Grace Stinton described her factory duties during employment that summer in Providence, Rhode Island.

> I was working in the American Screw Company. We were making rivets. They took me through on a tour, and first of all, metal comes through on wires, and they had them extruded into different dimensions. Then there was a place where they were cut. And then in my department, they were making the little circular pieces

---

[28] Wikipedia, "Rosie the Riveter," https://en.wikipedia.org/wiki/Rosie_the_Riveter

that would make a piece of metal into a screw. And those wires would come down, and all the excess wire would come down into a compartment into a machine they were working on, and my job was to take a great big long fork, like you would . . . use at a barbecue, and sit there and pull out all those extra shavings. I don't think it would even be allowed, now, with the security and the safety laws in the company. But I went around a whole long row of machines, and by the time I finished one row, it was time to go back and pull them out from the first machine, again. So, that was my job, just take that fork and pull those shavings out so that it wouldn't clog the machine. It was fun for just one summer, but it would be terrible if you had to do it all the time.

Many of the people I interviewed made the point that the jobs they held when they were young would be considered too dangerous to do today. Mary Lou Aukeman was one of them. She had a very similar job to Grace during her college years.

While I was at Calvin [College] I worked at Keeler Brass during the summer . . . It was a company that made door handles and all that. There were huge machines that would stamp. You would put a piece of metal on the table in front of you and the huge machine would come down and cut it. That was old technology, I would say, because if you happened to have your hand in the way, you could lose your fingers. So, I was glad I only had to do that for only three months. I preferred teaching. [laughs]

Have our standards changed because the need for the risky task has gone away? Nearly every male in my dad's family worked in the steel mills near Pittsburgh in the mid-20th century. These jobs were dangerous, not just due to the possibility of burns. Yet, no one gave the job a second glance. It was normal work for everyone in the family.

Steel mills, as they were then, aren't the only mainstream career that would be considered dangerous without today's safety precautions. The conditions found in Detroit during the height of the automotive assembly lines in the 1950s would also be considered far too dangerous by today's standards. Having grown up at the turn of the century, my image of a car being spray painted involved a robot. Anyone who has visited Epcot in Orlando, Florida, may have experienced this first hand on a ride that simulates the Ford Automotive Plant. Mid-century workers, however, were spray painting the cars themselves with paints and chemicals that permeated most protective equipment.

Dot Hornsby reminds us of this and of the potential of drones to make working conditions even safer.

> I think technology is good because it's made a lot of our repetitive tasks easier, like on the automotive line, spray painting a car instead of having a human in there to spray paint. I think drones are going to be good if they're used in the right way. I worry about them, as a pilot [myself], but having a drone go into a tanker and inspect if the chemical's gone [is good] . . . Can we clean it with drones? Inspect lines, power lines, with drones? So, I think there's so much good [with technology].

I don't think that societal norms alone can account for the shift toward more safety in the workplace. As Dot pointed out, now that we have the technology to avoid dangerous working conditions, why would we consider doing anything else?

For Gerrie Powell (b. 1932) of West Bloomfield, Michigan, technological advancements in chemical development made her job safer. Gerrie has spent her life in salons, tending to women's hair and mixing the chemicals to color, bleach, and perm. As the Environmental Protection Agency and the Food and Drug Administration developed guidelines for what was safe for human contact and chemical engineering became more advanced, so did what was and wasn't acceptable for long-term topical use.

> I got . . . my cosmetology license in 1954, and back then things were so different than they were today. We started out with a . . . machine perm wave. People were connected to what looked like a hair dryer with wires coming down, and they wound the hair around these metal curlers and it looked like you'd get electrocuted, but obviously you didn't.
>
> And then it went to machineless perms . . . and they were kind of tricky. You had to be very, very careful because there were chemicals involved that would burn the scalp if you didn't do it right. So, we had little leather pads that had sheepskin underneath, and there was a slit that you pulled the hair through and then wind it around these metal rods, and then you'd take a chemical that was encased in aluminum foil and you would put this on the metal rod after you dip it in water, and then put a clamp on it, and it would curl the hair. You couldn't do the whole head of hair at one time. You just did it in sections.
>
> And then, thank goodness, it went to cold waves where we rolled the hair with plastic rollers. At first, we rolled the hair with the solution, but today, you don't roll with the solution. You just roll with water, add the solution, and then time it for 20 minutes or whatever time you want, and then you rinse it well and then put on the neutralizer which sets the curl. So, there are no chemicals involved other than the liquid chemical which will not burn the scalp, thank goodness . . .

They used to have a state inspector come once a year. Never ever did they announce when they were coming. So, you had to keep your equipment clean, and you had to have your license exposed somewhere . . . You would get fined, even with me shampooing today. You're supposed to be licensed . . . I saw in the paper that [a local salon owner] was not checking everybody's license, and when the inspector came through she was fined $500 because one of the hairdresser's licenses had expired. Now they don't even have inspectors that come around that we are aware of. We've been in this salon with Charlie for 24 years . . . and they inspected when we first moved in and they haven't been back since.

With [regard to] sanitary things, when we were first doing hair in the 50s, we sanitized with formaldehyde. We kept cotton soaked with formaldehyde in a drawer and that's where we kept our combs. And now they have the comb jars with the Barbicide in it, and you change it at least once a week, and that sanitizes the combs and brushes . . . I was glad when we got rid of [the formaldehyde] because then we didn't have that odor, and we didn't even like to get it on [our] hands.

I don't know about you, but I certainly wouldn't want to touch formaldehyde every day. During my work as a first responder after Hurricane Katrina, formaldehyde was a major problem for those that had been issued FEMA Trailers. People were getting sick because the trailers had been cleaned with formaldehyde before being sent south. We weren't allowed to spend much time in the trailers as first responders, something I felt conflicted about. We were able to sleep in safety, but those who had no home but the trailer, could not. Technology has affected the salon industry not just through detailed chemical engineering, but also through our ability to understand how certain chemicals affect us. Today we know that formaldehyde is carcinogenic, and so another compound was invented that is safer to handle and use on the skin.

What we consider reasonable working hours has also changed over the past century. Overtime laws were enacted in 1938, but they were rolled out slowly and still didn't cover everyone in the country's workforce. Even today, nearly 30% of the workforce remains exempt from overtime.[29] Yet, overtime is more than a legal decision enacted for workforce safety. It is a concept that has permeated our working culture. When a friend messages me to say they worked a nine- or ten-hour day, my gut reaction is "ouch," because the eight-hour workday developed by Henry Ford[30] is now our cultural norm.

This brings me to Ann Atkin's description of her dad's working hours during World War II. Keep in mind that most men of working age were sent overseas. Ann's father held a job that was deemed "critical" because he worked for the railroad and so was exempt from the draft. Goods had to be transported from inland manufacturers to the coast to be sent overseas to our soldiers. Yet, with so few men to handle the job, he ended up working an extraordinary amount.

> [My dad] worked incredible hours that people today would not believe. He worked at night. He worked from ten at night until eight in the morning . . . He worked 28 days a month and got two days off. Which, of course, the first day was spent sleeping because he

---

[29] Don't Quit Your Day Job, "Estimates on How Many People the New Overtime Rules Will Affect," https://dqydj.com/how-many-people-the-new-overtime-rules-will-affect/

[30] CNBC, "A brief history of the 8-hour workday, which changed how Americans work," https://www.cnbc.com/2017/05/03/how-the-8-hour-workday-changed-how-americans-work.html

had worked all night, so he really only got one day during the month. And that went on for years.

OFFICE COMMUNICATION & ETHICS

"It's interesting to me when I go to a place and I see people applying for a job, and they can't fill out the form with a pencil and a paper. They got to go to the corner over there and try to fill it out on the computer. Some are able to do it, and some aren't able to do it, and those who aren't able to do it get up and walk out the door."

— Sydney Rushing

Betty Segal saw the evolution of technology during her years at the Centers for Disease Control. Typewriters evolved into word processors and she did her best to adjust, not just for her career, but for her love of writing.

In my work, it was fabulous. When I started working at the CDC, they were still under some old-fashioned male ideas about who did what. Professionals didn't type, but I was a writer. They wouldn't give me a typewriter.

We had a secretary. [I was] trying to design training materials, with illustrations, with a secretary who didn't understand what we were doing. And also, you had to get in line because we didn't have enough secretaries for all the writers. I begged for a typewriter. Finally, they had a spare typewriter they let me have, and so I could type a draft up and show them what I wanted, and then they had to do whatever they wanted to with it. That was fabulous. It helped tremendously.

But you couldn't correct a mistake and you had to have it looking good.

I had a typewriter for a while and then they got something in called a Wang Word Processor, but they gave them to the secretaries. And I worked with a group of mostly women but some men. We wanted one of these Wang Word Processors so badly. So, we would stay after work to use the machine, so we could create stuff. Finally, I went to the boss above the boss above the boss and they had a spare Wang sitting in an office in his area. We plotted and said, 'Anytime you need to use it, go upstairs and ask the boss' secretary if you can use the spare Wang.' So, I was up there, and the big boss came in and said, 'What are you doing?' And I said, 'Oh, we don't have word processors for the writers.' 'You need word processors?' So, we got one, you know, and we sort of circulated using it . . .

That was fabulous. Getting use of a machine that you could correct immediately, you could experiment with layout, was just wonderful. The typewriter alone probably increased my production by a third. The word processor went up above that. Technology is a blessing to a writer. Typewriters are fine, but no thank you. No, I went from typewriters, [which] I learned when I was still in high school. I had a class of 50 and we [learned] shorthand and typing and things. We had one electric typewriter and the others were manual at the time. I never got to use the electric typewriter and I didn't mind. So, I learned on the manual typewriter.

I worked my way through college typing, mostly summers, worked for the government in Washington . . . I worked for the justice system there . . . where you had to type five carbons. That's another thing that has improved life for people who have to create things: being able to print a document out and print as many as you want. Because if a congressman made an inquiry to the agency, first we had all these drafts — this was in the '50s — on yellow draft paper. And everybody marked it up and we went through several drafts. And then they wanted a final copy, and you had to have one perfect copy — no erasures, no corrections, of any sort — three pages, usually, and you had to have ten carbons, but you couldn't do ten carbons at once . . . so you had two chances to get a perfect original because you had to type it twice. What was very frustrating was you sent it back for signatures, and along the way somebody would decide to make a correction on page two, and then it came back, and you had to go through it all again . . .

And then when I discovered the Internet. The first time I was able to download a document from Sweden in five minutes, I thought I'd died and gone to heaven. You didn't have to go to the library, you didn't have to get a library loan. You went online, and you had it. I thought that was just absolutely fabulous.

I have eye problems. I was able to change the darkness of the screen, so it didn't blind me. I could change size on the screen, so I could see. Now I have a Kindle, that's the original Kindle that isn't backlit, that's fabulous for people who have eye problems. So, now I read mostly on screen, but not on computer. The lit computer bothers me.

As is illustrated by Betty, technology has deeply affected what a job, work environment, and career means. Roddy LeBlanc (b. 1975), son-in-law of the elder named Bones I interviewed in Mississippi, has seen the effect of technology in his work on the oil rigs of the Gulf Coast. You'll meet his family in the chapter on Child Development. They chimed in as Bones discussed how technology has changed work, and Roddy had this to say about his own experience.

> Work has changed a lot, too. We had a slide rule. We had to figure stuff out at work. Now you do everything on the computer. You punch in a few numbers on the computer and it's done for you. So, it's changed at my work, too.
>
> I work offshore . . . Everything that we do we do on the computer now. No more handwritten stuff. Everything on the computer. And the government looks at it, now. They don't come out and say, 'I want to see your handwritten file.' They say, 'Where's your computer-generated files at? Do you have it online? Where do you store it at?' Everything is computer-based.

So, many of the elders I interviewed illustrated this as I asked them about their careers, and not all of them have been enthusiastic. Sylvia Gutierrez (b. 1932) of Tampa, Florida, described her discomfort with the shift in technology at her banking job when she lived in New York City.

> I was supposed to use the computer [at the bank in the 1980s] to send to Argentina certain information. But I would do it the old way, until one day my boss, [he] was American, he said, 'From now on you aren't going to do it anymore . . . you are going to use this.' . . . I wasn't comfortable using the computer. Everything was by hand . . . You see children five or six using the computer, but for us, no.

Sylvia, and many others, had to push through the discomfort of adopting new technology in her job, but no one I interviewed had the vantage point Ray Green did as technology changed employment. As we learned in the chapter on Communication, Ray ran an employment agency in Detroit. He did his best to stay on top of tech, adopting it to the office as it developed. His company evolved as snail mail and typewriters evolved into fax machines and word processors. He tried it all, despite misgivings. He watched as technology changed not only the day-to-day office process, but the way we hire employees.

> Teletype. Many of the offices were connected with teletype, and they were supposed to share the job requisitions between all the units. And of course, they didn't. They kept the best ones for themselves and teletyped the garbage. But that's the first time I got involved at all with any type of technology, though my secretary took care of sending the messages . . .
>
> At some point, let's see . . . about 1995, the employers were getting more interested in getting resumes. I didn't want to send resumes. And I prevailed on a lot of my customers to have the applicant hand carry the resume. Well, that worked for a while. Then they wanted it sent. And I had refused to buy a fax. I said I'm not getting into technology.
>
> So, eventually I bought a fax. And what happened with a lot of these resumes is very disgusting, really. They'd get zillions of resumes. So, who do they look at first? I had one employer tell me that they got so many resumes they just took the top half off and threw them away.
>
> Anyway, it got to the point that they didn't even want us to interview the applicants. They wanted the resumes. So, what's the point? See, when I'm interviewing you, I'm getting a picture of what you're about, you know? Facial expressions, body movement, the whole business. And then, actual talking about it, you're getting a feeling of what they're like.

'Cause I liked to make referrals that were good. I didn't like to throw mud on a wall, as they used to say. For example, I can give you a perfect example, is Arby's. One of my customers. Not a technological [company], not a stamping or injection molding or anything. [This guy] was one of my big success stories . . . Arby's at that time had just five stores. And they had one district manager. This manager calls me and gives me the specs, and, basically, they wanted a decent looking guy who could talk, you know, a high school graduate, that's all they asked for. And this guy comes in to see me, he's got nothing, absolutely nothing. But I looked at this guy — he's very intense was the feeling I got from him. Intense. I thought, 'This guy's going to be a great manager.' So, I made the referral. So, he was an assistant for one year, became a manager for two years, then he became a district manager as they opened more stores. Ultimately, he became regional manager, then he became regional vice president. This is a guy with no education, and you know what he did for a living when he came in to see me? He was selling tickets on the Bob-Lo Boat. Now, a year later they would never look at this guy because they came up with all these specs. College graduate, blah blah blah. But eventually he left his job as a regional vice president [and] bought two stores . . .

Ray is right that one used to be able to get a job on merit or demonstrated cognitive ability, not just by a piece of paper that says "degree" on it. Betty Segal's neighbor, Delores Duncan, told me how her father got his job during the Great Depression in just this way.

It was during the early Depression and my dad was looking for work, and he was fortunate, when I was about six years old, to find a good job. My dad was very handy, and back then you didn't go to school to get a certificate to be an automobile mechanic, he fell into a job with a fella who gave him a chance.

Betty Segal echoes Ray's feelings on today's standard of sending everyone to college without considering the person or their intentions.

We have more people going to college, so in a sense we are better educated, but I sometimes question the purpose of sending everybody to college. Thinking that you can't do without college, because I've seen many evidence of people who do quite well to learn and are productive citizens without having to go through the drudgery of four years of college and the expense of it, which is, I think, one of the main problems of our educational system today, and the job market, that businesses have learned that colleges and universities do the screening for them. So, they say, 'Ok, they get through college, they're smart enough to come and work for me.' It's not that they learned anything, necessarily. It's just a screening device. An expensive screening device.

It used to be that people went to high school, they actually learned something, and they were able to go out into a business, and manage a business, and apply their native intelligence to what they knew. If they could read, and write, and do math, and today if you can deal with computers, you use what you have in your head to contribute to life without coming out of college with a burden of debt, with a health care system that is adding another burden of debt, with parents that are living forever that you're going to have to take care of. I think our children today face a very difficult future. And partly it's because of technology and partly it's because of how we have let our education system develop.

Education, four-year college education, shouldn't be for everybody. It should be for the people who need the things that are taught there, and the things that are taught there doesn't have to be geared to something that's here today and gone tomorrow. It should be a broad education that prepares them to deal with the things that come and go. The things that are here today and gone tomorrow you learn from training, which I dealt with for 30-some years. It is short-term training, that can be given on the job, to people who have a good high school education, maybe a two-year college education to learn the things that weren't taught in high school, some specialty, but the university shouldn't be teaching them. If you want to develop somebody who can create things, an engineer, who can go further and develop technology, then they can go to the university and get a bigger degree. I think education is too expensive.

We'll follow up with Betty's thoughts on education in the chapters on Money and Child Development, but I'd like to close this section with an offhand comment from Donald Wensel, born just miles from the steel mills my family worked in, now living in Detroit. It perfectly summarizes Ray's sentiment of the changing employment landscape.

"The age of employers being loyal to employees, and vice versa, is gone."

ECONOMY & WORK ETHIC

I was referred to Richard Paquin (b. 1936), a door-to-door salesman in Rhode Island, by Grace Stinton. He used to go door-to-door to sell insurance. In fact, it's through door-to-door sales that he made his career and started his own multigenerational insurance firm. With today's technology, especially the Internet, door-to-door sales isn't necessary, and in some ways is now considered invasive. The only door-to-door jobs still active today are either religious or political. For Richard, this method of selling wasn't just normal, but critical.

January 1st, 1963, I went full time as an insurance man. I stayed with the Nationwide Insurance Company for 18 years. Unbeknownst to me at that time, I was the largest Nationwide agent . . . in the State of Rhode Island, coming from a little hick town like Tiverton, population at that time maybe 10,000.

I had a disagreement with management. I wanted more freedom to expand, I wanted to open a branch, and they did not like that. They didn't want that, and they threatened to terminate my contract . . .

[When I left Nationwide] we sent a letter to every policyholder [of mine] asking them to come with us. We converted 96.4%. They didn't buy Nationwide, they bought us — me and my boys . . .

This young lady, by the way [*points to his daughter sitting with us*] . . . duplicated every document in my [Nationwide] office. That was a lot of files, a lot of paper. She spent the summer doing that . . .

[When I struck out on my own] I would take a street, go up one side just to introduce myself, and come down the other side. Knocking on doors. We called it 'cold canvas.' Just introducing myself and saying, 'When your insurance comes up for review, think of me, give me a call, give me a chance to bid,' and left my card. It works out that out of 12 households, you're going to hit one that the insurance is due now! And that's how it worked.

> So, I would go out nights and I would come home around eight, eight-thirty, and I would sometimes be up until three o'clock in the morning. I would be typing policies. Because in those days, you typed the policy. You had the policy in your office and you typed them up and delivered them . . .
>
> That's how I built the agency. You can't do that today . . . times have changed.

Indeed, if someone came to my door offering me his card and a chance to bid on my insurance policy, I'd be a little stumped. I just go to the Internet if I'm looking for a new policy. Even more, my policy can be changed at any time. My insurance company will prorate any advance-paid funds. Richard's methodology is obsolete, but it made all the difference to his career.

Ruth Harper's father, too, created a business out of seemingly nothing. Governmental and workforce regulations today may be wholly preventative to his ability to do what he did. He kept the family afloat during the Depression and World War II by his clever work.

> I regard us as having been very fortunate in growing up . . . In the first place, my dad was a machinist, and that job that he'd had when they put the union in, the drafting job that he quit, he came home, and my mother says, 'It's 1932. We have a Model A Ford, a mortgage on the house, and a year-old baby, and you quit your job.' And he says, 'Calm down. I've been thinking about this for a while.' He knew [the union] could go either way. He said, 'I've always wanted to be in business for myself.'
>
> We were really fortunate because we had five acres and because my Pa started his own business. He had a shop of his own. He was able to get really cheap machinery because a new thing had happened.

Machines used to all be run from a central power plant, whether in the factory or whatever, and they would run on belts. There were belts and pulleys all across [the ceiling] and then down [to each machine]. You can see it if you want at Wright Brothers Shop in Greenfield Village, [Detroit], you can see that type of set up. Anyway, they had gotten rid of those and had individual motors on the more modern machines. So, he would go to the junkyard and pay scrap prices for whole machines and set them up. And some of them had been there for a while and had gotten rusty, but he'd rub 'em off with oil and treatment and so on and paint them up and polish anything that was brass or steel that was supposed to be bright. He'd get that all polished up . . . We were welcome in his shop any time, but we were not to touch things because our sweaty young hands would immediately rust up those shiny things, the very things we would want to touch. [laughs]

But anyway, there was [his] machine shop, and that was just a quick run from the back porch. It was set up originally in the existing barn, because of course my folks came up during the horse and buggy days, and then moved into automotive, and so on. But there was a barn there, and they probably had a horse and a cow at that location . . . The horse to pull the buggy into town, or go to church, or whatever. Anyway, about the time I was born, actually, he added on because there were a lot of demands being made on him by the army, [who] wanted his machines. He had patents on two machines . . .

There were probably many times in the night that Pa woke up and wondered, 'When the war is over will I be out of business?' And I'm sure it wore on him during those years.

Not only has our economy changed due to regulations affecting the way one might start such a business, but the entire structure of one's career has changed. Marge Darger of Midland, Michigan, points out that only a generation ago one could expect to have a single job their entire life, with growth meaning a raise or promotion. Today, career growth may mean leaving one company for another, or even one industry for another.

As Ruth alluded in her previous comment, the economy was booming during and directly after World War II. The war made demands on the country that allowed new businesses to start and grow, and it was much easier to get a job one could depend on. The war created the economic growth necessary to pull us out of the Great Depression, and soldiers came home to a booming America. Marge explains that period of economic growth.

> I would say that, in the '50s, you know, it was after the Second World War and the economy was just bubbling, and there was this, I'm going to call it, a Golden Age. People went to work. Everybody had a job for the most part. People had pensions that they could count on, jobs they could count on . . .
>
> It really isn't that long ago that the idea of having a job for your lifetime and a pension you could count on [was normal]. Really, I think probably, even through 2000 . . . people have not been able to count on having a job all their [lives]. I mean, they could get a job and then it could end in ten years and that's the way it is.

Ruth Harper carries Marge's thought further, describing how careers have changed as a result of big box stores.

> [Technology] affects all of us when we want to do business. It used to be, for pretty much what you wanted,

you could find it certainly in Grand Rapids. In fact, Pa used to say, 'If you can't find it on Leonard Street it's not worth having.' [*laughs*] That was almost true. Down the street from us there was a lumber company, there [were] a couple dairies . . . things were more separate. Grocery store, meat market, beverage store, dime store. So, there were four or five family's livelihood and income and stuff.

Now, those four or five families may be at Meijer, each doing their thing. It's different because when you went to the meat market, they actually got in slabs of meat. And if for some peculiar reason, like for your bird feeder, you wanted suet, they would chop off some suet for you. And depending on the needs of the candle makers or anyone else, they may just say, 'Just take it. Get it out of here. Otherwise, I'll have to pay somebody else to haul it out,' depending.

Nowadays you go to a pet store and you buy a nylon tube of something that's got stuffed food in it . . . So, we end up with a society that, other than the people that make needlepoint and sell it in their shop and make arts and crafts and so on, people don't know how to do anything. That's just sad.

Now, it's true that the Internet can make it a lot faster for you. I know people, with the rate that new cars are coming out, even guys in the 60s were rebuilding engines on their hot rods so they could do 170. [*laughs*] Now the car stops, and they got to get a diagnostic tool and it'll say it's a sensor between here and here, and they go to the Internet to find out how to change whatever it is or put in a new serpentine belt or whatever. So, there are potential advantages, but it seems like when there's the good possibility and the bad possibility, all too often what's going to win out is the more negative one, the one that doesn't involve learning. So, you take it to somebody or junk it or whatever.

You try to find something now and you've got it in your hand and you turn it every which way. And what you've got for an address, phone number, anything, you may find a phone number and then it's a call center in India, but otherwise you'll find 'www' and you have no idea if you're talking Dayton, Ohio, or Japan, or China, or California. I mean, where is this thing made and why aren't you willing to put your address where I can find it? I'd really like to write to you about this. I actually have an idea for how this could be improved. This little part keeps breaking. Everybody says so. In fact, it's probably on the 'Net that this part breaks.

The types of small, family-owned businesses that Ruth describes were common for the Greatest Generation, but not all were as legitimate, with proper storefronts and regulated affairs. Today, one typically has to have a license and meet certain regulations to operate a business. However, there still exist unregistered markets to make money. Websites like Craigslist, Facebook Marketplace, or Airbnb might be our versions of what Onalee's family would do for income.

Onalee Cable grew up in a different kind of family business on Mackinac Island. One that was covert, ran out of the home, and certainly didn't meet any regulations. What is important to note is that no one was getting hurt.

I grew up in a gambling house. Dad had worked as a Euchre [card game] man in the gambling hall on [Mackinac] Island. Then they bought this yellow house . . . and he had a big pool table with all the things up above to keep track. They paid to play pool, and he would run a card game. My mother would run the card game in the afternoon, nickel or penny or whatever, and . . . [sell pies]. My dad would run the card game at night and play poker. That's how we lived . . . Not much money, but it kept us in bread and milk and eggs.

So, has technology been good for our work? Many argue yes, especially from a safety and efficiency perspective. But, like many, Adrienne Bard of New York cautions us to pause before we assume it has been 100% beneficial. As with everything, tech has had its side effects.

There are so many more conveniences, now, than there used to be, but people still don't have any more time . . . They see less of their neighbors and friends than they did years ago. You [may] bump into them while you're Christmas shopping or you're in the grocery store.

Yes, tech has sped our tasking, freeing up time. But humans don't do well when bored, and we naturally fill that 'new' time with more things. Is the ease of communicating over the Internet training us to reach out less in person?

MEDICINE

"I had a brother who died at four. He had rather an interesting situation, because today I don't think that would have happened. He had whooping cough following another disease like diphtheria, and he coughed so hard he broke a blood vessel in his head, bled to death. And that's why I say, today, they would have been able to take care of the disease in the first place and that wouldn't have happened. That would have been around the time of World War I."

— Ruth Blair

"If we can figure out how to put a man on the moon, why can't we figure out how to fix my knees?" Harriet Berg exclaimed during our interview in front of a food truck outside Wayne State University downtown Detroit.

As easy as it is to complain, the truth is that Western medicine has exploded over the past century. We've gone from home visits using only the tools one could carry to massive MRI machines clicking above a patient who might otherwise die of an unknown "natural cause." To reference *The Death of Ivan Ilych* by Leo Tolstoy, the main character's injuries are ones that might easily be survived today. A ruptured kidney is serious, but with surgery and care, Ilych would have survived his forties.[31]

Just so, Delores Duncan of Illinois demonstrates that her family would have fared better had they had access to today's technology.

---

[31] Leo Tolstoy, *The Death of Ivan Ilych*, (New York: Everyman's Library, orig. 1886, 2001).

Technology affecting my life . . . [is] a medical change, because of the facts that they couldn't find, or didn't. My mother's sister died of a brain tumor, and she had been treated nine years for migraines. This day and age, they would have found that brain tumor. My mother [may have] died of breast cancer. She had a breaking out on her breast, and the doctor sent her to a dermatologist who treated her for eczema of the breast. She had breast cancer. So, technology of the medical field is one of the greatest advantages that we have. I feel very strongly about that.

In spite of frustrations with over-prescribing and preventative care, life expectancy has nearly doubled, with the promise of a centennial generation already living, today. Stem cells and 3D printing provide solutions that would be called miracles by our predecessors.

This creates an interesting conundrum for one of the elders I interviewed, one that many more of us may experience in the coming decades. Rhea Currie (b. 1916) was one of the oldest people I interviewed, aged 99 at the time of our meeting. I was welcomed into her home in Midland, Michigan, to the smell of fresh-baked cookies. During her interview, she told me she loves baking cookies, and that she'd made some just for me. Her hospitality caught me off guard. My generation doesn't tend to bake cookies for a stranger. Whenever I have brought muffins or cookies to a neighbor, I have been greeted with a curious look.

Rhea told me she finds herself at an impasse with an organization that provides volunteer companions to those who are ill or in need of intensive medical care.

I never think of myself as being 99 years old. I still drive. I still am very active.

There's a group of volunteers who visit patients, and the gal who's head of that group keeps saying, 'Why won't you join our service?' I replied, 'Because I am too old.' And she says, 'What do you mean you're too old?' And I said, 'I could not go into the room of a 60-year-old woman who's dying of cancer and try to cheer her up. She's not going to be happy, I don't think . . . nor do I want to go into the room of a very ill 30-year-old, who sees me as this healthy old lady with white hair.' Am I wrong?

I replied that I didn't think she was wrong, but that I also thought that some people might find her presence soothing. Personally, I would feel her visit comforting exactly because she is older, like a grandmother, someone who has seen more than me and can watch over me as I dealt with illness.

INTERNAL IMAGING

I became familiar with internal imaging at a fairly young age. My mother, a Baby Boomer, started her career as an X-ray technician at one of Detroit's largest hospitals. Through a series of events early in her career, she had the opportunity to join the hospital's first ultrasound team, consisting of only herself and two others. In her college training, only a few years prior, there was no such thing as ultrasound. Suddenly she was able to use a new technology to find clots, tumors, and, of course, see babies moving in real time, all without the radiation of X-rays.

In Portland, Oregon, there is a community called Bridge Meadows, a sister community to Hope Meadows in Illinois. There, retired people live nearby foster families, becoming foster grandparents of sorts. I interviewed a woman named Juanita Laush, whom I was surprised to learn worked directly with the development of internal imaging.

Juanita was born in 1923. The development of medicine over her lifetime is even more drastic than my mother's experience.

X-rays were discovered in the 1880s, forty years before Juanita's birth. X-ray as a tool of medicine became prevalent during the early 1900s but was still somewhat feared and unreliable — much like stem cell research, today. Ten years before Juanita's birth, the X-ray method we continue to use was invented.

Juanita's career was much like my mother's. She was a medical assistant on the forefront of a new technology, in the right place at the right time. She helped write a textbook on X-ray and saw its true impact on history.

> My first job was as a medical assistant . . . I had been a secretary in the Navy for years, as a civilian, so I sought a job part-time because I had two kids by then and they said, 'Well, Dr. Barco needs a receptionist.' And I said, 'I don't do medical. I haven't any experience.' 'Oh, he'll teach you. His wife is doing it now and she'll teach you.' And boy, did they teach me. She wanted out, she wanted to quit, so I took X-rays, I gave shots. It was amazing what I learned.
>
> And it was also amazing that, along with that . . . I had been a Red Cross nurse's aide during the war, so I had that medical experience which was hands on as a volunteer in the naval hospital and the Royal Journal hospital, so I had that much background. So, I knew about medical ethics and I knew that this doctor was not ethical.
>
> He had very little room, his patient relationship was nil, and it pained me that he was the only doctor on the coast that was a specialist in ear, nose, and throat, and so he had many patients, loggers, children . . .
>
> He would line them up. We had a hall and we would line up nasal irrigations, and he'd start with the anesthesia and go down the line, and if this patient wasn't numb, too bad, it was his turn. He just didn't have any compassion for his patients.

So, anyway, I was privileged to have worked for a radiologist from New York. It was the only X-ray machine on the coast and so again the logging accidents would come direct to our office. And it was the beginning of cancer treatments for our office, and we wrote a textbook together. So, I learned transcription . . . and I transcribed a textbook for X-ray technicians. There wasn't one, but he wrote one. I was going to be a journalist, so that was really a passion that I enjoyed. So, then I kind of specialized in medical things after that.

Let's rewind a bit. Not only was X-Ray technology brand new at the time of Juanita's birth, but antibiotics hadn't even been invented. Can you imagine your life without antibiotics? A world where pink eye meant crossing your fingers and hoping it doesn't blind you. A world in which I would have died from the pneumonia I fell ill with when I was age 14 which was partially resistant to antibiotics and still left a whistle in my lungs despite modern medicine. This was our grandparents' reality.

Juanita continues,

My father was a veteran of World War I, and he married his nurse, my mom. And he was recovering from battle wounds, and tuberculosis was a World War I given. If you were in the trenches, you got it. There were no antibiotics, nothing medical they could do. So, my dad was in a military hospital in Colorado and they [said] that fresh air, sunshine, and dry air wasn't a cure, but you could function. He was in and out [of the hospital] for a couple years. He could have stayed in a veteran's hospital for the rest of his life, but one day he said, 'I'm taking off my pajamas and I'm going out of there.' So, with his pension from the world war, he bought a cotton farm in New Mexico . . .

In California we lived in a tar paper house with a concrete floor and I had one ear infection after another. And finally, at ten, I had ear surgery, which was the beginning of my hearing impairment because there was no medicine.

Antibiotics [were a] big thing. Wonderful thing. I had ear infection in the mastoid bone of my ear. There was no way to fix it but by surgery. So, they just scraped all the hearing mechanism out. But I still have pretty good hearing.

World War II brought penicillin and antibiotics, so [then] my ear problems stopped. I had one last surgery. I think penicillin is one of the big, wonderful things.

My parents' generation, the Baby Boomers, still experienced measles and mumps, polio and smallpox. Vaccination was the radical new medical technology for them, just as X-ray imaging was for Juanita. My father had measles as a boy. It was normal for him and it's something I can't fathom experiencing. Today, I am amazed at what seems like radical results through stem cell research and 3D printing of tissues. In 50 years, our children will find many of the medical issues these technologies correct unfathomable, too.

Hal Royer of Colorado experienced the changes due to polio vaccines first hand. He knows how important vaccinations have been to him, his children, and to medicine.

In 1952, I contracted polio. That was before antibiotics and I was in the hospital 28 days. The first week, they told my wife that I wouldn't live, but if I did live, I'd never walk again. Well, I fooled 'em! [*laughs*] But, when they came out with the serum for polio, I already had [had the disease]. I didn't want to go get a shot. The doctor called me up and said get your butt over here. Why? Because there's several different varieties of it. You're very likely to get a different polio. So, I had to go over and stand in line with women and children and get my polio shot. [laughs] We mustn't forget that technology which saved so many lives. And, of course, penicillin, which we didn't have at that time. What a difference that would have made in World War II. That would have saved a lot of people.

Ann House Veren adds that we know so much more that helps children in this day and age. Instead of suffering through a condition, we can identify and predict how it will affect their future medical care.

The medical is phenomenal. What they have learned that they had no idea of at all when I was growing up. My own health situation — I had surgery in October because my spine was collapsing. Which is a very serious surgery. It was in a 'C.' And I know now that when I would go to the doctor when I was a child, I don't know if it was a physical or what, but he would tell me to back up against the wall and he could put his arm through my back and he'd say to my mother, 'She's just sway-backed.' I didn't know I had scoliosis. They didn't even know what it was. And scoliosis played an important part in this and everything else in the hospital. Everything I had ended in 'osis' when I had an MRI. Wasn't just scoliosis but osteoporosis, and stenosis, I mean about ten different words that ended in o-s-i-s. So, I mean, [technology is] phenomenal for health. Phenomenal. That's a major, major gain.

THE CUTTING EDGE

"The 3D printers for body parts . . . that blows me away. That someone took a 3D printer for guns and decided at the last minute 'oh wait, this little girl needs a hand, maybe we can help her out here' . . . "

— Dagmar Booth

"I had some illnesses that I almost died, as a baby, a couple of times. I had pneumonia, and I had whooping cough as a baby. Those things were very common back in the 40s and 50s. You don't see those things, hardly, in this country [today]," explained Tom Lawson (b. 1943) at the restaurant in Louisiana, whom we met with his wife Charlotte in the chapter on Rights. He then began to tell me about his own experience in today's experimental medical technology.

I have been treated six of seven times with different chemotherapy drugs. Two years ago my leukemia went into lymphoma. I have leukemia and lymphoma. I got on a drug over a year ago called Imbruvica, which is a new drug. They conducted clinical trials at MD Anderson a couple years ago and I was able to get on that drug. I feel great, I feel like a normal person, sometimes. It's keeping my leukemia and lymphoma in check, and I can function pretty much as a normal person. I get tired a lot, I get pain in my back. That's one of the things that is so wonderful about how fast technology is moving, because they can develop these new drugs so quickly, now, as opposed to in the past it would take them years to come out with a new drug and have it tested and all that stuff.

Sadly, Tom lost the battle with his cancer two years after his interview. Losing him reminded me of the dual purpose of this project. Not only do I wish to understand the story arch of technological development across the past 100 years, but I want to preserve these histories and the perspective of the Greatest Generation. We will lose them if they are not recorded.

During our interview at the library in Midland, Michigan, Marge Darger told me about her son's own medical battle and the cutting-edge technology that surrounds his healing.

> My 47-year-old son [Tom] . . . had a lung transplant when he was about 24. Then, last April, he had a re-transplant. Now, I think that, probably, technology has had some impact on that . . . Well, for instance, they fly airplanes to get to where the lung is, to fly it back to Pittsburgh, where he's had his two lung transplants.
>
> And so, when I was in Pittsburgh when Tom was recovering from the lung transplant, we'd be going on the elevator, and there would be this little robot that was taking up, either he or she was taking up, either trays or taking up something to the different floors. So, there's robots! It wasn't spooky, it was fascinating . . .

I find it interesting that Marge stopped to place a gender on the robot before finishing her thought. I don't know what that means for how we will accept robots into our lives and homes, but it is certain that gendering both humans and objects is comforting for many, even when it's arbitrary.

Ruth Harper continues where Marge Darger left off and reminds us there's even more to her son's experience. One thing that I felt Marge didn't say is the level of medical advancement that was required in order to do a lung transplant in the first place. In 1951, early in the Greatest Generation's lives, King George VI of England, arguably one of the only people in the world with access to the best medical care possible at the time, had no choice but have a lung removed — not replaced — due to his condition.[32] Today, we would have known the condition was cancer and that radiation, not replacement, would be necessary. Back then, all that could be done was remove the troubled lung and hope for the best.

Ruth reminds us that removal and replacement is not the only advancement technology has provided medicine. Reattachment is one of the greatest advances in our medical technology. The amount of detail that a surgeon must attend to in order to do this kind of work is mind-blowing. I am confident in stating that there are thousands of people around the world who are thankful for the work that was done over the past century to develop this technology.

> All my life, I've thought about this stuff about reattachment. Well, they're doing it, now. Stuff I read about as a little kid, somebody fell off the back of the tractor and got their hand cut off. And I'd say why couldn't they just rescue the hand . . . and put it back together? Well, it took a lot of inventions to get there.
>
> The first thing about it is, we're put together, well, picture the old dolls with the arms and legs held together with rubber bands, and there's a kind of central wireframe, and there's the rubber bands going from the moveable arms and legs. Well, we're a lot like that, and what happens when you break a rubber band? It goes ffttt! [*gestures a rubber band retracting*] So, we had to have the technology to get it and hold it and not kill it and get that stuff reattached. And in the Civil War our technology went as far as, what, a hot stove lid to cauterize and seal things so nothing could . . . [*I wince*] yeah — and that's where the whiskey came in. [*laughs*]

---

[32] BBC, "1951: King Has Lung Transplant," http://news.bbc.co.uk/onthisday/hi/dates/stories/september/23/newsid_3083000/3083301.stm

There is one technology that was not released as a medical tool, yet has proven to be one of the most critical tools for communicating with those who are on the autism spectrum — the iPad. When the iPad came out, it was hailed as a more portable computer, easy to use and able to display your favorite photographs or take down notes while still containing a large enough screen to navigate easily. Soon, it was discovered that its ease of use made it available to non-verbal autistic people as a tool for communication. Fran Biederman (b. 1934) of Hope Meadows told me how her own grandson is using the iPad for just this purpose.

> [My grandson] will be 13 next month and he has autism and Down syndrome, and he doesn't talk. So, he uses the computer to talk. They've tried everything. They've tried the flash cards and the sign language, and he doesn't focus long enough [to use them]. But he'll know what button to push to [start] a certain game that he wants to listen to or music that he wants to hear. He'll push the buttons until he gets to the one he wants. It has helped him . . . I don't know how much he uses it at school.
>
> First, they wanted him to carry [a computer]. I think it was $10,000. The federal government would have supplied it, but it was huge. He would have had to carry it in a backpack on his back. My son said he can't do that! But they have the little iPad thing . . . I just wish he could talk, but he doesn't.

MENTAL HEALTH

"We think that more and more people are having . . . mental health [issues]. Mental health is, either we're hearing more about it . . . or there are more people, but there's so much more mental health problems, and we've got to start doing something

about it. And I think they are. I think they're thinking about it,
now, but who knows."

— Chris Smith

I was really scared when I was driving across Idaho after having left Missoula, Montana, and the two centennials I interviewed there, Ella and Emma. I had driven through the mountains and into the snow, entering Idaho and rounding mountain passes to get to the flatlands once more. The sun had already set and the landscape was pitch black. I didn't like to drive at night. I hadn't yet realized that it was because my eyesight was failing despite having had Lasik.

I was still two hours away from where I wanted to stop for the night. I had set a stopping point goal each day of the trip so I could manage my wake time and arrival time for each interview. What I didn't drive tonight I would have to drive tomorrow.

I was driving across the Idaho Panhandle National Forest and every few miles there were elk crossing signs. I live in the Lower Peninsula of Michigan — we don't have elk. I don't know their migration patterns, if they move at night after the sun has gone down, or how to spot them so to avoid hitting them with my car.

I called a friend to talk it through. I told him which mile marker I was passing and asked if he could tell me how far I had to go to the end of the preserve. It turned out it spanned for miles in all directions and it was another hour to the next town with lodgings.

This was not the news I wanted. Still, I had no choice. I was not going to pitch a tent by the side of the road in the middle of a forest that I did not understand, where my car could easily be hit by one of the few vehicles using the very dark interstate that night.

I pressed on, finally arriving in a small city. I chose to stay at a Motel 6, where the government would house us when I was doing disaster relief for the National Civilian Community Corps after Hurricane Katrina. It was a familiar brand and I didn't remember it being that bad.

Maybe it was the exhaustion or maybe I wasn't used to staying in such spartan conditions, anymore, but this Motel 6 did not make me feel safe or rested. The sheets were like sandpaper, the room smelled like smoke despite being marked non-smoking, and the shower head didn't spray straight. Still, I hoped that my weary state would make it easy to sleep. I put in earplugs, donned my eye mask, and dropped to the bed.

I didn't sleep. I couldn't. The bed was too hard or maybe I was too tired — past the point of being able to fall asleep. Whatever the reason, this was the moment of my breaking point. I was only a week and a half into my travel, but I'd had no true rest, no time for myself, no peace or meditation outside of a short detour to Arches National Park. My mind and my body were exhausted.

I started crying at 2:30am after three hours of trying to sleep. My tears were at first born of frustration at the inability to sleep, but quickly were added my general exhaustion and fear that I would not succeed. To this day, I wish I'd had more time and support on the road so I could have reached more people to interview. I know that my exhaustion played into this sentiment of failure.

When I realized I couldn't stop crying or stop the negative thoughts, I called a friend. I admitted I felt I couldn't do it anymore, that I just wanted to come home. I expected my friend to push me forward, to encourage me to keep going on this epic project. Instead, he said he thought that sounded reasonable. I could go home, wait out the winter, and then resume the work in spring.

Immediately, my mind rebelled. What about everyone who knew I was on the way? The people who had funded the Kickstarter campaign and were following my progress on the road? What about the money I'd spent on the car rental that couldn't be refunded? What about me? My dream? Above all, I couldn't let myself down like that. I had to keep going.

I told my friend "no," that I'd be fine, that I just needed a good cry, and hung up. I lied to him and myself that night, but the tears had helped, and I managed to sleep five hours before I had to get back on the road.

The plains of Washington were next, and they were a beautiful sight after such a difficult night. Still, despite my stubborn disposition to press on, I knew I could not continue the way I had. I called my therapist, with whom I had not spoken in many months. I tearfully told him how ragged I felt, and he immediately asked me about my self-care.

What self-care? I wasn't doing morning yoga, no meditation, my food was instant oatmeal, coffee, and snack bars from the trunk of a rental car. I rested when I reached the hotel and kept driving until I reached the destination. There was no time for self-care. There was no room for it, either.

I would be in Olympia in a day and I decided to take time in the rainforest. The silence of nature would help, I was sure. So, I said that would be my solution and his concern was sated. I was lying to everyone, including myself. This was the same initiative that pushed me through experiencing a natural disaster in order to continue case working in 2009, eventually resulting in post-traumatic stress injury. I couldn't stop — the mission was bigger than me.

Our stigma of disease and mental illness has changed over the years. The above story is one I never would have told, even ten years ago. Self-care is now an open topic on social media, at conferences, and amongst friends, and one of my favorite workshops to teach to entrepreneurs. Mainstream media promotes therapy as natural, while, in the past, it had been stigmatized as 'only for the broken.'

Before many physical illnesses were treatable or understood, taboo surrounded them and the people that carried them.

By avoiding an ill person, the spread of the disease was also avoided. That was all that was understood, and there was no difference in approach between a person mad with a contagious fever and a person who was mentally ill.

Unfortunately, it has taken a long time for mental illnesses to be normalized. Those who experience mental illness still undergo societal stigma, despite better understanding and treatments. Mental illness, untreated, can ruin the life of the person it affects and overtake the lives of their friends and family. Yet, as a stigmatized illness, many avoid the self-recognition necessary to take the step to get help, let alone reaching out to a practitioner.

My own mental health story goes exactly this way. I spent the first three years of my career in the disaster relief sector. That meant a lot of exposure to the trauma of others, and, eventually, being subject to a tsunami warning that had us running up a mountain to safety in American Samoa. The result was post-traumatic stress injury (PTSI/PTSD), but it took many months and breakdowns for me to realize something was wrong.

Unfortunately, this was during a time when army personnel were committing mass shootings that were blamed on PTSI. I didn't want to be associated with that — I wasn't being driven to harm others or myself. I hid for years, making everything worse. It was through the support of good friends and realizing I couldn't thrive without help that I finally got professional support.

Ann House Veren openly described to me what happens when mental illness is left unchecked, and how our society needs to change its mind about the issue.

> I have a daughter that's in a mental hospital, 56 years old. She's been there off and on several times. Her husband died a year before mine. She never had a child. And she's schizophrenic, bipolar, and I forget what the other one is. Three things. She's very, very delusional . . .

There's a lot of mental illness and people don't want to recognize it, and people don't understand how I can talk about it and not be upset. Honey, if crying tears would help anything, I'd cry enough to float a boat. But it doesn't change things.

If history has demonstrated anything, it is that social stigma only prevents the help, support, and growth of a person. In today's day and age, when we understand that mental illness is not the fault of the person affected, nor is it contagious, there is no reason for us to fear nor shun it. Yes, the unknown can be scary, but overwhelmingly all anyone needs is the support and love of others. If you are not a medical professional, you *can* offer that.

RELATIONSHIPS

"Social skills are being greatly affected. You know, they're side by side, and yet they're talking to each other on the telephone. Or they're walking side by side but they're talking to somebody else on the phone. The intimacy of people seem to be greatly affected by that . . ."

— Urcell Schulterbrandt

Our relationships have changed, haven't they? It seems that everyone says so, regardless of age or generation. I was speaking with a Millennial about the subject of this book and she held up her smartphone and responded, "These things are pulling us apart — they add distance to our lives."

Part of the purpose of this project is to see if we're right. It's often said that technology is coming between us in articles and newscasts, but most of the people saying it are between the ages of 25 and 50. Though cell phones, smartphones, and the Internet haven't been around that long, most of us didn't experience a pure adulthood devoid of the influence of tech. By the 1980s, communication had already been altered by many forms of technology.

This chapter is really about that one facet of technology. How does it affect our relationships? Has it actually added distance, despite its ease? Today, I can pick up a phone and talk to anyone in the world, free of additional charge. I can open my computer and do the same. I can buy a plane ticket today and see someone in Paris or Istanbul tomorrow. Technology has facilitated an ease of communication, but has it equally gotten in the way of closeness?

I was 13 when AOL Instant Messenger (AIM) gained traction. Those were the days when AOL (America Online) was the main computer program for "logging on" to the Internet, and you knew it by the sheer number of CD-ROMs they mailed to each household every year. There were so many circulating that, at its peak, 50% of all existing CDs had the AOL logo printed on them.[33] That's a lot of plastic. Today, they're collectors' items. Back then, my family used one to install the software, and the rest I used for art.

When AIM was released, it was an instant addiction for me. I could talk to my friends after school without tying up the phone line because my dad had purchased a second phone line for Internet and fax for his work. Many young people today don't realize that the Internet had to go through a phone line when it first debuted. Instant messaging also allowed me to talk to anyone I wanted without getting my strict parents involved in a vetting process to investigate my "potential" friends and their parents before I could see them in person. Plus, I could talk to boys. I never would have managed a long-distance boyfriend at a high school an hour away without it, though I may have missed opportunities in my own school because of it.

Instant messaging is part of the reason I took typing class in high school. If I could type faster than my friends, then I could win arguments and debates. It's the number one reason I'm a speed typist at 116 WPM. Today, the same rings true. Type more words and you're more likely to win your argument.

I remember when I started at university, we were instructed to *not* instant message our roommates when we were sitting in the same dorm room. We laughed because the concept of instant messaging was so new it seemed ludicrous to message someone sitting next to you, yet I find myself doing exactly that in my office, today.

---

[33] TechCrunch, "More on AOL's Disc Strategy: $1.19 Floppies, 50% of all CDs Made, and Precision Bomb-ing," https://techcrunch.com/2010/12/28/aol-floppy-disk/

Instant messaging, chat, and social media now means you can talk to your friends without leaving the house. I know I'm thankful for that in the dead of winter when all I want is to stay wrapped cozy under a blanket on the couch.

Except I'm not. Yes, it's nice to avoid a brief encounter with frigid air. It seems a relief when there's ten inches of snow outside and you've already cleared the car twice that day (once to go to work, once to come home). It's easy to focus on the "relief" part of the exchange and not consider the other half — the cost. Nothing is free. There is always a tradeoff, and in this example, the cost is cabin fever. It's so easy to glance outside and think, "Brrr, no," and stay in to message friends from under a blanket.

The homo sapiens mind was wired 200,000 years ago. Tech communication was wired only 40 years ago. We're not equipped to understand the subtle but compounding effects it has on society.

A survey called "What Do Happy People Do?" conducted in 2008 found that, no matter one's background, the activity that leaves us feeling most dissatisfied is Television.[34] As Adele Jones will describe in a moment, people may be physically in the room together, but their minds are elsewhere, following the story. In her book, "Zoobiquity",[35] a comparison of human and animal wellness, Dr. Barbara Natterson-Horowitz explains the impact of this mentally isolating activity.

> The problem may be worsened by technology that isolates even as it entertains and informs. Even those of us who love these activities recognize that watching television, playing video games, and "social" networking alone in a room can leave us feeling disconnected from

---

[34] John P. Robinson and Steven Martin, "What Do Happy People Do?," *Social Indicators Research* 89 (2008): pp. 565-71.
[35] Natterson-Horowitz, MD and Kathryn Bowers, *Zoobiquity: The astonishing connection between human and animal health* (Vintage Books: 2013) p. 223.

real people. A survey comparing free-time activities and contentment found that the only pastime that consistently left people of all ages and socioeconomic groups feeling unhappy was watching TV. While bird owners and others with common problems can find solace in online gatherings of people with the same issues, this phenomenon also has a dark side. The Internet provides cutters (and those in other self-injuring subcultures, including anorexics) with the *wrong* kinds of peer groups — ones that enable and support behavior, offer tips for "improving technique," post poetry praising it, and describe tactics for hiding it.

My theory is this. We talk to our friends online. Our brains check off the "socialize" need — the drive to interact with other humans — and we think we feel fulfilled. But the endorphin dump and DNA healing[36] we get from hearing a voice, seeing a face smile at us, and from the physical contact that comes with in-person human interaction doesn't happen. With the mental box ticked we don't think we require further friend time, but our physical state slowly degrades. Could this be why depression and anxiety are on the rise?[37]

The elders I interviewed for this book reinforce our suspicions that technology is disrupting relationships. I found Adele Jones (b. 1945), who lives only half an hour away from me in Mich-

---

[36] The Lancet, "Effect of comprehensive lifestyle changes on telomerase activity and telomere length in men with biopsy-proven low-risk prostate cancer: 5-year follow-up of a descriptive pilot study," http://www.thelancet.com/journals/lanonc/article/PIIS1470-2045(13)70366-8/abstract

[37] NY Mag, "For 80 Years, Young Americans Have Been Getting More Anxious and Depressed, and No One Is Quite Sure Why," http://nymag.com/scienceofus/2016/03/for-80-years-young-americans-have-been-getting-more-anxious-and-depressed.html

igan, through Virgil Westdale. They had been dancing partners some years ago.

Adele had me feeling a bit sad during our interview as she reflected on her and her husband's interactions since they bought tablets and laptops, originally purchased as added convenience and access to the news and books online.

> I can even see it in my own home . . . I have a Kindle Fire, and I watch Facebook on there, and I read on there. My husband has a laptop, and so we're sitting in the living room in the evenings on our own handheld computers and watching the 50-inch TV, and we don't talk as much. If the power goes out, we find ourselves talking about a lot of things that we haven't in a while.
>
> I make him go out to dinner with me enough that that's a time we leave our phones aside and talk.

Adele told me that, during those dates, she notices what many other elders have as well — that couples sit at a table together at the restaurant and don't interact.

> I see young people not using verbal communication. It's very sad to go to a restaurant and see a mother and dad and two little children looking at their phones instead of talking. I see that quite a bit.

If anyone can critique the effects of technology on relationships, it's Bob Johnson. We met him and his horse in the chapter on Transportation. He is a family and couple's psychologist in Salt Lake City and has something very acute to say about how Facebook and texting have affected our relationships. He starts where Adele left off.

> To tell the truth, some of the technology, now, I just want to vomit on it. I see young couples having dinner

together, and they're working on their damn phones! They're not even talking to each other. And you don't see a teenager walking down the street just walking down the street. They've got their phone in front of them and they're checking their mail or they're texting [while walking]. And, you know, they're texting while they're driving, which is crazy. It's just a different time period.

We have four grandchildren, and it's amazed me because all of them, by the time they were two, were more technically competent than I was. The sad part is . . . one of my grandsons, I mean, he would spend 26 hours a day playing Minecraft. Playing a game of some type. It is just the culture we're in. People talk about the wonderful thing about the information that flows, now. And I guess it's wonderful. Sometimes it seems that people are saying things that they wish they hadn't, but see, that's the opinion of an older person. So, it is what it is.

I met Jim Hayes Jr. at Hope Meadows, the same community as Betty Segal. Though I interviewed him before I interviewed Bob, his words agree exactly with what Bob says about families, technology, and restaurants. In fact, so many of those I interviewed made the same observation, that they don't all fit in this chapter.

A lot of people lost their reasons for associating with people where we used to associate with other people. You know, a lot of them are hooked into the iPad and all these other kinds of things. You can see mom, dad, siblings, going to the restaurant one right after the other and they all got their damn iPad, and you wonder when do people get a chance to relate to each other.

Jim's neighbor, Delores Duncan, makes a fabulous point about the distraction of smartphones in a single sentence.

> If I you can't sit and hold a conversation, why bother to go out to dinner with somebody?

Betty Segal, a neighbor of Jim's and Delores' at Hope Meadows, doesn't understand why her family comes to visit her but doesn't interact with her. It's the same issue that Adele has noticed happening between her and her husband, but there's something else to it. Her niece and husband grew up without the socializing that Betty, Adele, and the rest of the Greatest Generation had. This may be why they don't realize they are being rude by keeping their phones out instead of visiting with someone they haven't seen in a while.

> Oh, I think social media is ruining, ruining social life. I had, this summer, three people visit me, friends and family, for several weeks. A very good friend, she's about 60, she lives on Facebook. When you have a guest, you can't pick up a book and read, but your guest can pick up her cell phone and send messages out to friends far away, in your presence, and ignore you.
>
> My niece came with her husband, and she has become enamored [with her smartphone]. She didn't want it. He bought her this wonderful phone, but she has become enamored with social media. So, she has friends that she has never met. She's busy talking to her friends! She says, 'I'm talking to my friends.' And what can I do? I'm sitting there, her hostess, you know. We could chat, we could play a word game, but . . . somebody she doesn't know she's busy talking to.

My son came, and he was pretty good about it. He was pretty good about his phone. He did sometimes get on his phone. I did not get terribly offended by him. Sometimes he was doing research because he was busy building something . . .

And the other thing is you don't know what they're doing. You don't know. When my niece was here, and her husband was here, he would get on the phone and look up something for me, but he wouldn't say, 'Oh, I'm going to look up this something for you.' He just does it. So, they disappear. You're in a room with somebody and they have disappeared. Mentally. I find that it is a, I don't know, somehow people ought to be limited, or I don't know, they should learn not to be so rude. They didn't have that when they were children, and [so] no one taught them the management of it. And we haven't developed management for it.

Some of us are doing something about it. The moment I realized how distant I had become from my friends — and formulated my theory about the mental checkbox for socializing I spoke of at the beginning of this chapter — I decided to begin hosting monthly brunches. My friends are very busy, most of them being entrepreneurs and artists. Some are introverts, some have anxiety, and a regular event where they're familiar with the plan means they're more likely to attend. Some of my friends don't yet see how separating tech has been for us, so this ensures I see them, anyway.

Bob Johnson has begun doing something that I recommend to my coaching clients. He writes letters when he wants his words to have impact. This preserves the moment in which it was written, his words, and the profundity of the message through the time spent to craft something in one's own hand.

If something really means something to me, now, I will write a letter. And I hope I never stop doing that. If I want something to feel personal to one of my children on a birthday or something like that, it's my printing or my handwriting that does it. I get scared by the Millennial generation and the younger generation, now, are growing up not knowing how to have this kind of conversation.

I had a client a couple years ago who was engaged to a woman, and he broke up with her with a text message, and she committed suicide, and that's the reason he came in to see me . . . At the time, I thought, 'How could anyone even consider doing something like that?' And we did some work together and helped him get on, but as I told that story to other people and they say, 'Well, sure, that's just what we do.' Not the killing yourself, but 'Of course! What would be wrong with breaking up with a text message?' and to me it's incomprehensible.

The computer did that, too. I ran a staff of people when we were at Chevron, and we would have online meetings, and do things through the Internet. What I realized is we were losing personal contact with each other. And we were saying things in an email . . . we probably wished we hadn't said. And so, I worked it out so that once a quarter we all got together, even if it was bringing people in from even different countries. Because then we had the chance to sit face to face . . . What I realized is that I didn't want to lose that contact, and I think our culture is losing that. In fact, I know we are. To me, that's scary. I think that's a loss that will affect things in a variety of ways.

I do a lot of work with people in relationships, a lot of people will enter into relationships never having

learned how to look somebody in the eye and tell them
something that they don't like, or something that they
do like.

Writing is important to a good many of us. I love writing letters
in order to add the weight of importance to something that I need
to say. Writing takes time, which the reader knows, consciously
or subconsciously. Writing also creates something physical, permanent, which feels more important than an email. Writing a
letter also helps me ensure my thoughts stay in order if I need to
say something that makes me nervous.

As Jim Hayes Jr. told me what he thinks of seeing young
people and families on their phones in restaurants, he made an
interesting observation regarding the lack of cursive writing being taught in schools. The time spent to learn an art like cursive
may affect the ability to focus and communicate in the way Jim
describes.

> Cursive writing used to be a big thing back in the day,
> right? But the kids aren't doing too much writing,
> now. I got a letter from my granddaughter, and I could
> understand everything, but it wasn't like the kind of
> letters that we used to write, you know, years ago.
>
> I think the main thing we've lost is people's rela-
> tionships to each other. You gotta be careful . . . you
> watch what you say, you keep your hands to yourself,
> and you keep your feet on the ground. But when you
> try to relate to young people, and they believe in all
> this multitasking, and most of us don't multitask like
> the young folks, and you're trying to talk to them and
> they're doing all these other things, you don't know if
> they're paying attention to you or not, you know? You
> gotta get their attention, however, even if you need to
> take the gadget away in order to get their attention.

Adele Jones, like Bob Johnson, writes letters when she wants the meaning of what she's saying to be apparent.

> I hope the postal service never goes away. Letter writing, even if it's just thank yous, I think it's important ... something that we used to do a lot of. In fact, I have a terrific antique postcard collection that used to be my grandmother's and my mom's. It's really beautiful, and people had to send a postcard to communicate before the phone. I hope that writing things down is something that people realize needs to be done.
>
> I've even heard lately about schools not teaching cursive writing. That's just unbelievable to me. Will they even be able to read the letters [that were sent during the war]?
>
> Things that are saved on computers, nowadays, might just not be there [for future generations]. Even putting things on a flash drive, there will be a day not far down the road that that flash drive won't work, and your pictures will be lost on a computer.

What Adele speaks of is bit rot and planned depreciation. Bit rot is the destruction of information on a hard drive over time due to the natural corrosion of the metals. Planned deprecation is something many of us are familiar with. Apple often releases computers that no longer have technology like USB ports or CD-ROM readers. With the next generation of computers becoming slimmer as the extra ports go away, and prioritizing information storage in the cloud (online), we have less control over the location of our important memories.

I recently lost a video I recorded on Facebook Live due to a glitch in their database. It's just gone. It wasn't an important memory, but this reinforces the need to back up our images and computers in more than one way. I even like to print my best photographs so that I know the only way they'll be destroyed is by fire.

Adele told me after our interview was completed that she has another method of getting close to friends again, one similar to my own brunch parties — tea parties. Participants rotate homes so they're sure to see their homebody friends, and everyone has the chance to use their fancy china. They all agree to put down their phones and just talk. While this seems appropriate to older generations, up and coming generations may feel putting down the phone — the social safety barrier — may be daunting if their skills to socialize face-to-face aren't developed. With more and more pre-toddler-aged children being pacified with smartphones, this is a very real possibility.

FOOD

"At age 12, I went to work on a farm and I was like a farm girl for the wife of the farmer. And we got up at four in the morning and we started the breakfast because the field hands would come in to eat breakfast at six and go out and start haying and cutting wheat and everything else that they did. Then we would do the dishes, by hand of course back then, and . . . I would do laundry and hang [it] out on the line and then you'd have to iron it."

— Esther Gould

Our subsistence has dramatically altered since the development of machinery, manufacturing, science, and medicine. The current popular concern — Genetically Modified Organisms (GMOs) and organics — started in the late 1980s when GMOs were first approved for food production.[38] Packaging like airtight plastic and vacuum seals that keep foods fresh over the course of months, instead of days, became possible as plastics began mass production in the 1950s.[39] The development of long-distance shipping has enabled the transport of food items such as fruit to the United States from South America.

Ray Dirks had a front-row view of the evolution of our food production over the last century. He was born in 1932 at the height of the Great Depression on a dairy farm in central

---

[38] Bawa, A. S.; Anilakumar, K. R., "Genetically modified foods: safety, risks and public concerns – a re-view," *Journal of Food Science and Technology.* 50(6), 2016.
[39] Thompson RC, Swan SH, Moore CJ, vom Saal FS, "Our plastic age," *Philos. Trans. R. Soc. Lond. B Biol. Sci.* 364 (1526), 2009.

Colorado. His family were tenant farmers when he was young. In 1945, they made the decision to buy a dairy farm for financial security. That farm eventually expanded with the purchase of their neighbor's farm. They built additional cow barns and fences and moved the homestead at least once (an undertaking which is still no small feat even today). He spent his entire life on farms, only recently selling the last of the family land in order to retire. The homestead I visited when I met Ray was set on a piece of that family land, with a view out the back windows of what had been their farm.

In the chapter on Work, Ray described how the amount of work it takes to farm a number of acres changed dramatically throughout his life. The combines we use today can handle what once required several families to farm. A colleague of mine affirmed this change by describing farmers tearing out trees that lined their property in order to get to the land that was, until then, outside their reach.

Many of the elders I interviewed voiced opinions on how food has changed, but Ray experienced this change at its bottom line.

> There were some long hours [but] . . . it was exciting for me. You could see where you were making yourself better . . . You had to sell your crop, and the only way we could sell our crop was to milk cows. So, we milked cows for 40 years and got up to where we were about 400 cows . . . We just knew how to do that better than anything else.
>
> One time . . . the horse laid down on the [hay stacker] and broke it to smithereens, and my dad said, 'That's ok, son, we'll fix it.' That's basically the way we farmed. We just had things to do and we did 'em . . .
>
> We watched our neighbors go broke, and they worked harder than we did. 'Cause they bought the cattle too high and sold 'em too cheap. And I remember

buying a bunch of calves from a lady whose husband who worked for us and she said she wanted to buy those heifers back to breed them. I wouldn't sell 'em back . . . the market went down and she woulda lost a buncha money.

Hal Royer also grew up on a dairy farm. We heard a little of his story in the chapter on Amenities. His family's land was in Kansas at a time when they depended on a small electric train that carried their milk to Wichita for sale. As we talked, he often reflected that the amount of work and the lack of the technology we take for granted today was okay with them. They didn't lament it as we might do if we lost our access to tractors, tillers, and milkers today.

We sold fresh milk into Wichita. We shipped the milk on a little electric railroad that went from Newton, [Kansas] to Wichita, a distance of about 35 miles. My folks milked 12 to 14 fancy Holstein cows. We carried the milk in a cart in big ten-gallon cans up to the railroad every morning, and [the train would] make the milk run.

Dad would get up about four o'clock in the morning, go out to get the cows and get them in the barn, get them ready to milk. Mother'd get up about an hour later, or something, in that order, and go help. My job was to get out and start the fire in the cook stove. Then my sister would get up and I'd lay back down somewhere [*laughs*] and make breakfast for the whole family, so we'd have breakfast around seven or eight o'clock. Dad'd milk the cows by himself, by hand, mom'd finish up. In the evenings, I'd milk a couple cows. We were busy . . . In the farming community, tractors were only just becoming available. I drove a four-horse team as an eight-year-old kid. Boy, we thought nothing of it.

Ruth Harper reflects that our relationship to animals, one that was so critical and personal in both farming and private life, has changed.

> Oh, and that's another thing, life for animals has gotten a lot different. There used to be a lot of family farms, and your animals had names, even if you knew that they might eventually be slaughtered or whatever. At least, maybe it was imaginative kids that named them. Well, milk cows had names, you know, they were Daisy or Bossy or somebody. [*laughs*] They were healthy, they lived on the land in the way they were intended to live, and yes if you weren't a whole complete operation, you know, if you didn't grow your own hay fields and wheat fields and all that, you got that stuff somewhere else. There were various granaries and feed stores and things, but there were also individuals, so somebody out a little further, somebody that got rid of their animals but mowed their property for hay and baled it and stuff.
>
> We used to go out to old man Sanford's house and you could get two bales of hay into the trunk of a car . . . By then we had our '37 Ford, and so when [my sister] was in high school, every so often it would be time to go get hay, so we would go out there and talk to old man Sanford. He'd say funny things like, 'Oh, there was a raccoon in the something-or-other the other night, and I wondered how he got in there, so I put some corn outside and tried to lure him, and he went to this little place on the gate and he just squoze through there.' [*laughs*] Not squeezed, he 'squoze.' And we'd laugh uproariously and loved his stories and he loved that we loved them and I don't think he had any idea that it was a critical kind of loving him, maybe. But he was Mr. Sanford, it was ok if he spoke like that . . .

You didn't have to worry about factory farms and all the horrors that go with that kind of stuff nowadays. And as far as animals, you soon learned, or believed . . . that mutts were healthier and smarter and just better companions. I remember my Pa saying Collies were wonderful dogs. They were smart, they were shepherd dogs, but they bred the brains out of them nowadays. The AKC came out with the longer and narrower nose . . . but that's kind of how the Collies looked by the time I came along.

Of course, there's probably an upside as well as a downside in animals. You won't find rabid animals running around anymore because they made these laws, and so on. And I don't even think it's a great problem in the wild. I think rabies is in remission. [*laughs*] But on the other hand, they're way quick to take the animals to the pound and, in the more agrarian or small-town situation, you knew whose dog it was, or knew it belonged to one of those kids over the hill, or whatever, and so there wasn't all this dog snapping and so on going on by the pound if the animal got out. People weren't so uptight about things. They all saw animals regularly.

As far as things like cooking, mom made just about everything from scratch. Well, okay, the flour was already milled, we didn't have to do that, though grandma, on the other side, had grown up in a mill where they did do that.

Mary Lou Aukeman grew up in California, just north of Sacramento. When she was a little girl, it was her job to ride down to the nearby farm to get milk.

When I was, oh, I'll bet ya maybe ten or 11 years old, I had a bicycle, and about a mile down the road was a farm. I still have that little bucket. It's a can, looks like a milk can, but smaller. It's a gallon or two gallons. I would go down the road on my bike to get the milk from the farmer, straight from the farmer. At that time, they didn't have pasteurization, and it wasn't always safe. That's a lot different, now. Farmers can't sell milk right out of the barn.

Mary's husband, Owen, grew up on a farm. He was the fifth of nine children, and reflects that they were very poor, but because it was farm life, they never went hungry.

[We were] very poor. My dad made one dollar a day when he worked. We had just a few cows, and it was so poor. I'm sure people helped us, but I don't know . . . that piece . . . 1932 was a tough Depression . . . We always had food, because we had cattle, we had chickens. My dad bought 300 chickens, little baby chicks in the spring, and I never figured that out until just a few years ago. There's 365 days in a year. That would give us a chicken a day, and we had all the eggs we ever needed. And then we had pigs to clean up around the barn and farm, and we had cattle for milk, so we had milk, and mom baked a lot, constantly baking and cooking, and so we always had food. I never went to bed hungry. But it was poor.

One man I interviewed not only saw the development of the chemicals we use in factory farming today but helped create them. We met Etcyl Blair in the chapter on War as he told us about being assigned to chemical weapons development during World War II. He then told me how his post-war life evolved in the field of Chemistry.

The reason I went to the Dow Chemical Company, which I had never heard of [at graduation], was because they had a music program and a symphony orchestra, and I played in the symphony orchestra. I did that for 15 years. As a result, I've always been associated with the symphony, either as a player or, later on as a member of the board . . .

My life at Dow was a very exciting life. I never could have planned the life that I lived. I started work as just a chemist, and I was to work in the field of agriculture. Dow had many herbicides, and did not have insecticides, so I was asked by the head of the department if we could get into the insecticide business. I didn't know anything about this field; I had worked on the isolation and characterization of natural products out of agricultural products in Kansas. You know, extract certain things, irradiate them, try to create steroids, medicines, all that kind of stuff. I'm a very high-tech guy, so I'm always pushing technology.

Anyway, I end up being a synthesis chemist where you create things, you don't transform them. You take the basic elements and you convert them into other things. In this case it was organophosphate compounds, which you have to be sort of careful with because handling them can be very dangerous. I did that for ten or 15 years, and finally became head of the department, the Organic Chemistry Department.

Shortly after that I was asked to go into the agricultural department. I hadn't been in agricultural — I was just working in an organic chemistry laboratory . . . I was research director, and then I went all over the world; to everywhere, to have our products tested, to carry out testing, and all that. I did that for roughly five years.

And then the last 15 years really became very interesting for me, because Dow underwent an enormous change because a lot of new laws came out. EPA, OSHA, all kinds of new laws, and Dow was caught up in a lawsuit on 13 carcinogens. That word 'carcinogens' is kind of a bad word, but terribly misused because many of the things we do are carcinogenic and biologically we handle that, generally. And so, to defend ourselves, they asked me to lead the team. They weren't even [agricultural] products, they had nothing to do with agriculture. I'll never to this day know why I was selected to do this other than the fact that I had experience with the government because all agricultural products must be registered through the EPA and the Department of Agriculture. So, I had a little contact with government.

So, I led the group to Washington [*Etcyl pronounces it "war-shington"*] and when it was over I was then asked to reorganize the company worldwide and put everything on a sound footing where recognition of legislation and laws became paramount. Not just to lawyers, but to chemists working in the field so that there was a responsibility to what happened to the product, or the byproducts, or the waste. You can't just dump waste into the rivers . . . things like that.

As time and food has progressed, our bodies have changed. Etcyl alludes to the fact that our bodies are very able to manage all kinds of biological variants. That may be true on an individual basis, but we don't yet know how much chemicals and properties build up and pass across generations.

TECHNOLOGY'S EFFECTS ON FOOD PROCESSING AND NUTRITION

With the advent of industrialized agriculture came industrialized food processing. Quick mix cake batter requiring only water added, pasteurization of milk and eggs, and mass-produced bread products are some examples of how our subsistence has shifted.

With greater processing of our food came more processed sugars and starches, leading to the prevalence of diabetes.[40] Many find it difficult today to eat a sugar-free diet because of processed foods.

Eliminating gluten from meals is one of the latest fad diets. Changes in breeding our wheat, which began in the 1950s and continues to accelerate with the work of GMOs today, lead to an increase in gluten content in wheat. Gluten irritates the intestines of at least 1% of the American population, as they have a condition known as Celiac disease.[41] Though removing gluten from the diet of those with the disease is critical to their health, many more people choose the diet, mistaking gluten for a food property that harms us all.

Another major change we've seen with the evolution of our food is the average weight of our population. There are infinite ways to argue the issue, with many pointing fingers of blame at those who fight with their weight. Others relate to the plentiful growth, distribution, and processing of today's food supply.

Jim Hayes Jr. posits during our interview that food is too easy these days.

> I guess life is a lot, uh, I don't know if 'easier' is the right word or not, but you can do a lot of things, now, that you couldn't do before. You don't have to use the cook stove no more, [using] wood and coal. You can use gas or electric stove . . . You've got microwaves. I use the microwave — I haven't mastered it, but I use it . . . Boiling food, and meat, and using these cooking bags and stuff, that's beyond my comprehension. I

---

[40] University of California San Francisco, "Quantity of Sugar in Food Supply Linked to Diabetes Rates" https://www.ucsf.edu/news/2013/02/13591/quantity-sugar-food-supply-linked-diabetes-rates

[41] The New Yorker, "Against the Grain," https://www.newyorker.com/magazine/2014/11/03/grain

don't want to know about that, 'cause I like food the way it tastes the other way. But a lot of people take a lot of joy out of boiling stuff in a bag, or cooking in the oven in a bag, and all those kinds of things.

Is obesity a problem because cooking and food [has become] too easy?

The microwave is a tool that is under constant scrutiny for its presumed negative health effects. Many believe the microwave is responsible for cancer, destruction of nutrition, and other issues with our food today. I, like Jim, prefer the way food tastes when it comes off the stove, or when leftovers are reheated in the oven, and so do not own a microwave. It tastes more real to me, steeped in the traditional ways of preparing food through directly heating it. This is the way our grandparents heated their food.

In his book *Outlaw Cook*, John Thorne, culinary writer, states,

Microwave energy offers no equivalent experience to replace our intuitive understanding of heat; indeed, the body's inability to respond or protect itself means the cooking food must be locked away out of reach. Because microwaves cook food from the inside out, they are unable to provide us with any of radiant heat's familiar, helpful clues . . . what we never expected was that as kitchen experience in its entirety became progressively devalued, the aura that still clung to the stove would also necessarily fade. Unnoticed by us, the image of the chef before his range, sweat dripping down his face as hot fat shimmered in his sauté pan, was undergoing as radical a change for microwave users as the role of scullion had for us.[42]

---

[42] John Thorne, *Outlaw Cook* (North Point Press, 1994).

But, as Jim said, many people love the things a microwave can do for food and our time. Ruth Harper embraces her microwave and finds other's concerns unfounded.

> Some of [the technology] I really, really love. I think a microwave is super. I'm not afraid of it — there are people who circulate things, 'oh, it'll cause hydrogen peroxide in your food.' Come on! Whether you heat it by causing the molecules to jiggle against each other inside and heat it by friction, or you turn a fire under it, it's still turning on and it's not chemically changing. So, just, scrap these foolish ideas.
>
> Things have changed, but they're not necessarily way better. We used to wrap our sandwiches in wax paper. Well, there's definitely advantages to, maybe, a Ziploc bag. If your hot cocoa or thermos leaks out and your sandwich is in wax paper, you're going to have a done sandwich. I had one friend who said [she] had that happen so many times [she] just thought egg salad sandwiches were just better dunked in hot chocolate. [*laughs*]

Food has certainly become easier, not only at home but also because of fast food restaurants. Adrienne Bard adds,

> 'Course your fast food restaurants, McDonald's and all of those, are all brand new since I was young. To go to a restaurant to eat was, for us anyway, was almost unheard of, we never went . . .
>
> I don't know why I remember this so well, but [when we visited my uncle's homes nearby], before we went home, we always had something to eat. Sandwiches and so-forth, or something like that. And that's something that I remember about when we went to visit families.

Food sharing has historically been one of the most communal and symbolic methods of relationship building for humans. It once took a community to create the kind of healthful meals required for the growth of a group. This sharing also reinforced the relationships within the group. The plenty one may experience today in the United States by simply walking into a grocery store has, in some ways, spoiled us out of these traditions of sharing and feeding. Creating a meal no longer requires a person (or people) to spend hours in a kitchen, which means that meals can be had at any time during the day, and by anyone in the household, alone. Preservatives added in food processing plus household refrigeration lengthen the life of food, further enabling eating to happen at any time, rather than only at mealtime.

The role of visiting and being fed is one that restaurants have now filled in American culture. Yet, Adrienne touches on my own experience of traditional feeding by one's host with my family in the Old Country (Croatia). Whenever I visit, I am always stuffed to the brim with homemade foods of all kinds, made the same day, and I am implored to eat more. It is a personal glimpse into our caricature of the Old World, of the lengthy many-course meals that bring together the family in conversation and relationship development.

One of the most revelatory conversations I had regarding food access and community took place in Midland, Michigan, at the home of HJ Smith (b. 1942). HJ is known in her community as a sort of historian. A former teacher, she has a steel trap memory and has helped many people in her community develop books and other work regarding historical accuracy.

At the time of her interview, I'd already written about our relationships with neighbors being changed by food centralization at box stores like Walmart. Only recently has this reverted due to a resurgence in farmers' markets. When I go to the farmers' market, I expect to run into many people I know, and I make friends with vendors or other shoppers that are observing the same stand. That rarely happens at the store.

HJ told me of a song that perfectly describes this shift in food and neighborhoods. It's called "The Kelvinator," the original word for a refrigerator (Kelvin being a scientific measurement of temperature). With its invention, food stayed fresh longer, not only enabling reduced time in meal preparation and family access, but also enabling our ability to travel further from home and buy in bulk. By traveling miles instead of blocks, we stopped seeing our immediate neighbors on a regular basis, and the frequency of our grocery runs reduced to once a week instead of once a day.

> I heard a song on the radio a few years ago, it was called 'The Kelvinator.' Do you know what a Kelvinator was? It's a generic term for a refrigerator, and they were manufactured in Grand Rapids, [Michigan]. And this song was a folk song to the effect that our whole society has changed because we now have a Kelvinator. We can refrigerate our food, so we don't have to go to the market every day. So, the markets have moved away from our neighborhoods, and so we have to get in the car and go to the supermarket, so we stock up and we buy all the stuff that we bring home and put in our refrigerator, then we never see our neighbors because we're not going to the market, and we're not walking, so we're not exercising, and we're getting fat . . .
>
> That's pretty profound. I hadn't really thought of that, but in the old days, when my grandmother had an icebox with a block of ice delivered by the ice man, you couldn't keep food very long so you had to get out and get it. [The iceman also] spread the gossip, and the good news and the bad, so that's been an effect of technology.

Mary Muscatello remembers what it meant for her when that ice truck came. As a youth, it was less about hearing the latest gossip, and more about the ability to make Jell-O.

We used to make Jell-O to celebrate [my parent's] anniversary. Just a small tray of Jell-O. We had an icebox, but their anniversary was in March, and we were never sure if it would be real, real cold, real cold in March. So, what we did was set a tray of Jell-O out on the railing on the porch and set it there to make sure it would be nice and cold, and it just might gel. It just might gel . . . as long as we kept it out of the sun and there were no cats that came along on the railing. We would bring the Jell-O in and somehow, we managed to get a carton of heavy cream, and we would whip the heck out of it with an egg beater and put it on top of the Jell-O and it would taste like a million dollars. That was our celebration for my mom and dad's anniversary.

The icebox, we weren't sure if it would freeze our Jell-O. The icebox was usually wood on the outside, and it had many little box doors, like, and compartments, and so we could put in our vegetables and food to keep cool . . . We would wait for the iceman to come down the street and he would bring in big blocks of ice with the tongs, great big tongs, that would come in and he would set the ice into the icebox. 'Ice-a-box.' That was absolutely wonderful when we finally got an electric refrigerator.

For those families that kept a home garden, some of the issues that an icebox presented were less important. Ruth Harper explains how the home garden influenced their family meals. Her family also lived in Grand Rapids, Michigan, which meant that a good part of the year was cold. Ice boxes weren't critical during those times, and the dynamics of a heated home contributed to food's freshness.

My mother always kept a garden. She was a busy, active person despite liking to read. Anyway, we had a cow, we had a few chickens, so there was always fresh milk and fresh eggs. But that's good because we didn't own a refrigerator, we owned an icebox, so a couple times in the summer the ice man would come and would bring a big block of ice, and then he would, depending on the block size, because they were irregular, he would take it up and if it didn't fit he would take it on the back porch and chisel off some. And of course, the big kids always wanted to be there when that was going on because they wanted some ice to suck on. You know, it wasn't like there were popsicles in the freezer.

And then, conversely, in the winter time, all regular winters we'd have the fresh milk and it would come in warm [from the cow] and mother would set it on pans on the step because the upstairs was not heated. There were radiators running at the bottom, but this was a house built for a couple of old people, about three originally because great-grandmother had come over from Europe by then and was living there, but that was before my time. Anyway, so she'd set the milk on the stairway, so the cream could rise, and then she could skim some off for recipes or whatever cream sauces when they used real cream, and so on. And then we bought glass milk bottles, we could go down to the feed store and get those, and we'd get a whole stack of cardboard tops, you may have encountered them on Dixie Cups or something, where it's cardboard and it's pressed into . . . the top. [It] would fit in there and there'd be a little notch for it, and there'd be a tab and so when you wanted to open it you would dig your fingernail in there and then lift, and you could put that thing on and off as you used the milk or whatever. In the case of the Dixie Cup, you'd take the little wooden spoon [and eat the ice cream].

So, there were special things, as far as food, all this fresh good stuff from the garden, and you'd go to the grocery store and get 25 lbs. of flour and 25 lbs. of sugar and, you know, some other things, canned goods, of course. Although my mother, she canned maybe fruit though, maybe chili sauce, she'd make some other things, mainly she did jams and jellies and stuff, and also quarts and quarts and quarts of peaches and cherries and pears and plums, and we had a special place in the basement for those. The basement, too, was cool. You didn't vent heat into the basement. There was a boiler and it got plenty hot, but there were insulated pipes then going up to where each radiator was.

Many elders are worried that technology is removing our 'know-how' — our ability to fend for ourselves. This is most apparent with subsistence. Judith Blair of Ithaca, New York, describes what she's worried about as we get further and further from our personal food production.

It worries me because of climate change. I think that people are going to need to be more resourceful and more close to the earth. I think they're going to need to know how to forage for or grow their own food at some point. I think they're going to need to be creative about putting things together for their use for whatever needs they have because the energy grid is going to go down. You're not going to be able to press a button and have whatever you want to have happen. I worry that people who don't interact with the actual world, the physical world, I'm afraid that they're going to be very disadvantaged when the going gets rough.

I have one granddaughter who is really into gardening and growing food, preserving food. She's really little, she's only seven, but I'm thinking that's smart! I don't know about the rest of them, but that one's going to survive longer than the rest of them when the climate becomes disastrously different. I really think kids need to be out and interact with the rest of the world while it's still there, first of all, and second of all to learn how to use what's there in nature to do what they need to do so they've got survival skills. I don't think relying on tech is a survival skill . . .

The chemical agriculture thing, the whole business, not just the GMOs, though that's appalling . . . First, we put poison on the ground to kill everything, then we plant seeds that can withstand the poison, and we put pesticides on the seeds that will penetrate every cell of the plants so that no insects can eat the plants, and then because the plants can stand it we put more poison four more times during the growing season. That's terrible! The stuff they're putting on there, Roundup, it causes cancer, it kills all the beneficial microbes in the ground so the farmers have to buy packages of soil enhancement that contains microbes to replace what they've killed. The reason so many farmers in India have killed themselves is because they can't save their seed, and because they have to use all these other chemicals as a part of the whole GMO agriculture thing, and I think that's terrible . . . It's just dismaying to me to see all the intellect that's being used to do such terrible things to the planet, and technology is, in the end, going to destroy the planet.

Ruth Harper continues that not only are we farming in drastically different ways, we have created forced markets for our food prices. She told me a story of when farmers were destroying their crop in order to keep food prices high.

I had a friend, she's probably gone now . . . she had a farm down [south], but she called us up and said, 'Call your friends, call your neighbors, call everybody, and send them down and pick . . . cherries, because we aren't allowed to. They're afraid, it's a bumper crop, so they can't control the prices.'

Well, gee, if people got cherries cheap one year, how bad would that be? I mean, yeah, it's rough on the people if they're sole crop is cherries, but these people weren't that dumb, they had apples and they had other things, and why were all these cherries allowed to rot? And of course, you call your friends and they're busy, they can't all [go] 100 miles to pick cherries.

We each have a choice to make with regard to how much technology plays a role in our food. At a minimum, we have buying power. Each of us also has the right to vote or influence public officials on such issues. Many of us also have the ability to control our food directly by growing a small Victory Garden (coined during World War II when rationing was in effect). Food, like technology, can be a conscious choice.

MONEY

"And, of course, they have trouble making change. You give them a credit card, a lot of them don't know much about money."

— Kay McComb

If you were to ask anyone over the age of 70 if money has changed over their lifetime, they would likely respond, "Sure it has! I used to buy comic books for ten cents apiece!" Inflation is a fact of life in almost any country around the world, regardless of technology.

Credit, however, has changed by a lot over the past century. Before computers, credit generally referred to a running tab at the drugstore which was paid monthly. During periods of war, credit was especially important for families whose men, on whom household income largely depended, were abroad.

Even more, credit was (and still is for some) a fact of life for mining towns. In pre-1950s America, forms of credit were used at company stores. Company stores were provided in towns also owned by the same company, populated by said company's workers. Coal and oil towns are best known for this practice. The company also owned the housing, giving it a full monopoly on resources, allowing prices to be arbitrarily set and workers' income to funnel directly back to the company. This is the purest form of "wage slavery."

Workers in such towns may or may not have seen their paychecks. In many cases, the cost of living was greater than the wages paid, and workers always had an open line of credit which was paid for by more work. It is from such working conditions that the first unions were born. This passage from the book *Nine Women* describes these conditions.

Often, immigrants were recruited to work in the mines by the promise of free land to farm. When they arrived, there was no land, and there was no way to express grievances. They lived in a company house, bought their food from a company store, saw a company doctor if they were sick, and sent their children to a company school. Often, they were paid in company scrip instead of real money, so they couldn't leave town. If a worker expressed too much discontent, credit was cut off at the store, and he found an eviction notice at his house.[43]

Charge coins first appeared in the late 1800s. These little metal coins contained the logo of the store plus a customer number and had a hole in the center to hang on a keyring. This was a major step toward standardization and speed of transaction: no more looking up customer numbers or messy handwriting of said numbers on sales slips. Instead, the number on the disc was pressed on the carbon copy slip. In the 1930s stores began to move to the charge plate due to identity theft made possible by a lack of name on the coin. This was the first time a "credit card" appeared, but really it was a metal card with recessed name and identity information which was likewise pressed onto a carbon copy sales slip.[44]

In the 1950s, credit began to change with the first true credit card, different from charge cards which had to be paid in full each month. Carrying multiple credit account cards for different stores and merchants became cumbersome as the trend grew and made payment of debt tedious. The first consolidated merchant card was the Diner's Club, which was a charge card. In 1958,

---

[43] Judith Nies, *Nine Women* (London: University of California Press, 2002), 106.
[44] Wikipedia, "Credit Card," https://en.wikipedia.org/wiki/Credit_card

American Express was born but remained a charge card for some time. Credit as we know it today was developed in the same year by Bank of America as the BankAmericard. They started small, focusing only on Fresno, California, to prove their model to both merchants and customers. The program eventually expanded across the United States and consolidated in 1976 into what we know today as the Visa card.

Every generation has had those that struggle with over-spending, but with credit cards offering spending power far beyond most cardholders' means, the consequences to today's problem spenders is very different than that of our elders. Many argue it was the amount of debt Americans held that played a major part in the 2008 economic crash, including mishandled mortgage debt for homes larger and more extravagant than one could afford.

I know several such overspenders. Some are Baby Boomers and have a lifetime of sling-shotting from deep debt to settled accounts, from red to green, several destroying marriages along the way. But some are my age. I was shocked when I first learned of my college friend's debt. I had been taught to fear debt and didn't yet own a credit card at the time of our friendship. She'd opened her cards when she first got offers at 18, not fully un-derstanding the responsibility. By the time I knew her she was already thousands of dollars in credit card debt from spending on clothes, and she was only 21. She was so in debt she could only make minimum payments on all her cards. It would be years before she emerged free of the burden.

One elder in particular was passionate on this subject. Marion Graff (b. 1922) is a Navy veteran who served in World War II, came home, and eventually started an insurance business at which each of his children had interned or worked. It's likely that, due to his work and their involvement, the family practiced a low-debt lifestyle.

Marion can see what's happening to others, however, and he's mad about it. In his sailor's drawl, he exclaimed,

> The little plastic card that looks like this, they should
> have never invented it . . . We were taught, my mother
> and my dad, mostly my mother said, 'If you can't buy
> this, you don't buy it until you can pay for it.' All
> my kids have cards, but they all use them very very
> sparingly . . . [The credit card] is a damnation to the
> nation . . . Checking, you get that little thing that says
> 'insufficient funds'. But on that card, they open it up to
> what? $5,000? $10,000? . . . And one-third of what you
> pay is interest. To me, I look at it as a bad investment
> all the way through.

Ruth Harper developed similar spending habits — spend what you have, nothing more. These are the same principles that I was taught by my elders. My family's background is that of the working class, and the risk of credit just wasn't an option. Instead, I was taught reuse of resources by observing my grandmother keeping every food bag, cleaning containers which became her Tupperware, and using milk cartons whose wax lining made for a perfect food waste receptacle. Ruth explained to me how she managed her money, even as a child.

> I was very tight with my money. I would really debate
> spending a nickel for a Coke, or seven cents for a Cher-
> ry Coke. It didn't come easy. Although, I was kind of a
> regular at the little corner store a quarter-mile up from
> us . . . We'd go in there, usually with pennies, and you
> could get ten lemon drops for a penny, or two red beer
> barrels, or you could put the penny in the gum ma-
> chine and take your chances, and the interesting thing
> about that was that at one point the machine was mal-
> functioning. You'd put your penny in and run the little
> slide, and catch the gum ball, and maybe three would
> come out. And when the little compartment got full it
> would drop pennies out, so you could just feed it its

own pennies. [*laughs*] We finally told the guy. I think we really had a good time with it for three days and then we couldn't stand it anymore . . .

My parents were married months before the crash [starting the Depression]. So, definitely that was an influence. But, of course, they came from thrifty people, too. And, you know, a lot of the people that built these big houses [in Grand Rapids], they may have been lumber barons at some point, but they grew up thrifty, and that never totally leaves you. So, people who have a fortune tend to build it and keep it, and other people just never get near one.

I've observed this in my own family, too. My parents and their siblings made the transition from working class to middle class not only by getting educated in a different kind of work, but also by saving militantly. There is no reason to buy the latest gadget, the newest car, or a different house when the current item works just fine. Yes, little luxuries came and went, but it was through saving and its compounding interest that my family changed its standing.

Sadly, the Great Recession of 2008 has changed the landscape for many in Generations X, Y, and Millennial. Jim Tankersley of The New York Times described how this impacts our ability to save.

The sort of raises they were used to, especially in the late 1990s, just haven't happened in the wake of the Great Recession. So, for a lot of people, whether they're making the median or just under $100,000, they feel like 'hey, my quality of life just isn't advancing nearly as fast as I think it should be based on what I've seen in the past . . .' We see there are a large number of families who can't even get by if they've missed two paychecks. This is a problem that predates the

Recession. It's actually been a problem throughout the 2000s, where people borrowed, and they overspent, perhaps, relative to what they should have been saving just to keep pace with, again, with those quality-of-life improvements that they had been accustomed to in the past.[45]

STUDENT LOANS

"We didn't talk about the Depression in my home. I knew we had cut back on things . . . Of course, it was still Depression times when I went to college. It wasn't until a long time after I graduated from college and had gone on that I was going through some things of my dad's and discovered that when I went to college, he had borrowed money against his Life Insurance to pay my tuition. I had never known that until I found the papers among his things."

— Rhea Currie

There's something else about spending and credit that the Greatest Generation didn't experience in the way Millennials and Gen-Y are. Student Loans. Over the past two decades, state backing for colleges and universities has steadily decreased, increasing the cost to families and students.[46] Those friends of

---

[45] NPR Weekend Edition, "What Living on $100,000 a Year Looks Like," https://www.npr.org/templates/transcript/transcript.php?storyId=567602293, December 3, 2017.

[46] Center on Budget and Policy Priorities, "Funding Down, Tuition Up," https://www.cbpp.org/research/state-budget-and-tax/funding-down-tuition-up, August 15, 2016.

mine that took out loans to subsidize their education graduated from university with debt approximately equal to that of a small mortgage (students currently average $40,000 in debt by graduation[47]). However, these loans have higher interest rates than a mortgage and next to no ability to reduce the burden of debt in declaring bankruptcy. Even in death, private student loans are passed to the next of kin.

I have watched my friends struggle at entry-level jobs, unable to do more than make ends meet as they make payments on their loans rather than save a nest egg for their first home. Should a job not be the right fit, they are unable to risk a different career path or job transfer. The interest rates are so aggressive that the consequences of a new job not working out and loan payments being deferred are too high.

When I requested further understanding about the nuances of student debt from my Facebook friends, the responses were so numerous and emotional that I had to defer to hosting a tea party discussion at my home later that week. Student loans, according to many Millennials, are ruining lives.

One such Millennial said,

> I'm almost $30,000 in debt for going to Ferris [University] for two years as a single mom. I lived in student housing, so I got as much money as I possibly could to help me provide for my kids while I went to school, which is what I was advised to do. It was supposed to be Pell Grant money, but a back injury laid me up for a year and I could not finish school.

---

[47] Wall Street Journal, "Student Debt is About to Set Another Record," http://blogs.wsj.com/economics/2016/05/02/student-debt-is-about-to-set-another-record-but-the-picture-isnt-all-bad/, May 2, 2016.

No one reached out to tell me I could apply for an advocate or review or anything until after it was too late. I signed up for a program to make payments, but it only covered the interest charges. My credit is tanked. My debt to income ratio is so bad I am struggling to buy a decent home for my kids. I have an incomplete education and could not find a job doing anything other than retail or manufacturing and I cannot physically do that work. I applied for SSI [Supplemental Security Income] because of my physical issues and the inability to work and am still jumping through hoops trying to prove my need for help caring for my family. I am now diagnosed with bipolar depression and am on medication to help me not be suicidal.

My 15-year-old son informed me that he is not going to college and I felt like a failure, like it was my fault, somehow. I know it isn't, [but] when he was five his dream was to be a fish biologist. We have agreed that technical school might be his best option, [but] he's worried it won't even be worth [the] bother. The ability to work and pay off the debt of school, and also the ability to actually use any degree he works hard for are diminished to him. He sees going to technical school as more realistic, less expensive, [with] more possibility of income [and] therefore a higher payoff and greater reward for hard work. He now says he wants to work on music while eventually working towards running a business that gives back to the community. The job from a technical school would be just to live on. He's looking at it as playing the long game.

Another Millennial shared her experience with student loans preventing the hiring of good talent.

I have worked for six years in student recruiting for companies and the most impactful statement a student ever told me was, 'I would love to take your job, it's my dream, but with my loans I can't afford to take it.' Craziest part was I was offering $135,000 with $25,000 sign on bonus, but the cost of living in Boston was higher than Chicago, and that meant he couldn't afford to take my job and pay loans and provide for his family. This isn't just an undergraduate student, because he was getting his MBA from a top-20 university.

A member of Gen-Y once told me he deferred his loans for some years in order to pursue his dream of music. He was successful, playing in two signed bands and touring the world. When he began making payments, again, his loan had grown by two-thirds.

Even my friend who graduated from law school chose to live at home with his parents, rather than get his own apartment. He confided that the sum total of his debt after graduating from undergraduate and law school was $90,000. As an entry-level attorney, he preferred not to pay rent and focus on paying down his debt as quickly as possible. His payments for a debt that high equaled that of apartment rent but without the benefit of shelter. Should he, or any other person with student debt wish to marry, that debt responsibility would transfer to his spouse, a burden he didn't wish to pass on.

I'm an entrepreneur, and in my world the best way to change an industry is to disrupt that industry with a new or better option. So, I decided to found a student loan startup that had debt forgiveness built into the loans. Unfortunately, the company only survived to the strategy phase. When I ran the financials, I discovered not only that it was an uninvestable company, but a major reason as to why the industry is so out of control is the loans have no collateral, forcing interest rates high. They take an enormous financial critical mass in order to pay off investors, a critical mass that no individual investor or venture capitalist would risk. That is why the banking world rules the student loan industry.

That is not to absolve the industry of its harsh rules, but to simply explain what I know. I wrote a case study on my findings for those who are interested, and it can be found here: http://veronicakirin.com/student-loan

Now, technically, student loans have been around since after World War II. However, many in Marion Graff's generation returned from the war backed by the GI Bill.[48] They attended college or university when they otherwise might not have been able to afford it, changing education and employment standards for generations to come. Those who didn't go to war due to youth or other reasons (illness, last namesake) suddenly had to compete in a job market not only flooded by the men and women who'd served in the war, but by more college level educated persons in the market than ever before. And so, those who didn't serve began entering college and university to compete. Without the GI Bill or family backing, a student loan may have been necessary.

When my father, aged 70 at the time of this writing, took his bachelor's degree in the '60s he paid a total of $13,000 for all four years. If you haven't thrown this book across the room in exasperation at that number, keep reading. In 1965, the United States government took note of the loans necessary for many to attend college and began backing banks and nonprofit foundation loans. This was the birth of what we know as the student loan industry, a debt otherwise unknown by previous generations. As Marion Graff stated,

> The rule of thumb is you bring up your children, [and] your children should do better than you. Well, the four

---

[48] History, "GI Bill," https://www.history.com/topics/world-war-ii/gi-bill

living children did as good if not better than I did . . .
But the generation coming up now I don't know . . . It's
coming to the point where if you don't have that piece
of paper that says 'Degree' on it, you're lost. You're
going to work for a 8.50- or ten-dollar job . . .

Charlie Rusher of Kansas City illustrated the difficulty of student
loans and how they likewise transfer to one's spouse upon marriage. This is exactly what my friend worked to avoid by living
with his parents post-law school.

Another thing . . . relatives, I've been to their wedding,
and they'll have a big meal, and I'll find out later they
went and hawked for, say, maybe $2,000. And it's a big
drag on them, I think. And our minister said the same
thing. He said we just got to get off of this thing of having a whole meal for people and stuff like that. Because
in most cases of people he's talked to, they're already
having a hard time making it, the two of them. And
they will have, also, expenses for school, if they went
to school. I mean, they're really in the hole when they
start, too far. When the first one got married, I don't
know what it was back then. But when the second one
got married, I asked [her] (my wife didn't like it), 'Can
I just give you a thousand dollars?' At that time that's
all it was, get married, just invite us and her parents.
She wouldn't do it, and they made it alright, but I worry about that.

Charlie's story reminds me of my friends who will be getting
married at the time of this book's publishing. They are not asking for wedding presents. Instead, they're asking for money they
can put toward paying off their student loans, which, combined,
amount to $90,000. They want a home of their own but can-
not get a mortgage because their debt-to-income ratio is out of

range, and their credit along with it. As Charlie said, my generation is starting two steps back from previous generations.

SOCIAL SECURITY INSURANCE

Another pressing financial issue for younger generations is social security. I was particularly appreciative of Owen Aukeman's description of what he's seen happen to social security over his lifetime.

> I don't know what happened in Washington. social security started when I was born, in '32 or '33, and there were 30-50 people working for social security. Paying in, and the government was taking in the money all the time. But now, I just heard the other night, again . . . [retired] people like us are making our money on dividends, stocks, we're making more money today than when we were working. But they're not taking anything off from our check. In fact, we're getting our social security. So, they're not taking anything from us, except that we do pay our taxes, we probably give back to the government every year as much as they give us, but it's really not fair.
>
> Every check you get they take money out for your social security, and [Millennials] probably will never get it back, because at the end of the day it's going to be bankrupt. And so, I hear a conversation about how are we going to resolve that. I don't know how it's going to be resolved, but it has to be resolved, because what's happening . . . at that time people lived until 50 to 60 years old. 65 was old! Here I'm 83, and the doctor told me the other day we're going to give you five to ten more years. Well, guess what's going to happen? We're going to be collecting social security, and it's not fair.

So, it was a wonderful thing, and about 90% of the people still collecting social security need that money, but there's not going to be enough there . . . Somebody has to get really serious about correcting some of those things.

This comes full circle to the discussion had in the chapter on Work — that employers now have high standards of education, but the payoff isn't being seen by students or workers. Even for those who get what is considered a 'good job' their first year out of university, the total earnings may be below minimum wage due to their student loan payments. This was a major topic of the most recent presidential election and continues to this day in the renewed focus on learning a trade over getting a bachelor's degree.

My cousin, Barbara Markess (b. 1932), who grew up on a shared property with my dad in the working-class steel mill towns north of Pittsburgh, summarizes the urgency many in my own generation feel about this shift in education and career opportunity.

First you had to go to high school, then you had to go to college, now it's beyond college, which is good, to a degree. But some people have all these degrees, spend all this money, and can't find jobs . . . It's sad. I mean, I feel bad for them. They spent all this money, all this time, and I feel bad for them because it must be discouraging to some of them. Some of them have moved on and found different areas to expand, but it's hard.

POVERTY

"I think when you have come from an environment in which you don't have very much, everybody else is poor also, so you don't feel that stigma of being poor. But I can remember men knocking on our back door [to ask] if there was a job they could do because they would like some food, they were hungry . . . I think it made us more appreciative, and I think a lot of people today don't have that. We take care of things, and I wonder about that today in our throwaway society."

— Ruth Blair

Mershon Neisner (b. 1945) grew up in a family she simultaneously describes as middle class and poor. She never wanted for anything, but today's standards have changed society's expectations for what a childhood must look like, and it surely affects her view of her upbringing.

> I have just great memories. It was a very small town at the time, Grand Island was about 25,000. Now it's double that, probably. It was the ideal childhood. I played outside. I had lots of friends. We were very middle class, if that. At the time it was very middle class. Today it would be like, 'Oh my gosh, we were poor,' but we didn't feel that way at all, and we probably weren't. My dad and my mom both had college degrees, and my dad was a hospital administrator.

Ruth Harper grew up in Grand Rapids, Michigan, in a family that self-subsisted, though they lived in a city. She explains that a plethora of toys and things for the children wasn't standard in that era.

> We had relatively few things because things weren't that in. A few decorative trinkets, a few pictures on the wall. There were lots of books, my family were always readers, and at one point in my fairly early childhood I counted 700 books . . . We had old furniture. Shoes you got once a year. You got a pair for school. Some folks also got Girl Scout patent leather [shoes] for Sundays. We didn't. We just polished our saddle shoes and wore them to church if we went . . .
>
> Clothing, I was the youngest of three girls, I got lots of hand-me-downs [*laughs*] and I didn't mind that a bit. My mother also made clothes, so as a little kid I was almost always in homemade play clothes. Little pants things with the bib and the straps and the buttons, all linen and over a shirt. I don't know. She might have made some of the shirts, too.

Today, poverty means something very different compared to our elders. Most of the Greatest Generation had only a few wooden toys, and that was okay. Some didn't have electricity or indoor plumbing, as in the case of Onalee Cable. Today, children grow up with many amenities and so many toys they seem overwhelmed. In fact, emerging studies suggest too many toys may be related to anxiety, ADD, and underdevelopment of creativity.[49]

In many cases, it was the family unit as a whole that carried them through an impoverished situation. Shirley Tate

---

[49] Kim John Payne, *Simplicity Parenting* (Ballantine Books, 2010) https://amzn. to/2xxmXok

describes what it was like for her family during the Great Depression. Despite the extreme hardship, everyone was taken care of.

> . . . We were all very close. The sisters helped each other. What one had, the other one had. There on the farms, they raised cows for milk and beef, and they rose pigs for their pork, and they had chickens for eggs and chicken on Sunday. They swapped out food from the garden as well as the animals. When somebody killed a pig everybody got pork, and like I said, it was a Depression going on, but we didn't know it. We had things good in comparison to the other people. I attribute some of that to the big family and the way they were raised. The way my mother was raised, the way my grandma raised them, and the way momma raised us . . .
>
> We were poor, there was a lot of things we didn't have, but we didn't know it. We were well-fed, and had a lot of company, and a big family, and everybody in the same church, and things just went along like that until I was 14.

Parents just did the best they could with what they had, and for the Greatest Generation, it seems that knowing one's parents were focused on one's wellbeing was enough. Mary Muscatello grew up in a very poor family by today's standards, but she knew her father loved her and her siblings and wanted the best for her. A lack of things did not set them back in life.

> We never had the best car, we never had a new car, and [my father] would pick up some of these jitney's, we called them jitney's, but there was always some kind of motor to jump into, and sometimes a rumble seat. [My father] would take us out. I think he was a kind

of naturalist. He loved the outdoors. He wanted us to flourish, I get the sense.

It was kind of sad how we [a family of nine children] had to go from a small little house, at one time, to an upstairs flat that didn't have a full bathroom, and we had to take baths on Saturday night in a big galvanized tub, so that was an ordeal. But I knew, I always felt that it was a kind of temporary thing. But there were a lot of sacrifices that were made, but we knew it was okay. We felt it was an okay thing.

My father would take [us on picnics in a big field] . . . We'd go out there with the intention of picking dandelion greens because they were supposed to be so healthy for you. [He'd take] a kettle and fill it with water, and he'd start a fire with a few stones or brick around and then he'd put pasta in there, and we would have a dish of pasta and some sauce and then we would enjoy eating that. After, he would take the pan down to the brook or stream nearby and cleaned it. He picked up a handful of mud from the stream and he'd be cleaning the inside of the kettle, and I . . . thought it was defeating the purpose. He said, 'I need this because it's abrasive.' And that was my first exposure to the word abrasive, and I was seven or eight years old.

Hal Royer grew up during the Great Depression in the Dust Bowl. The conditions which he described in the chapters on Amenities and Transportation, conditions in which countless others were reared, would likely be grounds for removal from the home by Child Protective Services today.

As Jim Hayes Jr. puts it,

I guess at that time, everybody was poor, but we never . . . wanted for anything . . . I don't ever remember being without.

COMPUTERS & SCHOOL

"We never should have put the test questions on the computers if there weren't enough [to go around]!"
— Charlie Rusher

Today, to be impoverished often means a lack of updated technology or reliable Internet connection, not a lack of running water or indoor plumbing. Teachers that I interviewed for this book, like Urcell Schulterbrandt, reinforced this fact.

> I think that technology has hurt minority students more than anything else. Not because of access, but because there comes a time that you don't need a computer, you need to speak to someone . . . there comes a time when you have to interface with someone . . . That's the trouble of them having technology because it affected people's [social skills] who can less afford to be affected by such advancement of technology.

My education, and probably that of many others, hid this problem from view. The first school I attended with a computer lab was my second elementary (a new building built halfway through my primary school years). This was in the mid-1990s. Every so often, my class would book an hour in the lab to learn a computer program or complete an assignment.

Our library had computers as well. While we learned to do bibliography from book pages, our exposure to card catalogs and the Dewey Decimal System was limited due to the new computer system. Because of my age, I didn't think twice about using computers to find books. With no prior experience, it seemed normal. This is the experience of any youth growing up in what may be a unique set of circumstances if they are not told there is any other way, a role I hope this book will fill.

Middle school was my first experience with mobile computer carts full of laptops. Our class would rent a cart when we needed computers to complete a project. I thought the carts were silly and awkward, preferring the organized environment of the computer lab. I was too young to realize that carts symbolized the growth of using computers for education — there were too many classes competing for the computer labs and computer carts bridged that gap.

My family also had a computer at home thanks to my dad's career in computer software sales. By then, it was mandatory that one use a Word Processor to complete one's schoolwork. When school papers came due, I was able to write them at home. No handwriting or typewriting necessary. (In fact, the first typewriter I had full access to was a brilliant birthday gift from a past partner to encourage me in finishing my novel — I still have the olive-green Olympia and continue to use it to write my books.) All the while, I didn't realize that this was a unique set of circumstances, even within my own extended family.

Contrast my unlimited computer access to that of the boy I tutored 15 years later in 2010 while working for the National Civilian Community Corps. By then I had my own laptop and cell phone (no smartphone for another year, however). The school at which I tutored was in Woodland, California, the fourth poorest district in California at the time, and one of the greatest migrant worker populations in the country.

I was instructed to rotate between students, but one in particular seemed to need me more than others. This boy, son of migrant workers, stayed after school because he had a paper due about World War II.

The paper wasn't the reason he had to stay after school. If he'd had it his way, he would have gone home to write the paper in the comfort of a familiar space with the encouragement of his parents. The paper needed to be researched and typed, and the family didn't have a computer, Internet, or any of the 'old school' tools like an encyclopedia.

The value of learning to search Google for the answers one seeks, something I sometimes have to teach my entrepreneur clients, is invaluable today. I literally started my website development business and learned to code because I searched online — I didn't take design courses, first. That was one of the main lessons I attempted to impart on him.

My tutee's dedication to his paper was understandably lacking. He didn't want to spend more time at school, especially with a strange woman who didn't share his background, to complete homework in an environment that resembled detention. I could tell that, in addition to his lack of enthusiasm, he didn't know how to use Google — or to conduct the critical thinking to formulate a basic research question. Some may blame today's education system, some the language barrier, some his moving locations often in chase of work causing a lack of stability or consistency, and some the Internet itself. Whatever the reason, it was obvious to me that the lack of a computer in the home directly correlated to this boy's success in school, which would ultimately influence his further success in life.

Charlie Rusher is still active in his neighborhood association, which was formed to quell crime in the area and help the school, which had fallen behind on averages. When the association was formed, they asked the school what they could do to support its student population in getting back on track with national averages. They started by putting a walkway in the neighborhood, so students could safely cross a highway and walk to school directly from the neighborhood, drastically shortening the walk.

> [Now] it's only a half a block to the school.
> And then . . . they don't have shampoo. They don't have lip balm . . . toothpaste, combs, toothbrushes. Three times I've taken 100 down there. I go to garage sales and get 'em. They don't sell so [I get them for] 25 cents apiece. I have got some wonderful thanks from

the school . . . that's one thing we do . . . and I'm not the only one.

[So] we asked them what [else] we could do, and they said they didn't have enough computers for all [the students] to have computers when they're taking the test, [which is timed] so that counts against them . . . We get the grant [for the computers] and the people at the grant say, 'Well, can they afford to be hooked up once you get them?' No . . . So, they can't take them home to use.

We should have never put the [test] questions on the computers to begin with if everybody didn't have them. That's common sense, you know? My daughters both have to teach, and there's things just like that.

Another thing . . . they give them meals and a lot of people complain about that, but a lot of kids don't get [a meal otherwise]. They're better students when they get a breakfast.

My oldest daughter teaches at an all-black school, and there she's taught six grades . . . They have put disabled children all in with the other kids. Which is a good thing in one sense. But it takes away too much from the kids, because they're very disruptive, you know? I don't have a child like that, and I can see why they do it, because they get along better in life if they [are integrated], but with my daughters they both say the whole class . . . will get [held up] because they just go wild sometimes, and they talk out loud and the whole class laughs, and they're not disciplined at all, I mean you can't do it. I wonder if we're losing some good kids to the bad kids.

With changes in what poverty means to Americans comes something else — changes in what safety means.

SAFETY

"Things were easier back then. We didn't have to worry about being up at night, and our doors locked. Playing outside at night, walking home from a friend's house not worrying like we do, now. It's sad we have to worry about that, now, as much as we do."

— Adele Jones

I waited until late in my writing to tackle this chapter. It's a complicated topic, made even more complicated by technology and population growth. Consider this; the world's population was just above 2 billion in the 1950s. We just passed 7.5 billion in 2017. That's a massive difference, and it influences everything.

With more people comes more activity. That's just a fact. And so, regardless if crime's prevalence has actually increased, it will seem so to the Greatest Generation, just as everything else will seem to happen more often. Technically, it is happening more, because there are nearly four times more people doing more things on this planet.

Now add the ability to gain access to information at a moment's notice due to the radio, television, and Internet. We learn when something happens in nearly the same hour of its occurrence. As Jubal Hershaw states in *Stranger in a Strange Land*, "... most neuroses can be traced to the unhealthy habit of wallowing in the troubles of 5 billion strangers."[50]

---

[50] Robert A. Heinlein, *Stranger in a Strange Land* (New York: G.P. Putnam's Sons, 1961), 98.

In 2014, my small city of Grand Rapids, Michigan, made national headlines for an awful crime. That June, Charles Oppenneer was found in a park, dead and headless. Soon after, his girlfriend was also discovered dead, too late for their unborn child, in the trunk of their killer's car who committed suicide during police apprehension.[51]

A friends' dad, a detective for the local force, worked the case. She told me how disturbed he was by the proceedings. Indeed, if this wasn't the biggest murder story to ever occur in the area, it was absolutely the most disturbing in memory.

Adele Jones continues her opening remarks on how her feeling of safety has changed in her small town.

> Well, like I said earlier, being more fearful of taking walks and having your doors unlocked, that has changed. If I'm alone I don't feel safe even having the doors unlocked and the windows open. It's just the way it is these days.

Chris Smith acknowledges the very real increase in violence in one specific area — mass shootings. Yet, another school shooting was reported the morning of this writing, the 16th school shooting of the year, the highest number at this point in the year since 1999.[52] As we explored in the chapter on War, weapons are technologically advanced, just like every other tool. Yet, they aren't regulated in a way that prevents mass shootings, affecting not only the safety of the children schools are intended to protect, but the general public.

---

[51] MLive, "Craigslist Murders," http://www.mlive.com/news/grand-rapids/index.ssf/2014/08/craigslist_murders_wyoming_pol.html

[52] CBS News, "16 School Shootings in 2018 Alone," https://www.cbsnews.com/news/generation-lockdown-16-school-shootings-in-2018-alone/

> The things I don't like [today] is going on with the guns. I've always had guns, I've never carried one with me, but I had a concealed permit to carry if I wanted to . . . I don't know . . . as far as I'm concerned, why the government doesn't come in and take, especially these automatic rifles, and destroy them, get rid of them . . . The guns in the schools is just unbelievable. The reason for it I just don't understand.

So, what happened to the couple in Grand Rapids? Brady Oestrike, the man responsible for these crimes, was responding to a Craigslist ad posted by the couple.

Craigslist is a free online classifieds site where users can post jobs, sales, and other interests. I've used it dozens of times to buy and sell furniture, hire tradesmen or new employees, and give away free stuff (called "curb alerts"). Have I become more cautious in using the program since the awful murders that took place only five miles from my home? No.

Thelma Gale lives a mile north of my home at an assisted living home, one mile further from the attacks. I feel incredibly secure where I am, and just as secure walking around downtown alone. Her sentiment, influenced by both age and the news, is very different.

> I know if I'm in the city I'm afraid. Now that we're here [in assisted living], we feel very secure, and the people take very good care of us here. But as an older person, I have to use a walker, I would be afraid to walk downtown, because some ruffian would take advantage of an older person. I don't remember ever hearing of people being robbed, and I'm sure they were when I was a child . . .
>
> [Newspapers] were the technology, then. We had a radio, but it was a little tiny radio sitting in the corner of our breakfast nook, and my mother would put it on,

sometimes, but there weren't the constant newscasts that we have, now. I mean, something's happening and within ten minutes it's on television. But we do have a TV. We watch it too much. Especially now that we're here, living in one room.

Eva Amundson (b. 1911) of Missoula, Montana, one of the eldest people I interviewed aged 104 at the time, echoed what Thelma said about personal security and the shared community of assisted living.

> Well, we're getting to be a fearful society. When I was growing up we didn't have to worry about people coming in and robbing you or stealing or anything like that. We never locked our doors. We were too trusting, I guess, and I guess our generation still trusts people . . . When I go to lunch, I lock my [apartment] door, because when people come in you don't know who it is. You have friends, but very few. You get so . . . you don't trust people, anymore. You have that in the back of your mind.

I wasn't able to study whether Eva's statement about trust is true. However, the gap created by technology between generations has created a market for preying on our elders. The lack of knowledge of some about how technology affects banking, taxes, and medicine has left them vulnerable. This usually comes in the form of a phone call requesting social security numbers without authorization or donations to fake organizations. It is such a shame that we value our elders so little in our culture that an entire industry has sprung up around scamming them out of their fixed income.

I've chosen not to watch the news. I've realized that television media is in the business of ratings, and the more macabre a story equals more viewers and higher ratings. When I do watch the news, I feel immediately unsafe and fearful. There is so much horror right in my backyard! With the television off, I can remember the truth: I bought a house in the safest neighborhood in my city; Greater Grand Rapids has seen a crime rate drop of 20% over the past 20 years;[53] and the United States' violent crime rate has likewise gone down by 50% over the past 20 years.[54] I am safer than I've ever been.

THE TECHNOLOGY OF NEWS

"I think we have gained confidence . . . and security."
— Mary Muscatello

Let's take a step back. Remember this is a book about technology, not crime statistics. Technology has improved communication immensely, making it infinitely easier for media outlets to get hold of any story, no matter its locale. Rather than needing employees to watch the ticker tape and hope something big comes through, news syndicates have computer programs that watch Twitter and other websites for keywords. 911 calls are now recorded, placing viewers right at the scene when the story is replayed on the six o'clock news.

Kenny Ladner (b. 1947) of Mississippi explains how the advent of the radio has played a massive role in the apprehension of a criminal.

---

[53] MLive, "Grand Rapids Area Crime Drops," http://www.mlive.com/news/grand-rapids/index.ssf/2013/08/grand_rapids_area_crime_drops.html
[54] Pew Research Center, "5 Facts About Crime In The US," http://www.pewresearch.org/fact-tank/2017/02/21/5-facts-about-crime-in-the-u-s/

> [You know] the CB Radios? Well, the radios are way ahead of where an individual might be [because of the network]. You take a criminal trying to hop on the highway, most of your law enforcement is behind him, but we've got radios way ahead, so we can catch him on ahead. So, that's technology.

We have smartphones that take video, which can be instantly uploaded to the web or sent directly to media agencies for a finder's fee, and digital cameras that capture photos that are easily duplicated by a click. We have left the world of secondhand reporting and entered an era wherein crime doesn't feel so far away because we can see and hear it as if we were there. With the Google Pixel™ (and other smartphones) being issued with virtual reality goggles and products like Google Glass™ a growing market, it may not be long before we can actually view a crime scene in 3D, as if we were really there. Crime rates are down, but we feel like they're up because a private dispute-turned-shooting in Santa Fe can be televised to Long Island, usually with hype and spin on the incident so viewers don't turn off the program even though the event took place 1,000 miles away.

Renee Scott of Portland explains that not only does technology play a role in the closeness of news, but it also can generate the news. Technology is a tool, and people will use it how they wish. If someone is negative in nature, they will use technology to that extent.

> I think there's a lot of predatory people out there, and they are misusing what was meant to be a good thing. You see it every day on the news, and a lot of this has to do with people posting pictures, posting their children's pictures, that type of thing. I don't think it's a good thing, you know?
> I think the loss is as great as the gain, but when you, say, watch the news, and I like the news, I like the

local news as well as the world news, you see where technology is doing a lot of harm. Even airplane crashes they say could have been caused by somebody with a laser, you know? It's terrible. People are dying from some of this stuff.

Recall the beheading that took place only five miles from my house. Five miles seems awfully close. Yet, in a densely populated area like a city, it is a considerable distance. In fact, the crime was far enough away that it was in a different municipality entirely. It's easy to forget that when the information is so accessible, but the reality is even a break-in two blocks from my house is many, many homes away.

COMMUNITY

"In those days, if the neighbors saw [you misbehaving], they would call and say, 'Do you know what your granddaughter was doing?' So, you couldn't get away with much in those days."

— Dagmar Booth

Airbnb, the online rental community founded in 2008 that enables users to rent or lease their couch, spare bedroom, or entire apartment, has taken root in communities around the world. In doing so, tourists and visitors are able to stay in what were otherwise private homes, blurring the lines between commercial and private residences and altering how community is formed. In a tourist hotspot like New Orleans, Airbnb is a gold mine for residents with extra space in their homes. Unfortunately, the website became popular at a time when the city was still vulnerable after Hurricane Katrina. The 2005 hurricane significantly altered the neighborhoods of the region, including ownership of homes that were previously owned through inheritance for generations. Opportunists purchased many of the homes to flip them. Those that retained their new properties could use Airbnb to provide a steady stream of guests at a higher rate than a typical renter.[55]

New hotels and bed-and-breakfasts have been tightly restricted or banned for many years in New Orleans' French

---

[55] New York Times, "Airbnb Pits neighbor against neighbor in tourist friendly New Orleans," https://www.nytimes.com/2016/03/06/business/airbnb-pits-neighbor-against-neighbor-in-tourist-friendly-new-orleans.html?_r=0

Quarter to preserve some degree of the residential character that is part of its attraction. Regulations for short-term rentals are even tighter (nothing under 30 days, in theory), but Airbnb and other online services have provided an easy workaround. The technology that has disrupted the hospitality industry has also disrupted civic life and public policymaking.

To this point, Barbara Markess (my elder cousin in Pennsylvania) makes a point that is reflective of the disruption that Airbnb creates for our communities. However, it seems that it's not just Airbnb that has had an effect. In fact, towns and cities that don't have a large rental turnover are still experiencing less neighborliness.

> Neighbors used to get along, and now you don't even know your neighbors . . . People are more afraid, now. Some people. They're not as open as they used to be. You know, you could trust everybody. You knew your neighbors. You knew who was selling things . . . you just knew everybody, and you knew who to trust. And neighbors watched out for neighbors. I mean, if someone came to the door [when I was little] and you didn't know them, you would close the door. But the neighbors would know your parents weren't home [and] somebody would come over to see what was going on. It's a different world, today.

I want to take a step back to recall the conversation I had with HJ Smith about refrigeration and farmer's markets in the Food chapter. Her comments about the Kelvinator (refrigerator) are similar to another story Marge Darger of Midland, Michigan, told about garage doors. Neighbors were almost guaranteed to see each other every day and have an opportunity to say hello because they had to get out of their cars twice a day to open and close their garage doors. Automatic doors were invented in

1926 but weren't popularized until after World War II.[56] Add to that machines like loud gas-powered lawn mowers as opposed to the quiet reel mowers, and our opportunities to see and interact with each other as a natural course of the day dwindle.

> Garage door openers, so people go into their garages, so they don't [talk]. They use the dryers instead of hanging clothes out in the back yard, so there's no natural ways for neighbors to connect. And they're busy, so they don't connect. I think the impact on neighborhoods — well, I know there's been a tremendous impact on neighborhoods because . . . our Mayor has been pushing neighbors to neighbor. I mean, she has had all these different programs going, and she's picked them up from all these programs around the country. So, it's obviously a problem.

Many of those I interviewed told me stories of running around town, freely exploring, during their childhood. There weren't any video games to keep kids indoors, so after school and on weekends they would all turn out of the house to invent games, ride bikes, and play together.

Rhea Currie, whom we met in the chapter on Medicine, loved her roller skates, and was free to go where she wanted, but within certain boundaries. One night, she pushed that boundary, and got in trouble.

> We just skated around town. One evening, three other girls and I got in a bit of trouble because there was a

---

[56] Wikipedia, "Garage Door Opener," https://en.wikipedia.org/wiki/Garage_door_opener

new highway, and the last thing my father said to me was . . . don't go out on the new highway. And the next thing I know, we were way, way out on that highway, and it was getting a little dark. One of the girls had brought her little sister along, and she was getting to the whining stage. She was getting tired! [*laughs*] I was probably 12 . . .

Anyway, we turn around to go home and we saw a car coming toward us and we were so excited. It was my father, and the father of the sisters, and so we start scrambling into the car, and my father says, 'I'm sorry, but you were not to come out here, tonight. You skated out, and you will have to skate home, but I will not leave you.' So, he drove beside me all the way home.

Ruth Harper told me stories at length of running around her neighborhood in Grand Rapids, getting dirty and scraped up, with the other kids on her block. She summed up the experience compared to today's children with this.

Kids weren't thought of as these little things to put in a jar until they're 18 and then let them out and see if they can climb a ladder. We were all over the place. I was running up and down ladders handing my Pa . . . more nails . . . if he had to fix the roof . . .

Carol Ann Lesert (b. 1932) lived very near to where Ruth grew up in Grand Rapids. She remembers her local police sergeant being kind and a trusted figure in the neighborhood. Someone that one could approach in a friendly and familiar manner. Today, that familiarity is gone, and, in many cases, is reversed.

On the corner . . . there was a police precinct. There was this . . . Sergeant . . . and he took over watching the kids a lot, in the neighborhood. He gave me my first pair of roller skates . . . those kinds that you [strap] onto your shoes. He gave my three brothers these toy trucks to play with. He was just like a summertime Santa Clause. He was great . . . Nowadays, it is [unusual] . . . People were much more together . . . and that's one thing your [smartphone] did. It did good, and it did bad. It did some of both.

Donald Wensel, who grew up in the town adjacent to my dad in Pennsylvania, continues Ruth and Carol's commentary.

[We've lost] togetherness. When I was a kid I lived atop of a hill. There was two streets that came up, and there was a little street that came across. It was about half a mile down from my street to the next major cross street. And I think I knew everybody on those two streets and maybe the next street over.

Now nobody knows anybody, and they don't care. Even right here, people across my cul-de-sac [*points to the apartments across the parking lot*] they don't speak to us. It's just a different world. And that I don't like. 'Cause it used to be close. It's gone.

There are stories of barn raisings in our past, typically seen by our younger generations only in books or in movies. It used to be that the entire neighborhood would turn out with food and drink and help lift those walls into place, no questions asked, because they knew the favor would be returned. In those days, it wasn't seen as a favor. It seems that it's not just family that has moved apart, but communities as a whole.

Edwin Gould, pioneer in developing the cameras in our first spy satellites, remembers what it was like.

The generation before me, the previous owners of [our] cabin, if anything needed to get done they got together and did it. Now, if anything needs to get done, we all chip in money and hire someone to go do it. Community getting together to do things happened in my growing up years in New Hampshire as well. If you were going to build a garage all the neighbors came over and helped you build the garage. Nowadays you go and hire a contractor to do it. Almost no one builds their own, and certainly all the neighbors don't come . . . I mean, that was normal. That wasn't an unusual thing, that was normal, that everybody chipped in to help everybody. You helped this guy plow his garden. He helped you plow yours. We lost some sense of community by our technology.

Not only was it conventional to help each other with work, but it wasn't unusual to watch each other's kids, or to share tools and resources. Bones' family lives this way, today, but they feel isolated by the fact that they help each other.

Fifty years ago, a hundred years ago, every house had a porch, and people sat on the porch. Now, if a house has a porch today, it's for looks. No one goes outside and sits on the porch. No one knows who their neighbors are. No one knows what their neighbors do. No one knows what their kids do.

When [my daughter] grew up, she grew up in a house full of people, in an extended family of hippies, and there was what, a hundred of us? And at any given time, our house was the central place because her mom and I were the first two to get married and the first two to have kids . . . and every night it was a house full of people. And we never locked the doors. To this day we never lock the doors. I don't have keys to my house; I don't even know if I have keys to my house. I don't take the keys out of my truck. We go to bed, it doesn't matter who was there, you'd go to bed and there was a house full of people, and you'd wake up and there was a house full of people you'd never seen before and it was okay, because everybody was good. Everybody took care of everybody's kids. If you went somewhere you went with eight kids and you only had one [of your own]. You took a crew of them. If you had to discipline you'd spank 'em all.

Everyone took care of everybody else's building. If you had something, you shared . . . and it's not like that anymore. There's no sharing or caring . . . It's all very much 'me me me me me'.

When did it stop? Was it because of the safety concerns discussed in the previous chapter? Or, like some elders imply, echoed in a recent music video released by Moby titled *Are you Lost in the World?*,[57] are we too distracted by our bright LED displays to notice our neighbors?

Pauline Attisani, sister of Barbara Markess, suggests its beginning.

People don't enjoy people anymore. We used to play charades a lot — people don't even know what charades is anymore. [We used to play] all kinds of games. People don't do that anymore. It's sad. You know, [now] you almost live your life around the television . . .

Dagmar Booth made the same point during her interview. She reminds us that life is unpredictable, and that these gatherings are important not only for connection and celebration, but also to draw closer to loved ones when they age.

---

[57] Moby & the Void Pacific Choir, "Are You Lost In The World Like Me?," https://www.youtube.com/watch?v=VASywEuqFd8

Who gets together and talks anymore? You know, in the 50s you'd go to these dinner parties, on the weekend families would have the card games. Someone's birthday party would be a big thing. Sometimes it was a themed birthday party.

One year, John's birthday was coming up, and I said well are we going to do it this weekend? And he says no, it's going to be too hot, and we almost cancelled it. At the last minute he says oh come on let's get everybody together . . . It's a good thing we did, because that was Sunday, on Monday he got the call that his dad had had a massive stroke and had died.

The Booths are thankful for this last interaction with a loved one before they passed. I, myself, have my own thankful story. A dear friend passed away at age 38 from a heart attack. It was a genetic condition that we knew about, but thought was managed. Though I will always wish I had spent more time with him, prioritizing time together over our busy schedules, I thank my stars that he dropped in on me on his way home from a black-tie event three weeks before his death. I got to spend time with him, hear about his work and romance, and enjoy his presence one last time.

David Netterfield (b. 1938) grew up talking to his grandfather while dangling his legs out the window of the family gas station. He illustrated the need for these connections during his interview. You'll read more touching stories about spending time with his grandfather in the following chapters. He says he's been writing about this, because it seems like something we've lost. In his mind, it's more important than some of the other things technology has altered.

I've written a few articles about the benefits of living here at Hope [Meadows]. The neighborliness of the folks that are living here with us and the fact that you can walk around and know everybody in a few block area. We speak to them by name and they speak to us by name. I thought that my real accomplishment in that regard was when I became able to start calling pets by name.

That used to be the way it was when we lived in Midland, [Michigan], and we lived on Burgess Street. We knew everybody on this small street. Several of them were school friends of mine. The older folks loved to have us all come and visit with them, to sit and chat. But after I left there . . . I lost some of that. When I was in the military . . . I often didn't know the people who lived on either side of us. I can think of one town in California while I was going to school out there, and I knew people three or four doors down from ours, and we were friends. They had kids about the same age as ours, but I didn't know the people who lived immediately around me. I found that frustrating as I got older. It's very difficult. It's not at all comfortable.

That was one of the things that appealed to us about Hope Meadows. When we came here to visit, to inquire about the community, we met some people who were just darling. I remember standing over there on the other side of Fran's house one afternoon, talking to the gal who lives in the next house beyond her, and she was just such a wonderful, open person, that tried to encourage us to come. And as the conversation went on, her son arrived back on the school bus, and he came over to talk to us, and he said, 'Oh, would you please move here? Would you move into this house right here? Because nobody lives in there and we'd love to have a neighbor there, somebody we can come and visit with.'

Later, when we ultimately moved here, I spent several years taking that young man to doctor's visits in another community an hour, hour and a half from here, one day a week, and then coming home by way of a restaurant where we could combine dinner and enjoy his company. It's just so different from my military experience, and even post-military experience . . . There were many years in my life, and probably many other people's lives, where you just lived here by yourself, you went about and did your things, but you had no idea who the other people were in your life.

Dave Chicoring, who described some of this at length in the Communication chapter, returns us to what he coins the 'acceleration factor'. The idea that technological development is exponential, to which point not only do we have trouble integrating it into our lives in a healthy manner, we have trouble predicting careers since there are new industries developing each day. This disrupts both family and community.

We've lost stability, for whatever that's worth. Community, you might call it. We've lost community. We probably don't know our neighbors. We knew everything about our neighbors, good and bad, back in country school. Now, it's a very impersonal world, and that can have its good and bad, too. We've lost the sense of community, and we've lost the stability.

What are you going to do? I'm going to be a doctor, I'm going to be a veterinarian, I'm going to be this, I'm going to be that. Things are changing so rapidly, now, how the hell can we predict? We can't predict the stock market. We can't predict a lot of things. It's the acceleration factor.

GENERATIONAL PROXIMITY

"It was a quieter time. People stayed put more than they do, now."

— Rhea Currie

Generations are living further and further from each other. It's likely that the majority of those reading this book grew up with only two generations in the home, yourselves and your parents, with your elders living outside your neighborhood. One set of my grandparents lived two cities away, a half hour drive. The other set lived two states and a four-hour drive away. I saw one side several times a month, and the other several times a year.

Rhea Currie grew up on a farm with family that rotated in and out of the house. Someone was always around to help with the children, and they never felt alone.

> We were fortunate. One of my aunts' children were older enough that . . . one of them always lived with us, when we were young. It was their job to get us off to school . . . [We had a] very family-oriented upbringing with so many of my mother's siblings near to us. They were the people that we really associated with.

Today's children may receive similar care, but from a babysitter or nanny who is ultimately a stranger to the family connections that each household has. Relatives are often too far away or too busy to offer regular support.

Ever since transportation became faster, safer, and more reliable for the consumer market, generations have been moving further apart. In some cases, it's for career opportunity (like my father), in others it's simply because they can (myself). In the

20th century, the ease of travel to visit family after migration helps maintain family connections and has released many more to make a move they might not have otherwise. The advent of the telephone, computer, Internet, and smartphone has further affected our ability to maintain family across state and country lines.

HJ Smith explains how easy it is to visit her children thanks to modern technology.

> It certainly has aided us in the fact that our families are more spread out and we can visit people. We can go visit our son in New York, we can go down to our daughter in Mississippi, they can come here, we can go to the local airport and we can fly, so that's wonderful.
>
> I sometimes think about those people who came here in the 1600s and the 1700s never to see their families again and maybe never to hear from them. I mean, if they were illiterate, they couldn't write, they couldn't read, and then if they sent a letter on a ship and it sank or pirates got it, you know?
>
> And that provided, too, an outlet for people if they needed to get away, if they were outlaws and they needed to find the frontier and just go, then they weren't murdering their friends and neighbors, wherever, so it's a double-sided thing. Now there's no frontier, there's no place to go — well, maybe Alaska. But if a young person needs to find a means of support to feed himself, where does he go if he has no skills? You can't go out on the frontier. But then there are [new] ways to get skills.

So, how recent is this evolution away from multi-generational homes as a norm? Many in the Greatest Generation had live-in grandparents. Sonee Lapadot of Detroit dove right into this topic during our interview.

My grandfather had a stroke — he was a surgeon — and the whole left side was gone. Both families sold their homes and moved into one big enough to have his sick room in the office behind the dining room, so we could all work together. People don't do that today, either, I guess. My grandmother ran the house and my mother ran the dance studio. So, my dad went off to war, and Nana did the cooking and my mother taught the dancing.

Grace Stinton, too, grew up in a community full of multi-generational homes, hers included.

When I was home in Tiverton, [Rhode Island], before I went to college, families were a lot closer, I think. Generations stayed together. So, often there would be an older grandparent or an older aunt or uncle staying with someone, and they just lived there. In fact, at my grandmother's house, there was always an older relative who helped out . . . My great-grandmother wanted to help, so when my grandfather, who did the dishes at night, did the dishes, he would take the silverware and put it on the table and she would dry the silverware, and she thought she was helping.

So, I think people were a lot, maybe not more considerate of the older people in the family, but there were so many farm families. It wouldn't be an easy thing to do, now. Because if a husband and wife are working, you don't really have the space, you don't really have the opportunity to care for an older person in the family.

I don't know of anyone who went into a nursing home when I was a kid. They were all taken care of by relatives. And I don't think it's because people aren't as considerate, now. It's just a different set of circumstances. You just can't do it at this point.

Well, about families, um, there was radio, there was no television, so there was a closeness, because that was all there was to do, was to talk to each other. You didn't. You weren't disconnected by television or something like that. There was a lot more interaction between the generations.

TECHNOLOGY AND SHARED TIME WITH ELDERS

Grace Stinton alluded to one of the biggest trends of today: retirement and nursing homes. Nursing homes have filled an important void for many who require complex medical care in their old age, but it can easily be argued that they are overused. As I sat with Lillian Carrara in her dining room on Long Island, New York, I saw "the old ways," as Charlotte Lawson implied in the Rights chapter, firsthand.

Lillian's husband has Alzheimer's disease. My grandmother had it, too, so I immediately recognized the hardship Lillian was experiencing. As Seth Rogen stated, "I think until you see [Alzheimer's] firsthand, it's kind of hard to conceive how brutal it is."[58]

Lillian's husband seemed lost and needed to be steered as he navigated the home. Alzheimer's is not an illness that allows for in-home care after a certain stage — the person may get lost, hurt themselves, or hurt others because they just don't recognize things anymore — but Lillian chose to try for a time. It's easy to argue that their connection as husband and wife pushed Lillian to do what many today do not try, but perhaps, as a culture, we have forgotten how to try.

---

[58] CNN, "Seth Rogen: Alzheimer's Is Brutal," http://www.cnn.com/2011/HEALTH/04/27/seth.rogen.alzheimer/index.html, (April 27, 2011).

Even more, home life has significantly changed over the past 50 years. Our lives are less centralized, as Sister Plattie stated. We are also arguably busier these days, as we heard in the chapter on how work and tasking has changed with technology. One hundred and 50 years ago, Leo Tolstoy explored this 'business' of relating to death amid busy lives in *The Death of Ivan Ilych*. In the book, friends were too caught in their own lives to stop, care, or relate as the main character perished.

> Ivan Ilych had been a colleague of the gentlemen present and was liked by them all. He had been ill for some weeks with an illness said to be incurable. His post had been kept open for him, but there had been conjectures that in case of his death Alexeev might receive his appointment, and that either Vinnikov or Shtabel would succeed Alexeev. So, on receiving the news of Ivan Ilych's death, the first thought of each of the gentlemen in that private room was of the changes and promotions it might occasion among themselves or their acquaintances . . .
>
> Each one thought or felt, 'Well, he's dead, but I'm alive!' But the more intimate of Ivan Ilych's acquaintances, his so-called friends, could not help thinking also that they would now have to fulfill the very tiresome demands of propriety by attending the funeral service and paying a visit of condolence to the widow.[59]

I prefer to think that America has culturally forgotten how to care for our relatives in need since an easier option has emerged, rather than the self-centered scenario of Ivan Ilych's friends.

---

[59] Leo Tolstoy, *The Death of Ivan Ilych*, (New York: Everyman's Library, orig. 1886, 2001), 2.

Lillian Carrara knows all too well that family proximity has changed, even in the midst of caring for her husband with the help of her sons who live nearby.

> I grew up in Pittsburgh, on a street where, next door, is the house my mother grew up in, and my grandmothers lived in there while I was growing up, and my aunt and uncle lived in the same house, and two doors away was my aunt Barbie, and another house was my aunt Mary, and then my aunt Zora, and my aunt Charlotte and my uncle Matt. They all lived on the street where they initially grew up, themselves. And so, it was wonderful growing up there, because I never worried about anything. I had so many cousins and we all played together. If my parents had to go out or go shopping, they'd say, 'Stay in the yard, Tete [aunt] Mary is going to be watching, you'd better behave.' You always knew there was going to be an aunt around watching what you did so you didn't get into trouble . . .
>
> Growing up, everybody lived in the same community. As years changed, everybody moved to different places, and the fact that everybody is traveling around the world, now, which, actually was not that common way back when I was young, now you hardly meet anyone who hasn't traveled outside the United States — everybody travels, today.

Elders living apart from us today is mainstream American and very Western. Families of immigrant, ethnic, or minority backgrounds tend not to follow this trend. In fact, a study by Pew Research in 2013 found that families who continue to have live-in grandparents were unlikely to be of Caucasian descent.

Most of my family in Croatia has multiple generations living in the home. One set of relatives live separate from their elders, but they are right next door on land that has been used by the family for generations. My cousins' home has apartments that were added for them as they entered adulthood, with both grandmothers living in the home. Single 30-year-olds still living with their parents and grandparents is frowned upon in the United States due to our value of independence, but in the Old Country, it's still the norm.

One of the most touching stories I was told involving intergenerational relationships was that of David Netterfield and his childhood with his grandfather. I touched on David's story of visiting with his grandfather at the family-owned gas station in the previous chapter.

David's family lived in extreme proximity to each other by today's standards: three generations living together in a travel trailer. While uncomfortable at times, it was this proximity and the care of a family business that allowed David an intimacy with his grandfather that is the stuff of storybooks.

> I used to really enjoy working nights with my grandfather. My grandfather lost both legs at a young age, just above the knee . . . He and I used to have wonderful conversations at the station when we would work nights. The two of us would be alone, we weren't real busy, and so we could talk a lot. So, that was another of my favorite activities.
>
> But I remember when I was, I don't know, three or four, we moved to Midland from Dearborn, [Michigan] — we had a stay in Dearborn for a while, my dad worked at one of the car manufacturers, and after that, when he went into the Navy we moved up to Midland to be with other family, grandparents specifically.
>
> They lived in a, I would guess, 30x6 foot mobile home. Nowadays we call these things travel trailers. You can imagine, in that particular home, there weren't

a lot of bedrooms. So, my mom had the bedroom in the back of the trailer, and I think that my middle sister slept with her. My grandparents had a mattress or some kind of a padding situation that [they] could drop the table down and it would extend between the two bench seats and over the table top, and they stayed there. So, that's the middle of the trailer. We were in bunks above the front window. So, my grandparents were, obviously, within my eyesight.

My grandmother used to get up every morning, and her routine was that she'd get a dish or pan of water, and she'd come in and give my grandfather a sponge bath. And at some point, early on in that relationship, I looked over and saw that his knees were cut off here [*gestures to his leg*], and so as a young boy, what do I know, I said to her, 'Grandma, how did that happen?' She says, 'Well, one day, a long time ago, I was giving Grandpa a bath,' which is what she was doing with this bowl of water, 'and he started to pull out of my arms, and so I grabbed his legs to stop him, and as he fell they just popped right off.' And so, for a number of years I believed that's why he didn't have full legs like the rest of us. Now it sounds ridiculous, but I didn't know any better at that age.

I think that he was working for the CCC and they had some sort of industrial accident that caused that. It wasn't a frequent topic of conversation in the family. It was so easy to just accept him for who he was. He was just a very lovable guy, and that's where this whole conversation started.

Though standards of living have changed so that such family closeness is highly unlikely, David is appreciative of today's technology. He points out that, without it, he wouldn't have the opportunity to meet his grandchildren within 24 hours of their birth. Yes, proximity has changed drastically, but technology also offers the tools to bridge the distance.

> [My son] has a brand new [son] and a not too much older [daughter]. By means of all of our new electronics, I've been able to gather pictures of the two kids as they have grown . . . that's one of the things that keeps me excited about the electronics that's going on.

David wasn't the only one to make this point about technology bringing us closer together. Harriet Berg's comments included in the chapter on Communication highlight the many uses for Skype when family is far away, as did HJ Smith as she considered trying to live without her iPhone.

> It's kind of hard to think about not having one. It's just so neat to see pictures of my grandchildren pop up. Videos of my grandchildren playing their musical instruments 'cause I won't see them that often. So, that's wonderful. I had a granddaughter who went to her first camp, she went to an art camp, so I could text her, and that was wonderful. She'd have mail in her mailbox every day or so. So, that's cool.

When I asked Sylvia Gutierrez about how technology has changed our society, she responded that she misses "the family. The proximity of the children, the grandchildren . . . My children I miss more than anything . . ."

I met Barbara Blake (b. 1936) of Wilmington, North Carolina, courtesy of my friend, Diadra Blake Cooley. Barbara is her grandmother, and I visited her as I drove up the East Coast. Barbara says she, too, believes that family was just closer when she was young.

> We were always close . . . I just think people were clos-
> er when I was coming up than what it is now. I mean
> families were just closer.

Sister Ardeth Plattie observes that generational closeness has
changed both in distance and in relationship. Her words remind
me of the previous chapter on Community, and those of Charlotte Lawson when she talked about caring for her cousin who
was 'slow.' It was common to care for each other as a community, rather than quietly in the family.

> We never drove far distances. We had a very simple
> lifestyle. We seldom could go long distances, just in-
> tentionally, because we didn't have the money to do it.
> Families all lived closer together, in the village. People
> got to know their neighbors very deeply, and caring for
> each other . . .
>
> Definitely, that is one of the things that I've no-
> ticed is that, growing up, any person that was ill, the
> people of the village took care of them. There were
> children in need, like myself. There was always care. If
> it didn't come out of the Sisters at the school, it came
> out of neighbors who knew me and loved me and took
> care of me. You know. So, I think the neighborliness
> was closer, I think communication was deeper, I think
> that there was a concentration on simple ways and
> simple means. I think that, as technology has escalated
> into, you know, various areas, like planes and cars, and
> even mass transit, things became used, and then may-
> be they became abused, instead of being used for just
> basic human need, they became used for such luxury.

Personally, I wish my grandparents had been closer. My maternal
grandmother was diagnosed with Alzheimer's disease so early
in my life that I didn't get to know her, and my paternal grand-

mother was too far away for a familiar relationship to be built. Both passed away when I was 19.

I would have liked to have known them better, and even with the help of today's technology, I don't think I would have known them like I wished. There is something that happens when one shares space and time with another in a relaxed manner. I don't think my family would have worked well living under one roof, but having the ability to spend time at a grandparent's house without time limits offers a familiarity that technology just can't give us.

And so, how has technology changed what family actually means to us as a society?

FAMILY

"What does it do to families? Breaks them up. You got three or four siblings, and they live three or four places in the country, and they're doing wildly different things. And they've probably changed their vocation three or four times in their lifetime."
— Dave Chicoring

What it means to be a family has certainly evolved over the term of human existence. As was demonstrated in the last chapter, family once included multiple generations and a full span of cousins. For those who have read *Gone with the Wind*, there is a moment of pride as Scarlett describes her ability to identify up to her 14th cousin twice removed.[60] I can only handle third cousin thrice removed.

Family meant helping with the family business, even if one was still a child, and family absolutely meant taking care of one another, first. For Rhea Currie, it's unfathomable that families don't stick together, today. Even at a distance, like her and her sons, she feels family should still work on their relationships.

> I couldn't imagine going on TV and saying, 'I hate my mother.' This sort of thing. People don't work on their relationships. They just, I don't know, give up or don't try. I noticed that so much, that families just don't seem to have the same bond.

---

[60] Margaret Mitchell, *Gone with the Wind* (New York: The Macmillan Company, 1936).

What left us crying at the end of Charlotte Lawson's interview in Louisiana was just this. After an hour of rousing skeletons from the family closet and reflecting with her sister that it was the full spread of generations and cousins that helped each other through those hard times, Charlotte realized what had been lost, and what needed to be rekindled.

> Since I talked to you, I've been doing a lot of thinking, and thinking back, and I've thought about things I haven't thought about in years, and it was upsetting. It really was. But I was driven to succeed in life, and I feel like I did . . .
>
> Talking with you . . . has had a big effect on me, personally. You made me think, and the things that I have thought about are going to be talked about in our family . . . We are going to pull together, again, like we did when momma was alive. I am who I am and what I am today because of her, and I'm very, very grateful for that. My daddy made it hard, but she hung in there . . .
>
> Families aren't the same anymore, not like when I was a child. Kids get married and go off. My sister called me last night, because one of momma's grandchildren just got out of a psychiatric hospital. That's not what we called it, but she needed help. And [my sister] said, 'Should I contact the church?' And I thought about it because I had been thinking about [doing this interview] and I said, 'No, let's do what we used to do when momma was alive. What would momma want us to do? Momma would want us to take care of her. You call everybody in the family and you tell them the situation.'

Recall David Netterfield and his family living in the small travel trailer with his grandparents in Midland, Michigan. His grandfather owned a gas station there, and David would help out after school. Not only did he learn valuable skills, but he had irreplaceable moments with his grandfather.

> We'd stand out in front of the station, 'cause there was no air conditioning, and at night it would be warm in there, and so we'd stand there and I remember bending my leg and hooking the heel of my shoe over the windowsill of the station while we were standing there. And some nights we'd spend hours out there, just chatting about who we were, what our goals were in life, what was important to us, and . . . I was basking in his knowledge and love. In spite of his leg problems, some nights he'd go out and pump the gas. He had a cane that he used to get around with, and he was pretty capable in that regard. [*He had prosthetics?*] Yeah. So, I was just so impressed.
>
> That may be part of what led me to get involved in the Special Ed training that I got later on, 'cause I knew that people with disabilities weren't in any way totally disabled. They were quite capable of being a loving, caring, working person. I used to love those nights he and I got to spend together.

Ruth Harper explains that any time one spoke with a family member they were doing more than just talking. There was history and family knowledge being passed on, piece by piece, across generations. I personally enjoy large family gatherings for this reason. It is at these events that stories of family origin are told as aunts, uncles, and older cousins begin reminiscing. Often, stories are told that my parents wouldn't otherwise have disclosed, themselves. These conversations fill in the lines, both of who my parents are, and also of where I come from. Ruth Harper explains,

> Conversation [in the family] was history lesson, basically. Any time they got to reminiscing, we're talking

a lot of years. And, of course, when grandma told her story, that took us back even more . . . That's another thing. Families just were closer. It's a negative influence of television and several other things.

Was family actually closer before technology? Family dinner was mandatory when I was young, as it was for many of those I interviewed, like Tom Lawson, and television or cell phones weren't allowed at the table. According to a 2016 study, this tradition is on the decline.[61]

I wish cell phones were never invented. Everybody is always on their cell phone. Families don't have dinner like they used to because the kids are online surfing the web emailing their friends, texting their friends on cell phones. I think cell phones have done more harm than good.

While television was not allowed during dinner, my dad would, at times, break this rule. For Barbara Blake, the television wasn't even a factor.

I just think that people were closer when I was coming up than what they are, now. I mean families were just closer . . . I think we've lost the closeness of family, because, I mean . . . when we were raising our children, I got up in the morning [with Guthrie] at about 5:30 because he'd have to commute back and forth to Jacksonville, to the Marine Corps base, 'cause that's where he

---

[61] Walton, K., Kleinman, K.P., Rifas-Shiman, S.L. et al, "Secular trends in family dinner frequency among adolescents," *BMC Res Notes* (2016) 9: 35. https://doi.org/10.1186/s13104-016-1856-2

worked. I got up every morning and fixed breakfast for him . . . My kids never went to school without breakfast, either . . . When Guthrie would come home . . . when the kids were little, at 5:30pm they were ready to sit down and have their dinner and . . . we wouldn't start unless he was here. We had television, [but] there was no television while we had dinner because that was our time to discuss what had happened that day and what someone had done wrong, so they would have to tell their daddy. [*laughs*] But it was just closer.

Adele Jones of Michigan echoes Barbara's story in retrospect. 'Families that eat together, stay together' comes to mind. It aids in closeness, communication, and supports long-term relationships.

You know what, I'll just say this, what it makes me think of — my favorite memories, even as a young adult and mother, is going back to my parents' home, sitting around the kitchen table, and family conversations. My favorite memories are being with family without telephones or anything interrupting the conversation and playing games and having fun.

Family spent time together in big ways. Barbara Blake resumes talking about her family.

In the summertime we would go to Masonboro Sound, because my grandfather had a sister that lived down there on the water, and we would go. The whole family would go, and we would stay maybe two or three weeks down there on the water and go fishing and clamming and shrimping and all kinds of things. So, we had a pretty good relationship. And now all my family is dead except one brother and my sister . . .

Adele, too, had regular visiting days with her extended family.

Sunday afternoons were going to your aunts and uncles and playing with your cousins.

Dagmar Booth continues what Adele and Barbara said about their family visiting customs. Dagmar grew up next door to her grandmother in a duplex, similar to my father's growing up in which his grandparents lived in the apartment next door to his parents in a duplex.

My childhood was a lot of fun. We lived next to my grandmother . . . and so every Sunday it was like a new set of playmates because you never knew which cousin was coming. Sometimes everybody would be there, and since you lived on a corner you basically took over a quarter of a block because, I think at one time we counted, we had 40 or more grandchildren, and when we all showed up we would have a ball playing outside, in the backyard, down the street, down the other street. So, it was a fun childhood. What can I say? Those were the good old days.

The families got together every Saturday night to play cards. Whereas people getting together with the families and playing on Friday or Saturday night, they'd play cards until 12 o'clock at night and the kids would be sleeping all over the floor in the living room or the first bedroom, because we lived in shotgun houses. My parents would play for a little bit, but since my dad had a business they would leave about 9:30. I would stay on that side because we lived on the other side of the house. We lived in a double [shotgun]. So, it was a nice childhood.

I didn't grow up with these visiting customs. I don't know if it's because my extended family was so large, or if it was because of the decade I grew up in, but it seems that weekend family visiting was common to many of those I interviewed, and it likely kept families closer. I'm not close to my cousins, for example. We follow each other on social media, but I never got to know them well. We only see each other for special weekends or holidays, so when we get together, we don't have much commonality to start with. We remain only acquaintances.

DIVORCE & SINGLE PARENTS

As Fran Biederman told me of her childhood when I visited her in Rantoul, Illinois, I felt I was listening to one of my grandmother's siblings. My grandmother was one of 14, and after the sixth child was born, her father passed away. My great-grandmother raised those children alone until she remarried and had the rest of the children. Even with a father-figure in the home, the kids were responsible for managing the house, and the eldest children became responsible for the new lot as they were born.

> I come from a family of ten children, eight girls and two boys, and my eldest brother was killed in the Second World War, and my mother raised the ten of us. My father left when the youngest was six months old, and never came back. My mom raised us the rest of our lives and the rest of her life as well. I was next to the youngest . . .
>
> My family was always so busy, there were so many of us. My mother would go out to work and we would do the cooking and the cleaning . . . There was always something going on in that large of a family . . .

It was hard on my mother. I look back now and wonder how she ever did it. She had a guaranteed income of $40 a month, and that's how she raised us. Of course, she took in the washing and the ironing and cleaned people's houses [for additional money].

Then she went to work for the federal government . . . She had to take a civil servant test and you had to have 72 to pass. Well, she got 62 — she only went to the eighth grade — and then she got ten points from my brother that was killed, so that gave her a passing grade, and they hired her in like she was a veteran . . . That was a lot easier for her. She died when she was 75.

Divorce has contributed to the disruption of the old family ways. Does that mean these customs have to disappear, or that family must break apart? It doesn't seem to, even for elders who grew up with a single parent. Barbara Blake, whose family would gather at a cabin property every summer, describes her family structure further.

My mother and dad divorced when I was about two, and my mother remarried when I was 11. Momma was from a large family, and . . . we were close, I guess you could say . . . My aunts and uncles and grandparents all took a lot of time out with us because we were being raised by momma by herself.

It was unusual for parents to be divorced in Barbara's time. This is something that we all acknowledge has changed. When I was younger, I dated someone whose parents had divorced in the 1980s, a time when it was still largely unaccepted, and he had borne ridicule for it at school. Today, divorce is more normalized, with 73% of America deeming it acceptable in a 2017 Gallup poll.[62] Yet, for some, it is a relief after years in a bad marriage. Social convention no longer compels us to stay where it is unhealthy. For others, however, it seems it's easy in, easy out. In the meantime, children are born, only to grow up in single parent homes or bouncing between houses. That is what concerns Charlie Rusher of Kansas City.

> I even worry about . . . people getting married and getting divorces. It might have been a little thing . . . but I knew [my wife] from the time she was a little girl, and there was nothing I didn't know about her she didn't know about me, and I wonder [how] people find out things, you know?
>
> I have a grandson that I asked him, 'Ben, when are you going to get married?' He's 31, now, I think. He said, 'Grandpa, I don't know. The guys that got married are all divorced practically. And they're tied down, too, if they had a child or two, they're paying for that the rest of their lives, and it's hard to get married again because you've got that. I'm almost afraid to get married.' It's sad.

I recently became familiar with a unique solution to the issue of children 'bouncing between homes.' A neighbor of a close friend explained that they, the parents, had decided to be the ones that rotate, rather than the children. They retained the same apartment the children had grown up in. This gives the young ones greater stability and very little change in environment during

---

[62] Gallup, "U.S. Divorce Rate Dips, but Moral Acceptability Hits New High," http://news.gallup.com/poll/213677/divorce-rate-dips-moral-acceptability-hits-new-high.aspx

and after the divorce process. They go to the same school, have one of everything instead of two, and see the same neighbors and friends every day.

Another solution for children of divorce is, in a big enough home, dividing the house as roommates. This also continues stability for the children, perhaps even more so because both parents are in the home. This takes an enormous amount diplomacy on the adult's part, placing the negotiating of a difficult situation on the adult, instead of the child. Every situation is unique, but these ideas might prove useful for a couple that remains amicable.

I interviewed Wanda Moore just before meeting Charlie Rusher in Kansas City, Missouri. She reflected on divorce and the effects technology has had on family and relationships after her comments about Race.

> Divorce was not really a good thing, at all. Nobody wanted to talk about anything like that. Nowadays, a couple can get together and live together and think nothing of it, that's fine. And that was, of course, taboo, when I was a young girl. We were much more, what do I want to say, we didn't have the freedom. Is it freedom? . . . We just weren't allowed to do a lot of the things that the kids seem to be allowed to do, today. I don't know. Maybe it's the electronics they come up with now?

Is the increase in divorces one of tech's effects, as Wanda implies? Not directly, but television stories and movies featuring separated families has certainly helped reduce the negative treatment of children of divorcees and the divorcees themselves. It has normalized the experience, allowing those who haven't experienced it a window into the lives of those that have. And that is what tech is lauded for most. Showing us what others experience, increasing empathy.

I will take the liberty of saying that, while technology may not have directly increased divorce, it has played a role in separating families. I've observed this in my own family's behaviors — that is, cousins have unfriended me over the simplest disagreements on social media. Articles describe couples who split up after one steals passwords and breaks into the other's Facebook profile to see who they're talking to in private. These are symptoms, not the cause, of issues that lead to family dissolution, but they are nonetheless amplified by technology.

Regardless of divorce, respecting one's elders was a capital tenant of family values. Even as a child in the 1980s, I was told over and over to respect my elders. Don't raise your voice to your parents, acknowledge them when you're spoken to, and obey. For some, that is a more rigid experience than others, but it reflects my parents' upbringing by the Greatest Generation and is echoed by many of the interviews I conducted. It was this respect that supported elders being cared for in the home.

Lillian Carrara, whom we met in the chapter on Medicine and heard from again in the previous chapter, can see how family values have changed. She practiced what she preached, taking care of her husband with Alzheimer's as long as she could with the help of her sons.

> Family values have changed a lot. Back in our day, you respected all your elders. You did what you were told, and you didn't question things. Today, it seems that parents don't have that control anymore over their children. Some do, and some don't . . .
>
> I think here in the United States, people have to go back to some of the more old-fashioned ways of family traditional things. Traditions are very important, and family connections are very important, I think. Because we're so spread out all over the world and all over the country, we're losing some of that. It's very important that we get back to some of those things.

Adele Jones agrees with Lillian, as do many of those that I interviewed.

> My family always had a good time. My parents were the type of parents you behaved [around] because you respected them, and that's something I don't see now as much. The kids are too spoiled, or something, that they don't treat their parents with respect.

Is it because children are spoiled, today? Perhaps it's something to do with the lack of discipline that Honey LeBlanc (b. 1972), daughter of Bones, will discuss in the upcoming chapter on Child Development and Education. Our educators have seen a change in the way children behave, and the way parents set boundaries, and both Honey and HJ Smith go deep on the topic.

CHILD DEVELOPMENT / PARENTING / EDUCATION

"Last night we went over [to my daughter's house] and Emma [my granddaughter] was doing her homework. It was all on computer. My other daughter, who lives with them, now, and she teaches school, but they were both on the computer all the time. I worry we're going to be computer smart but dumber than hell. [laughs] Even in conversations, here I'm talking to [them], and they're doing this [mimes texting] all the time, and I wonder why the hell I'm here! That's one of the biggest reasons I don't have a computer. I don't have anything in my house that is [a computer]. People that do it, it doesn't bother them because everyone else is doing it, but if you're not, [you're on the outside]."

— Charlie Rusher

TECHNOLOGY AND EDUCATION

It is natural to discuss education in relation to technology as it affects the welfare of our children. The elective classes I took in high school — shorthand and business letter writing — are no longer offered to today's students. Cursive, the method in which I wrote this book, is also no longer taught, nor is the memorization of times tables required.

Honey LeBlanc, the daughter of Bones and part of the family I interviewed in Mississippi, has seen how the removal of once-standard aspects of education has affected the children in her own classroom. Not only do they struggle in certain subjects, they struggle to make connections.

> My ninth graders cannot tell me, if I say six times eight, they all freeze up. They're like, 'How am I supposed to know that?' Third grade. That's when you're supposed to know that. Third grade. Times tables. They've been allowed to use calculators, and it makes them lazy and forgetful. And I don't really blame them. They're not bad kids, they're not inherently terrible . . . Why would you learn it if it's right there and all you have to do is push buttons?
>
> I used to pick up calculators and turn them on just to see what was the last thing on there, and sometimes I'd look at the screen and it would be something like eight divided by eight. You've gotta be freaking kidding me! You're 15 years old and you did eight divided by eight in the calculator? But they did, and it doesn't even occur to them that that is bizarre . . . And really, it's bad for them. It's so bad for them.

Sure, I was the student who complained about math class, questioning how I would use the skills in the real world. As an adult I use math thinking many times a week, even as a social scientist. Math education requirements are a great example of adults knowing better. The curriculum being pulled as it is today seems to be done by someone who hated math and never saw the benefit outside of school. As renowned educator E.D. Hirsch Jr. stated, "We cannot assume that young people today know the things that were known in the past by almost every literate person in the culture."[63]

I had the opportunity to interview three generations in one sitting while in Mississippi. Though I didn't set out to do so within the confines of the project, it was an opportunity I could

---

[63] Joshua Foer, *Moonwalking with Einstein*, (London: Penguin Books, 2011), 194.

not pass up. Charles "Bones" Rhodes (b. 1947) lives in Pass Christian, Mississippi. At his interview were his daughter, Honey, son-in-law, Roddy, and their son, Mark. As you have learned, Honey is a grade school teacher. During our time together, she told me that a psychology teacher at her school didn't teach the lobes of the brain (i.e., temporal lobe, occipital lobe, etc.). When asked why, the teacher responded that she doesn't teach anything that could be found online. Indeed, "Why bother loading up kids' memories with facts if you're ultimately preparing them for a world of externalized memories?"[64]

The problem with this thinking is that students won't know a topic exists in order to search for it if not first introduced via an educator, parent, or by another exposure. For example, if I hadn't been taught that Sigmund Freud is considered the father of psychology, I wouldn't know to search for quotes or information about his work, let alone understand the significance of any psychological breakthroughs that might cross my path. Similarly, one cannot look up the names of the lobes of the brain if he or she doesn't know there are lobes in the first place. Honey describes the effects of technology she's seen in her students.

> I feel like, as a teacher, I see the manifestation of years living this way, of students absolutely incapable of thought. They are absolutely, when I first get them, incapable of me giving them facts and then taking it to a conclusion. They want me to tell them. Like, in my US History classes, they want me to have to tell them why things have happened. And I train them over the time I have them, so that at the end I'll say, you know, unexpectedly 200,000 Chinese troops poured over the

---

[64] Joshua Foer, *Moonwalking with Einstein*, (London: Penguin Books, 2011), 191.

border into North Vietnam, why? And I'll tell them what happened, and they'll say it's because they were communist, they were helping North Vietnam, they were located right there . . .

This year I assigned my algebra class . . . there were strugglers. There's a website called Khan Academy where you can go on and there's a tutor. There's YouTube videos that tell you how to do it. There's practice questions. You can go home [and at] any time you can do your homework. You can go on and watch the video and it shows you color-coded step-by-step. They wouldn't do it. They couldn't do it. They never use it.

And our school uses technology. They said, 'Oh, kids can bring their own technology and you can use it.' They don't use it for that. They use it to Snapchat, they use it to say mean things about each other, they use it to be total assholes to each other. In my room, I've straight up said no phones. If I see it, it's mine. You will interact with one another. You will pay attention to me. We will do this the old-fashioned way. And I've had more kids in my classes come to me and say, 'I've learned so much in your class.' 'Cause I don't use technology in my class. I mean, I will hook up some cool things like show a video clip, but, you know, three to five minutes. I don't show a whole video and video teach, because they're not going to pay attention . . .

People say you can do web-based learning — they don't do it. They absolutely don't do it. They go online and watch videos of kittens. And it's amazing to me because I can remember using the Peer Reader's Guide to periodic literature . . . Monthly they would print out this huge index of all the articles printed in Magazines and if you were looking for research you had to go through this guide and try to find it. It was done by topic, it was done by magazine. And you had to physically dig through the old books with really thin paper to find that crap. Now you just Google a couple of words and bam there it is! And they still can't do it . . .

Typically, these kids have more information at their fingertips than any generation before, and they are more helpless. They can't do anything for themselves, they can't [even] make change.

Reflect back to the story Dagmar Booth told about her 12-year-old grandson when visiting the massive New Orleans World War II Museum. He couldn't read the old letters written by soldiers in cursive. To him, and many other young people, more than half of human history will be inaccessible.[65] The generations who aren't taught cursive won't be able to have an 'ah-hah' moment like my family did when reading a 1946 land contract between my great-grandfather and his brother in Croatia — all in cursive. They won't be able to read the letters written in cursive like I found in my great-grandmother's drawer from our relatives in the Old Country, to whom I remain connected by having those letters.

I think that many have begun to realize it's more than the communication of cursive writing we've stopped teaching, and that's why we care about its loss. We've stopped teaching a discipline — cursive isn't easy to adopt as a child — and an art form. We've removed a connection to our elders and our past. Not just practically — that historical letters may not be legible to future generations — but cursive was always considered very "adult" and brought to the minds of the learners much that goes with it. It made the child consider their parent's writing (there may have been a show and tell of their parent's handwriting with the unit

---

[65] "Half" is an estimate I made based on the time of the printing press invention and text translations on the web today.

at school), their grandparents' writing, history, adulthood, and when and where cursive may find its way into one's own practice as the student ages. What brings up this connection to our elders and past in cursive's stead? Nothing comes to this writer's mind. There may be small projects individual to a teacher or school, but they don't compete with the national and cultural scale of cursive writing.

Really, it's a rite of passage. When one was old enough and practiced enough, normally in the second grade, one could begin cursive training. One would go home and ideally practice with a parent or guardian, often being introduced to that person's individual style and the possibility of creating one's own.

Douglas Gale of Michigan brings up another issue due to a lack of cursive knowledge. Not only will young people not be able to read historical letters, they can't read signs.

> They're not learning to write cursive anymore. That's what I had on the side of my truck in the furniture business. That kind of print, on my truck door. Kids wouldn't be able to read that, today. If it's not block print, they can't read it.

Dagmar Booth told me of another issue with her grandson's education when I spoke with her on the phone to set up her interview. He wasn't taught to read an analogue clock, and so had to constantly ask for the time while visiting. The Booths have an analogue clock on the wall in their home, and the boy couldn't read it.

While I was visiting my family in Croatia recently, we toured some cities with clocks more than 1,000 years old whose faces show 24 hours instead of 12. Will future generations even appreciate such a unique design, or will they tear the 'useless' clock out in favor of a digital one? Being able to use does not always equal being able to value, but a lack of use absolutely devalues a thing.

My cousin Barbara in Pennsylvania reflected on this while we discussed the education of elementary-aged students, today. She, like many of those I interviewed, worries how the younger generations are going to fare without the tools we learned in school.

> So many things are so much more advanced, today. I mean, we did the A-B-C's and counted, but now there are so many other things that people do that we didn't do. Like, if there were multiplication tables, we didn't do them that high . . . lots of things we counted on our fingers or wrote them down, but now there are all those other [tools] that you can use.
>
> Some [kids] can go along with it, but some . . . don't know how to handle the changes.

HJ Smith retired from teaching only a few years before the writing of this book. She taught in the 1960s, and then returned to teaching in the 1990s after her children had grown. Her term away allowed for a stark contrast between the children she first taught and the Millennials she returned to, with both pros and cons.

> I think the schools have changed tremendously . . . from the time I first taught in the '60s to the time I taught in the last decade, with a lot more of individualized instruction, which is good, more multi-sensory kinds of approaches to subjects. My English students would sometimes [do something unique] for a final project . . . I had one do a stained-glass window to demonstrate what he'd learned. I had another write an opera. I know it sounds really weird, but that never could have happened in 1964. You would write a paper. Period. If you had a final project. If you wrote!
>
> I don't remember when I was in school as a public-school student really ever learning to write. By the

time I was teaching that's what English was all about, was learning to write. Write and write and rewrite and read and write some more. Express yourself and do it coherently. And maybe that's just the districts that I taught in, but my students, I mean, people say kids these days don't know anything, my kids wrote a whole lot better as eighth graders than I ever wrote as a high school student, even a college student. 'Cause they'd had background and they were used to it. I think that was a good change . . .

What I was seeing in schools was kind of a reversal of who was in charge of the house. When I was a child, back in the 'dark ages,' the parents were in charge and they ruled the roost, but I was beginning to have to give the parents of my students permission to discipline them. It's ok if you say no. And it was like the inmates were running the asylum and it was not necessarily a good thing. I think that a lot of the kids felt that they would really like their parents to be the heavy and to say no, and then they could say, 'My mother would kill me, I can't do that,' and they could put it off on her. But as it was, the mother was not saying no and the children were strapped with more responsibility than they were ready for in a lot of instances.

As a matter of fact, just as an illustration, I used to have my students write a journal from the point of view of somebody living through the Revolutionary War era, or the colonial era, and so they had to know about the culture and the society and the daily life and all of that. And one little girl was writing about how her mother felt guilty because she couldn't give her a new pair of shoes for her birthday. Her subject area was the Salem Witch Trials. I said, 'You don't understand. Parents didn't feel guilty in 1620! That was up to the children to feel guilty.' First of all, you wouldn't have a birthday party, but that was something she wouldn't necessarily know. Nowadays, I guess our children expect for us to feel guilty if we can't provide for every need.

I hadn't considered how much parenting styles had changed until I conducted these interviews. I certainly had noticed technology being used as a pacifier. Until these interviews, I wasn't sure if this use of tech was an addition to our parenting culture or a symptom of a more fundamental alteration. According to HJ, and many others, it is the latter. Parenting has become softer, sometimes to the detriment of important lessons a child might have learned. Ida Mae Harris (b. 1920), a neighbor of HJ's and the mother of a woman who provided a place to rest my head on my journey, said the same thing without knowing HJ's opinion.

> I think they expect too much. I think every kid expects too much. And, of course, your parents try to give you everything, now, that they could. And they're all so busy. Like my [great-grandchildren], each one of them is busier than a one-armed paper hanger. Busy, busy, busy . . . They just expect too much, and I think, in the long run, it might hinder them in getting to be what they want to be. [They] have to slow down and take it easy and let nature take its course.

Owen Aukeman agrees that younger generations are moving too fast, sometimes missing important lessons or cues in history.

> We have so much information, now, that we don't know how to use it . . . You just have to sit still, listen to the birds. Because it's rush, rush, rush, flying from one place to the other. Trying to catch up, trying to catch up. Sometimes it's just too fast.

261

It's going to be interesting to watch the Millennials. How are they going to take all of this information, and process it, and come up with a solution? And looking back at history and seeing where we have been, and now where we should go.

Are children actually busier? Many studies discuss filling children's time with sports, activities, after-school programs, and more. There is no idle time left. Yet, Dagmar Booth tells how her family kept her just as busy when she was a child.

In those days you were on a time schedule. As soon as you got up, my grandma would hear you moving around. You got up and went to her side of the house. You had to go over there and eat breakfast and help clean. You had chores to do. You either had to dust, pass the dust mop, dry dishes, you know, you had something to do. If one of the uncles went off and came back with a bushel of peas or something, you were expected to sit there and help them shuck these peas . . . You weren't allowed to go back on your side and watch TV . . .

We wanted to watch the scary movies . . . and guess what? Uh uh! You had to watch what [the adults] wanted to watch. Which, nowadays, I don't think kids are that disciplined. The young mothers nowadays ask a child, a baby, 18 months old, what do you want? Oh, come on, how stupid can you be? That kid doesn't know what it wants . . . We just can't have everything we want in life. I think the kids don't know that, yet.

There are personal parenting touches that may have been lost, as well. It seems that we have forgotten that the silly repetitive things our parents did to us that seem 'dumb' today were exactly what a young learning mind required. Repetitive peek-a-boos make an infant laugh in part because they don't yet understand that there is still a face behind the hands, and in part because repetition is how their minds are wired to learn. Ruth Harper explains that her mother would do these silly things which really aided her mental growth.

> My mother did something that was very helpful to my learning to read, and now they make it sound like it's a dumb thing to do, but it's actually not dumb at all. When you're reading something, follow along with your finger, and then drop down a notch, you know, to the next line. Because she did that, and she read very well aloud, it happened that, one day, that every time she came to the word f-o-r, she said 'for,' and I thought, 'Oh that's why it's important to know 'f' is for 'ffff,'' you know, it's like Click! So, I didn't instantly start [reading], but I think I started saying 'for' with her.

TECHNOLOGY AND PLAY

"What worries me is that kids have the attention span for cartoons on TV, but in the classroom we have to worry."
— Dot Hornsby

In the chapter on Poverty we looked at how technology has changed our perception of fundamental needs. Kenny Ladner's comments about his childhood development harkens to that, but also describes a version of roaming play many communities have outlawed.

> Today, in this time, most people would say that it was a horrible childhood. We grew up on a farm. We raised

263

all of our food supply. Vegetables, meat, syrup. Anything that was on that table was off of that property that we owned . . . Some people would say, 'Well, you never had a childhood, you never had time to play, that's the reason you work constantly,' and hey, to us, when we grew up we knew we had to work the gardens, we had to tend the animals. That was what we called our childhood, back then. Because we had fun doing it . . . Here's the thing, we had pecan trees and tung nut trees, and we would have wars with pecans and tung nuts. Believe me, when some of those tung nuts hit you, it left a bruise on you [*laughs*] . . . Another challenge that we had [was] we had livestock. We had hogs, we had goats, we had cows, we had horses, and we knew that horses were for riding. We would go and round up some of the livestock with the horses. Well, we knew it was a bigger challenge to get out there and ride some of the bulls. We knew it was a bigger challenge to get out there and ride some of the bigger hogs. It was one of those things. That was our childhood. When we got the chance to get out and do some of that, that's what we did. We didn't have the movies. We didn't go to the movies then. We didn't have parties. It was just a [bad] childhood for kids today . . . We were actually happy with that childhood.

The saying "it takes a village to raise a child" is still as true today as it was when the Greatest Generation was coming of age 70 years ago. As was discussed in the chapter on Community, children grew up knowing their neighbors, and neighbors were trusted. The police wouldn't bring your child home from the park saying the parents had abandoned them. It was the domain (and maybe even the obligation) of children to go out, explore, and get dirty. To learn their limits and who they are. Though we hate to think of our children getting into trouble, it is a necessary part of learning the reaches of what is possible, so that when stakes are higher as adults, those mistakes have already been made.

Many, many people I interviewed reinforced this point as we talked. Dave Chicoring, too, roamed free, learning his limits and discovering the world.

> Every day was an adventure. It was through this woods, or that woods, falling into this pond . . . we weren't watched out for like the current little children. 'Oh! God! You left your child!'
>
> We'd spend whole days making rafts and sailing across the pond, and inevitably getting wet clear up — clear up — that sort of thing on a cold day. Now you would say, 'My God! We were just cut loose,' but we survived. It was Darwin. [*laughs*]

Ruth Harper explains that parents were not expected to provide entertainment. It was up to the children to do so.

> We entertained ourselves, largely. By the time you were three or four you weren't expected to say, 'Mom, what's there to do, I'm bored' . . . I'd go outside and climb trees and I was perfectly happy with that kind of stuff. And learning to ride a bike, that opened up the world. Especially when I got a three-speed bike with the relatively skinny wheels, then I talked in terms of not just a mile or two miles but miles. I could go anywhere. And so, it wasn't long before I'd ridden [from Grand Rapids] to Lansing and East Lansing and Grand Haven.

It is the concern of many of our elders that children are not spending enough time outdoors during their youth. Not only are they not able to roam free, they are cooped up, and their energy left unspent. HJ Smith believes that the technology of television, smartphones, and gaming devices feeds this trend.

I think [kids] aren't spending as much time exercising. They're not spending as much time outside. If they've got a little iPad, it's addictive. I mean, I've seen my own grandchildren, who have to be torn away, or have to have, you know, deviceless days, or unplugged holidays. But it's no more addictive to them as it is to us, I guess. But it's kind of weird that they're so connected to it. I think it's nice for a child who's an introvert or a loner, might just enjoy writing on it or reading stuff, but I think it may damage their social life. I don't know. It's hard to tell.

I see kids out on the sidewalk in those little motorized cars. Have you seen those things? You go out and [drive] up and down the block — what kind of exercise is that?! Are you going to be sleepy at the end of the day and want to go to bed? Lay down during quiet time so your poor mother can get a rest? . . . To me it's damaging . . .

There is creativity developed by children who play outside. I used to make mud pies, and my best friend and I would steal discarded building supplies from the neighborhood homes under construction to make a fort. That fort was never completed but a finished fort wasn't the fun of it. The fun was the creation, deciding what might go where, and countless hours spent bonding with my best friend and learning how tools, physical force, and geometry worked. I was only 12.

Mershon Neisner explains that she passed the kind of independence she experienced while growing up on to her children. She attributes their independence and stability to the free range and early responsibility she gave them.

So, when my kids came along, I have three children, so they all . . . from the time they started junior high they started doing their own laundry, they all had allowances that they had to manage similarly. Now they're 40, 45, and 33 . . . and they're all responsible, financially responsible. They're really responsible and I think it's because I raised them in a similar way. They had lots of freedom. People now, when I tell people what I let my kids do, they're like 'AHHH' . . .

TECHNOLOGY AND MENTAL DEVELOPMENT

"I don't know if they take life seriously enough, like we were taught . . . I'll get the impression [watching TV] that they're not caring enough about life, or are serious enough about life, or are selfish . . . But then I've seen the wonderful young people here and that makes me feel really good, because the next generation is going to have to carry on."
— Yoko Mossner

Mike Dubuque (b. 1938) is a fast-talking retired truck driver and born-again Pastor living in Detroit, Michigan. Based on the speed of his speech, I am sure he has never sat still a day in his life. He describes the differences he's seeing between his childhood and that of today's youth.

I just don't like sitting around doing nothing . . . [*laughs*] Well, the kids are growing up today with too much stuff. You don't see kids playing outside, anymore, and doing things. They're always inside with their technology. You go into a restaurant and you see two or three kids sitting at a table and they're playing with their phone or their tablet. They're not conversing back and forth with one another. You don't see kids playing outside on the street. That's what we did, we played on the street. And we were out there all the time. My mother said be home by dark, when you see the streetlights come on, be home. There was no phone. They couldn't contact us. We just took off and ran . . . As long as we were back by dark. They couldn't keep track of us. Now, the parents are keeping track of them. I don't like how these young kids always have to have a cell phone, but I know they're all into this stuff.

Helicopter parenting is a phrase coined to describe the kind of parenting that keeps kids close, tethered, always in touch and never quite free to make their own mistakes.

Added to this is the discomfort I discussed at the beginning of this book — technology is everywhere. The "Internet of Things," a network of technological devices that is connected to the Internet and shares information with each other, is both a growing reality and an ideal, with new technology and things developed for network connectivity all the time. A Pew survey found that 77% of Americans owned a smartphone in 2016, with a growth of 35% over four years.[66] By the time of publishing this book, that number is predicted at 85% adoption. These phones are now able to be connected to cars, thermostats, lights, appliances, and more.

Smartphones are being hailed by our elders as the new pacifier — and not in a good way. Young parents are being conditioned by their children to continue this practice because they are quickly contained by handing them a smartphone or tablet. I've watched it in action as my own friends enter their parenting years. From their mouths I hear worry about screen time affecting development and the intent to limit it, but their actions

---

[66] Pew Research Center, "Record shares of Americans now own smartphones, have home broadband," http://www.pewresearch.org/fact-tank/2017/01/12/evolution-of-technology/, (Jan 12, 2017).

prioritize the ease of distracting a fussy kid over worry for their future.

Recently, I attended a friend's birthday party at a local brew pub. Shortly after my arrival, a couple joined us with their two-year-old son. I was shocked to see them hand him a smartphone immediately after settling him into the high chair. They didn't even give him a chance to interact with the guests, and we didn't have that chance, either.

Kids are restless. They need to be outdoors where they can play, explore, and break stuff. Yet, it seems the rise of fear for safety we discussed a few chapters ago is affecting today's parents' allowance of such play. Mary Muscatello remembers her free-reign play as a child.

> We had a little garage a couple of doors away from us, and the girls would go in the side door, and we would sit on little red wagons inside when it was raining outdoors, and we would have little needle and thread, and we would sew pieces of material while the boys went over to another side of the garage and they would have pieces of wood that they would pound nails into.
>
> We would sit there with our legs dangled over sewing our pieces of material, but it was the most wonderful and comfortable feeling to know we were just all kind of together, and we were busy talking. But that was one of my fondest memories of young childhood.
>
> We had a wonderful hill on the side of our neighborhood and we would go up and down that hill with snow suits on and just come home dripping wet and freezing cold and just had the best time . . .
>
> We played hide and seek, kick the can, we had the best, best summers ever. We would take [a] stone . . . and make hopscotch on the sidewalk . . . playing jacks and jump rope from the clothes line . . . and we would do double rope.

One of the most interesting narratives about technology's effect on children's development came from Dave Chicoring. His two children are raising his grandchildren with opposing philosophies about technology, and he's been observing the ramifications as they age. One set of grandchildren is allowed unlimited access to technology, the other isn't. He can see the differences, even before they reach a double-digit age.

I have some grandchildren, and they're being taught very traditionally. They're not allowed technology. They've got to learn to read before they're given it. They have cousins that have free reign, and they're developing differently. The ones that have free reign are becoming very independent. It's affecting the families, it's affecting relationships within the family . . . their whole focus. Their free time, and their values. You at the table don't matter, I'm tuned into this. And it stresses the families.

I would say that . . . the cousins of these others have rules. They generally accept them and go along with them. You have to sit down and play piano. Yeah, it's a pain to do that, but the kids with the technology, they're not as disciplined. It's maybe all part of discipline. Then again, that's how families evolve, and how families are changing, in other words. All you've got to do is go on a bus, go into a restaurant, and you can see some teenage kids, or some junior teens with a vacant look on their face, and they're someplace else. And they don't give a damn. That's what they're pursuing.

In terms of morality, however, you want to define morality, you see people listening to rap music with their technology, here. You can hear the thing for three blocks. And what are they saying? 'Slap that bitch!' And so, forth. And what does that say? It says they are affecting the attitudes about women, they're affecting attitudes about society, they're saying do what you wanna do, you don't have to listen to anybody, it's rejection of traditional . . . values and mores, so by definition it's accelerating the rate of change that, by itself, I think, there are a lot of problems that need to be worked out.

There's a lot of worry about access and distraction. Children have access to anything, including porn, at a very young age. They also are made vulnerable to predators. This has been an issue since chat rooms and instant messenger gained popularity. I was only 12 at the time AOL and access to chat rooms became popular, but fear of predators was well-developed in my parents. My access to the Internet was timed and monitored. I always wanted more and would frequently request that infinite 'five more minutes' when told to get off the computer. HJ Smith reflects that, even as a full-grown and disciplined adult, the Internet is addicting. Children haven't developed such discipline yet. Will they learn it with infinite access to the online world?

Sometimes it's a terrible distraction. I find it's a distraction for me, and I like to think I have some self-discipline, some direction in my life. [*laughs*] So, I wonder about it for children. It makes it hard to focus.

On the other hand, it makes it easy to find things out. It's wonderful! Just Google it. Can't do this? Well, Google it and I'll find out. So, that's good.

I think [the Internet], you can't trust it altogether, and I think it's hard to teach kids that, just because they saw it on the Internet, doesn't make it true, and it's hard to get them to withhold their judgment and look for multiple sources and credible sources, and I still think that books have gone through a process that a lot of things on the Internet haven't. What you can find out [in a book] has been edited and peer reviewed.

So, that's something that needs to be taught, needs to be emphasized.

Concern for what our children might access online adds to our questions about how technology will affect our children as they grow. The question of developmental factors like discipline and socializing are an important concern, one we may or may not realize for another 50 years.

I conducted an accidental interview in Grand Rapids with a former teacher named Kay McComb (b. 1921) while looking for another Kay in the same retirement center. I didn't have the room number and used the directory to determine where to go. I was sent to the wrong wing of the building, and met Kay Mc-Comb, who wanted to be interviewed despite the surprise. She told me she worries for today's children as they have so much information at their fingertips at an early age.

> They hear too much and see too much and have too many things too soon . . . Now [parents] want babies to walk out of their cribs. And, of course, if they're very smart, they can run all these electronic things better than adults, sometimes. They know things they don't really know about. I mean, they can quote them and use them in the right places, but they have no background for it, so they don't know why it's [important], and I think it's better that they know why.

All this brings us to one of the biggest talking points regarding technology in the media — child development. How much will growing up with technology affect today's youth? Does it affect empathy since they'll communicate or play games with digital friends who can't be injured? Will focusing forward at a screen diminish their ability to observe their surroundings? Slacken immune system development due to diminished exposure to 'dirty' things? What about the ability to learn or how they learn? With

ADHD on the rise,[67] Honey LeBlanc wanted to know the answers to these questions so she could manage its symptoms and cause in her classrooms.

> Our pediatrician . . . said that all that screen time is what causes ADHD. And so, our 11-year-old gets no screen time. There's no televisions in our house, there's no computer, no TVs, but as soon as Friday afternoon comes, he's like jonesing to get on. Like an addict. Like a junkie. I've gotten up before and he's sneaking it in the middle of the night, at three a.m., 11 years old, on YouTube, watching who the hell knows [what] . . .
>
> Teenagers have never had any impulse control, and now they have the whole world as their platform. And they have no impulse control, and they do things, too, like I love my boyfriend so much I'm going to send him a naked selfie. And now your boyfriend hates you, and your naked selfie has been seen by the whole soccer team. It's horrible. And the girls are dealing with that . . .

Tom Lawson truly worries about the bullying and loss of privacy that has come from technology, especially for our youth. They aren't equipped to deal with complex social problems like private images being made public and may not ask for help from an adult out of embarrassment.

---

[67] Centers for Disease Control, "Attention-Deficit/Hyperactivity Disorder Medication Prescription Claims Among Privately Insured Women Aged 15–44 Years — United States, 2003–2015," https://www.cdc.gov/mmwr/volumes/67/wr/mm6702a3.htm?s_cid=mm6702a3_w, (2018).

The boys are always on their cell phones, taking pictures under the girl's skirts and emailing them to their friends, and all that kind of stuff. We've all heard about kids who've committed suicide because pictures were taken in compromising or embarrassing positions and they were teased by their friends and bullied and so forth. I don't think cell phones in the hands of children has been a good thing. We all grew up here without cell phones and we made it through school just fine . . . I don't understand why kids, today, have to have a cell phone. I don't see it as a good thing. Now that doesn't mean things won't change in the future.

Millennials are already dubbed the "Generation of Me" by their elders, as social media taught them to start their sentences with "I" instead of "you." In an argument, this is a good habit to follow. In empathizing, it is destructive, and many elders feel alienated by the tendency.

How different will the next generation be in their socialization? And will we notice? Differences generation to generation are more of a gradient of change, rather than the stark contrast our elders in the Greatest Generation experience due to their age and distance from the youngest generations.

Our brains are developing from ages 0-25, after which adaptation is harder, preserving habits and a way of life.[68] In this way, the memories of the Greatest Generation are a time capsule. Their worldview was formed and generally settled by their mid-twenties. This contrast between the oldest remembered way of life and the shape of our lives today is our best

---

[68] CNN, "You're an adult, but your brain may not be," http://www.cnn.com/2016/12/21/health/adult-brain-development/index.html, (Dec 21, 2016).

chance at understanding how much technology has changed us as a society.

Dave Chicoring continues describing what he sees as the conflict between our youth and the online world.

> The kids are very into their smartphones, and I think we despair when they zone out anytime and anyplace, and that becomes the focus in terms of generational . . . family values. [They] haven't adjusted to the reality of the new media. And, of course, it's always ever-accelerating. The trouble with ever-accelerating is the same as when you're driving in an unknown place. And we're in an unknown place, in many ways. We had very, very slow evolution for so long . . .

Thelma Gale reflects the differences between the way she and her husband ran their business and how technology changed it. But she worries, like Chicoring, that young people are getting stuck in their gadgets and missing out on the rest of the world.

> Well, it's really sad to see these little fingers flying all the time. They're concentrating on these little instruments in their hands, and it's sad, because if they looked outside they might see a bird. They might see some flowers. They'd breathe some fresh air. It's sad. It's a shame.
>
> Technology is wonderful. I have a computer. I use it. But I don't sit at it for hours and hours and hours a day. I used it in my business. My bookkeeping I did it on the computer, and that was a real change. Because when we first started our stores I used to do it all by hand, and it was really slow because you had to fill out all the forms for the government . . .
>
> When [technology] controls a person, all their waking hours, that's sad.

Thelma's husband, Douglas, chimed in to reinforce her worry about the impact of computers.

> We've lost the ability to figure things out for ourselves. If it's not written down, do this, this, and this, you're out of it. And that's not good.

Judith Blair of Ithaca, New York, echoes Thelma's sentiment that children are missing out on real life by spending so much time on the computer.

> Just sitting in front of the screen, I just think you miss a lot of what life really is. That's not real life to me.

Eva Amundson of Missoula, Montana, also worries that kids have their noses stuck in technology and are missing out on the life going on around them.

> [Kids] can't visit each other anymore. You go some-place and here they have all their little [gadgets]. My great-great-granddaughter came up with her little computer. She's two years old, showing me how to run the computer. Most of the kids can't think for them-selves. They depend on pushing buttons, and that's not good . . . Technology is great, I think, but it's scary to think what would happen if the electricity went off, what would our young people do? They can't add two and two. I know some kids that can't add. And that's scary to me when you can't start thinking for yourself.

Eva echoes what many have said about technological depen-dence, whether it be a lack of knowledge in growing food or simply entertaining ourselves. Joan Pryor (b. 1934) follows this thinking with disappointment in our youth's interest in books.

In my day, they liked books. I understand children aren't too keen on regular print books anymore. They want the technology. They want what they can see on TV and what not . . . In that one instance, I'm really amazed that the interest in books has really fallen off.

With books, we don't need anything except the book itself and light by which to read it. That, too, is changing. Even at this writing, preparation of an eBook version is necessary to the publishing plan for this book. Paper alone isn't sufficient, anymore.

Ruth Harper used to ride her bicycle all over her city and most of the western half of the State of Michigan. She was independent and would find things for herself, just as Douglas Gale said above. She worries that the information available online, today, may not have the merit that asking her elders did when she needed something as a young woman.

In order to amuse themselves nowadays, they're not going into nature, seemingly. You don't see them climbing the trees and there's plenty of good climbable trees in this town. [laughs] There's a whole lot of things that aren't available to them that were to us, at least indirectly. When I was growing up we didn't all own horses, but you knew somebody that did. And if you went over to help [with] the horses, you might get to ride 'em. Or if it was your friend who had them, or whatever.

The toys and things that we were given were at least potentially education in and of themselves. An example, when [my older sister] was ten, she got a chemistry set but she could supplement the things in the chemistry set. It had lots of things in it, and it had a letter that said that because of the war effort we can't give you any of this or any of that — and I've still got the letter somewhere [laughs] and what's left of the chemistry set . . . So, she knew early on she wanted to be a chemist and she would read about things and say, 'Oh, I need sulfur for that — Pa, where do I get sulfur?' And he'd say, 'Ride your bike down to Odie's. They carry that because it's good for this or that.' And so, she'd go down there with a nickel and get a jar of sulfur.

And now kids' amusement typically comes out of their mother's purse and looks something like that [*points at my smartphone*] but it's got all kinds of abilities and keyboards and games and plays little songs and plays a movie for them, whatever. So, there's lost opportunities there. They don't observe people going to books for something. They probably observe people [saying] it's on the 'net, look it up. So, okay, you go to this box and you look it up. Now I've done that with some things and one of the things I've found is if you look up you'll find a number of sites that have the Gettysburg Address. Now, you memorized it when you were little, but you want to know where to put the commas in or something, so you read the first one and you say, 'Wait a minute, that's not right' [*begins reciting the full Address*]. No, no! This is wrong! Now you've got me confused, so you go to the next site . . . but they got this wrong! And you go to different sites until you find some that agree. And if you've got a book, and you go to the book and it's in there, the chances are pretty darn good that it's right. A magazine, not so much.

I don't want to leave the impression that technology is strictly bad for children. It is not. It is a wonderful tool that allows for ease of research, information, and global connection. But it's just that, a tool. The rest is what we make of it. Grace Stinton believes it facilitates a different kind of behavior that can be beneficial, and absolutely has helped kids get smarter at a younger age.

Our great-grandkids had a weekend last year at a park in Frankenmuth, here in Michigan, and the kids had a little alcove up in the cabin and they all went up for naptime, and they all went up and every one of them had some kind of gadget. That's so different, to see all those great-grandkids, four and five years old, all looking at their handheld [screens] and mechanized gadgets. Otherwise, years ago, they probably would have been up there fighting. [*laughs*] But they were all into their little electronic gadgets.

I think it makes a big difference. The kids don't interact quite so much, anymore, because they are so busy with their own little things that they are looking at. I think that [my generation] played a lot more games [together].

I think we've lost the interaction between same generation, between different generations. There's a closeness I think they've lost, a little bit.

[But] the kids are smarter. Much smarter. The kids are allowed to speak up a lot more than we were. When I was a kid, you sat there, and if the adults were there you'd have to break into a conversation, you probably weren't even included in the conversation. So, I think that a lot of it is due to the electronic things they have to work with. Even television. It's helped the generation. My grandkids are much smarter than I was as a kid.

Just the same, Bob Johnson, a psychologist who treats families and couples, feels our youth are much smarter and able than he was at the same age.

Well, the positive of it is young people, almost without exception, have technical skills that are way beyond anything I had as a child. I have a granddaughter, our oldest grandchild is 15, and I've watched her over the past ten years, and she would come home from school with an assignment and immediately go on the computer and Google what she needed to get for the assignment and I thought, 'Good heavens!' That is so different from the way I grew up. And she's not uncomfortable with it. So, I think that's a gift.

Wanda Moore agrees with Bob, as did many others in their interviews.

I have a great-grandson who picks up the iPod, and he's five years old, and away he goes, you know? And even the two-year-old is beginning to do the same thing. So, that is amazing, to me. Just amazing. So, that's a big difference, of course, but that's because of the electronics and technology we've made.

Jim Hayes Jr. doesn't use technology, himself. He has a flip phone (which went off during our interview) and doesn't want to get more technical than that. But he recognizes how his lack of technological engagement is leaving him behind, and the effect that may have on others in his generation should they do the same.

Education is an ongoing process, and technology is part of it. The people in the older generation need to be a part of it if they're going to be appreciated. 'Cause if you don't, then you're going to be lost. I don't feel lost [not using technology], but I know there's a lot of things missing, but it's not bothering me.

There is one more important facet to technology that is not often discussed due to our concern about the effect it will have on our brains. While I was sitting with Ann Veren in Birmingham, Alabama, she began to talk about our youth and the issue of our faces being so close to screens. She actually made me laugh because of her reference to our posture due to technology — it really is terrible. I have such back pain at times because I sit hunched over my computer. Even with my laptop eye level on a stand, I subconsciously lean toward it.

Well, for one thing, they're on [smartphones] all the time. They're going to have a serious problem with their neck when they're my age, when they're 80. Or they're into the computer all day, all night. Their shoulders. But what it's doing to them is that they're not outside, they're not playing, they're not being active, they're just glued to the screen. That's it. They miss a lot.

I don't know how well they communicate with others. You know, people are interesting, and you learn a lot from people. If you listen, you learn a lot. You probably think I'm nuts! [*laughs*]

[*I respond: What do you think I'm doing here?!*]

[*more laughter*] Really, it's true. There is a lot [to] communicating. You have to be able to communicate with the lowest human being on this Earth, as well as the very tip top . . . You've gotta be able to communicate. And you also have to have compassion, because not everybody is in the [rich] situation. There's a lot of poverty and a lot of children that are so neglected. A lack of love in the home, drugs . . . That's a lot of things that are being missed by the youth. See, there was a time people were scared, but now these young people aren't scared of anything anymore. They just think 'oh.' And they all want what we worked for all those years, and they don't want to work to get it. They do not. We all want our children to have more than we had, but it's not necessarily real good.

RELIGION & INTEGRITY

"I'd like everybody to know how much Jesus Christ means to me. Without him, I'd be overwhelmed with all the [technological] changes. But by praying and asking the Lord to help us, it gives me peace and contentment . . ."

— Thelma Gale

In 2015, the Pew Research Center found that religion, especially Christianity, is in decline in America. Of those born in the Greatest Generation, 85% identify as Christian. Contrast that with Millennials, identifying at only 57%.[69]

What does technology have to do with it? Most likely, access to a wider range of information outside what parents and guardians teach offers validation to any doubts. Estrangement or being alone in beliefs — even being shunned — is a major motivating factor in one's decision making. If someone fears family abandonment or non-acceptance, they will most likely choose to adhere to the status quo, maybe even on a subconscious level. Without a clear alternative, the option never truly exists, so the mind doesn't probe further. But if one is able to find community elsewhere, the option is then available.

Does that mean that, given the freedom from familial and cultural pressure, it's a 50/50 shot at religion taking root in the human mind? That is, were our elders duped? Not necessarily. Not only was communication with outsiders more difficult in

---

[69] Pew Research Center, "America's Changing Religious Landscape," http://www.pewforum.org/2015/05/12/americas-changing-religious-landscape/, (2015).

their day, but America's culture as a whole valued religion differently than it does today. Church was where community happened almost everywhere but in big cities, and by not attending gatherings one removed themselves from more than tradition.

> *"I was a convert . . . I went to mass [to please the girl I liked] and she explained it too well."*
>
> — Fr. Jaques DePaul

When I met the Gale's for their interview, they gave me a hard time about my own beliefs. They refused to speak with me until I told them of my religious standing. As an anthropologist, I've been trained not to insert myself into the lives of those I interview — I should be like a shadow, taking in information and not affecting my subjects' lives with my opinions. However, it is also my duty to make those I interview as comfortable as possible. And so, I discussed it with them, treading lightly. The questions I experienced were common in their region not two decades ago. Religious affiliation and church patronage was how people quickly identified each other and found a level footing from which to begin a conversation and relationship. Charlotte Lawson explains this evolving landscape further.

> This country needs to pull together, again, as a nation, as a country. We built this country for freedom of religion, and that is being taken away from us in many ways. People don't go to church like they used to. Those numbers have dropped off terribly. My generation was the last one in my family that held on to those roots of family . . . I said we went to church three times a week. That was our entertainment. Almost everybody who went to church was related somehow. And it was wonderful. Those were good days.

Charlotte's husband, Tom, followed her sentiment about seeing one's community regularly at church.

> I hated going to church as a kid. Later, just before [my wife] and I met, I joined a Methodist church in Baton Rouge, and I enjoy it. I look forward to going to church every Sunday because I have friends, and before that I was very shy. I had a few friends, but I was very, very shy and did not mix well with people, especially people I didn't know . . .

When I met Kay Rypkema (b. 1921), the Kay I was meant to interview when I accidentally interviewed Kay McComb, I didn't know she was a Jehovah's Witness. She eventually told me and gave me some of the materials she hands out to family and strangers. She, too, is surprised by the lack of religious practice in young people.

> The Bible is just lost . . . I see so many young people that don't even believe in marriage. That's unheard of, even in other countries . . . There just used to be more people listening to what the Creator said. I am a Bible teacher, and have been since I was 30 years old . . . I see all these young kids letting television get into their minds.

I had the wonderful opportunity to interview my mother's cousin, Father Jaques DePaul, before he passed away from cancer. He had dedicated his life to faith in Jesus as a monk, traveling the world to study his faith and becoming the lead expert in the story of St. Agnes.[70] He always had a sense of humor about things,

---

[70] The Michigan Catholic, "Fr Jaques DePaul Daley, OSB," http://www.themichigancatholic.org/2015/11/fr-jacques-depaul-daley-osb/

so even though he admits concern that we are too inundated in technology to care about faith, he quips at the end of his thought about his own love for his iPhone.

> I'd like to be remembered as somebody who fell in love with Jesus. He was the center of my life. It makes all the difference in your life. Even if you're married or not married, Jesus has a certain part of your heart. The Lord has a certain part of your heart which belongs to Him and if you're married or not it doesn't matter. It's like belonging to the Lord, and He's with you . . . Jesus wants our heart, that's what I tell people. Jesus is after our heart more than anything. And He begs for our love, but so many people are too busy. I think they're just too busy, you know? . . . [We have] a lot of distractions. But I must admit I love my iPhone.

TECHNOLOGY AND MANNERS

"In my day, you never swore. You never used swear words. I mean, that was really naughty. [laughs] And I don't think, nowadays, you hear these young kids and I don't think they think too much about that."

— Wanda Moore

Have we forgotten how to be kind? How to be polite to familiars and strangers? Does religion have anything to do with it?

I think the biggest concern for those I interviewed is that their own family doesn't pay them mind, especially their grandchildren. Here they are, full of love for their succeeding generations, willing to pass on knowledge and curious about their young relatives' lives, but their young relatives keep their noses 'pressed' to their screens during visits, just as we heard in the chapter on Child Development. Not only is it hurtful, it's impolite to ignore one's host or guest. It seems to elders like Barbara Blake, Millennials are downright rude.

> I was taught that if someone came into your house, if someone came to see you or see my mother or step-dad or brothers, you always spoke to them. You know, you didn't just come in and go to your room or go do whatever you wanted to do and didn't speak . . . But I've found that kids aren't brought up with a lot of the manners they should have.

I speak with my peers about the importance of listening to the stories of their grandparents (and great-grandparents for those who are so fortunate) before they're lost. By all accounts, young people don't mean to be rude. In fact, they love their elders very much. Unfortunately, their acknowledgment of this is almost always coupled with, "I just don't know how to talk to them."

This is heartbreaking, but not a surprise. Millennials are nicknamed 'Generation Me' for the tendency to begin sentences with "I," as trained by social media. If one only knows how to speak about themselves, and their world is predicated on tech that their elders don't use or know of, a barrier of understanding will form.

What we've culturally forgotten (and what I so often must teach my clients to improve their businesses) is how to speak to 'you.' That is, start with asking how 'your' day is, how are 'your' friends, what do 'you' think? This simple turn of mind will open a treasure trove of conversation and is the very vehicle I used to write this book. I, personally, don't know what it's like to live in a retirement community, but I can ask about 'your' experience and learn!

In addition to the ability to connect to our elders and be a polite host and guest, honesty and integrity seem to have changed. Bob Johnson, the psychologist living in Salt Lake City, describes the differences he sees in his clients and family. Not only this, Bob describes the issue with technology — it's not inherently good or bad. It's a tool. It is amazing when used for progress and terrible when used for terror.

> I don't think I would want to live anyplace other than America, but our capitalism is so corrupt, now . . . It's the thing with technology that allows us to invent the world, it's also the thing that causes us as human beings to say, 'I'm going to cheat you before you cheat me.' Because I've been in the drug industry, I look at that and it makes me want to vomit . . . And so, I struggle with, I mean, technology is all part of that, but I think in many ways it's bringing out the worst in people and not the best.
>
> I think we've lost integrity. I think it's interesting, there's a piece of me that's almost a socialist. And yet I realize for socialism to work, it would require the same integrity and honesty that capitalism would require. So, if people are just trying to take advantage of others, whether you're a capitalist or socialist, it's not going to work . . . My concern is . . . everything that I do is up there is in the sky someplace and being held up there someplace [on satellites], and there's so many opportunities for people to be taken advantage of.
>
> It was interesting. I got a virus on a computer one time, and I took it into the computer place to get it fixed, and I was talking to the guy about what kids write to break into your computer, and he says, well, they need a job, too. He was like what's wrong with that? I mean, they're technicians and they don't have a job, so why don't they have a right to break in? And he really thought that! He was just a young man who thought well, that's alright. If he can get away with it, why not?

Technology is a tool. A very efficient tool. Medicine has improved by leaps and bounds throughout the lifetimes of the Greatest Generation; likewise, the medical industry seems to focus on profits over truly helping others. Nuclear technology has powered hundreds of thousands of homes, benefiting large swaths of the world; it also can destroy the world in one fell swoop.

The Internet amplifies our actions to a greater extent than any technology before it, the good and the bad. Most of us understand that a blogger can say whatever they wish — nothing on the Internet requires fact-checking. Are some purposely misleading others? Certainly. But I think, on the whole, we're doing the best we can and sometimes get it wrong.

I see people taking care of each other on social media, standing up for one another, and doing what they see as right, all of which takes personal integrity. Social media has provided us with the vehicle for revolutions, greater awareness and acceptance of mental health conditions, and greater awareness of systemized prejudice. Survivors of sexual assault in Hollywood and politics no longer need hide — the Internet ensures their voices are heard. Because of all this, I don't think we're lost as a society. My cousin Barbara closed her interview by saying,

> I think some people are very nice with each other, some people are very nasty. People have to learn to get along, because it's one big wide world. I don't think that occupations or languages should be a deterrent to people getting along.

CONCLUSION

"I think the world is a bigger place. We've learned how other people live and have learned by that. We've learned how they live, how they lived, what they do, and that's interesting and makes us broader, and some things are alike that we've done, and even if the languages are different some things are similar. Some people are born to be free and other people will be slaves and that's sad, and we keep going back in history and it's still happening today. It's a big wide world. Some things change, but some things never change. They may change, but in a different way, a different approach, a different manner."

— Barbara Markess

As my research accelerated and I planned the Kickstarter fundraising campaign to conduct interviews on a national scale, a book came across my path that I found to be an eerie prediction of our future. It is called *Super Sad True Love Story* by Gary Shteyngart.[71] The story revolves around a 40-something male who falls for an early 20-something woman. Mildly dystopian, the plot takes place in a future Manhattan after the US Dollar has crashed and Yuan is the currency of power. It is clear that these two main characters will face more than financial hardship in their relationship, for the generational gap is made infinitely larger by the rapid development and adoption of personal technology.

Shteyngart takes the discomfort we have with tech's growth and pits it against the main character as he tries to get to know

---

[71] Gary Shteyngart, *Super Sad True Love Story* (Random House, 2011).

the young woman. Things like acronyms he doesn't know, online shopping he doesn't use, and public facing profiles that allow others to rate your standing compared to others at the bar all get in the way of his pursuit of his romantic interest.

As I read the book, it wasn't the characters I identified with. It was the way Shteyngart had envisioned technology would be adopted by society that kept my attention.

I had to giggle when the main character, Lenny, shows extreme discomfort (and some confusion) at the acronyms being used by his love interest Eunice and others in his life. Just as in our own society, technological communication spawned a new set of slang. Due to Lenny's hesitation to adopt this lingo, he is left out of many conversations.

The first time Eunice visits Lenny's home, she is repulsed by the smell. Lenny's apartment is full of books. The smell that both Lenny and I find terribly romantic is one foreign to the younger generations in this story and, to them, simply smells of must. Isn't it fitting that today's elders are stigmatized for smelling of strange things not often encountered by younger generations? Shteyngart is pointing at the grim fact that today's prime will be tomorrow's passé if we continue to devalue generations older than our own. As eBooks explode in popularity and tip the hand of the publishing industry, it may very well be that the "elder smell" of Generation-Y will be that of books and records.

Eunice is equally confused by Lenny's lack of an active online profile — she doesn't know how to identify his social standing without one since that is what her generation (and the public at large) use to understand their relationships. Social constructs have changed. She demands he create and curate a social media profile immediately, but Lenny is at a loss. His mind hasn't been trained to think in that way, and he bumbles through it to Eunice's further disappointment.

Even Lenny's workplace is teched up, and as his sales fall, they require he follow suit. Work no longer consists of soft skills and know how — it must be conducted through the technology their customers use, conveying a certain image of assimilation in the process. Are we not equally confused by someone still using a flip phone or, heaven forbid, a landline? There comes an awkwardness in relating to such a person. In fact, I had to juggle a bit to find a way to record a phone conversation with an elder in a situation where I would have normally used Skype and its affiliated recording programs. The elder didn't have a smartphone or computer on which she might use the app, and I had to pivot.

It's no surprise that Shteyngart reflects upon money as a significant player in the story since the writing took place during America's most recent recession and mortgage / credit crisis. The dollar had crashed in the book as we had feared it would in the early 2000s and money not tied to the Yuan was effectively worthless. Lenny's old-world money ethics instilled by his Russian immigrant parents led him to a frugal and conservative lifestyle in order to save money worth something. He thought often about the state of his accounts compared to his desires for the future.

Eunice, however, lived a credit-based lifestyle. Many of the scenes involving Eunice included her using her Äppäräti (jewelry that holographically projects what the user might find on a smartphone screen) to shop the web. She is utterly caught up in the consumerism that many of our elders call the "throwaway society." She displays many of the attributes of one who has accepted commercialism's assertion that the latest and greatest will solve one's problems, and that buying often will rescue the economy. As you saw in the chapter about Money, it is the opinion of participating elders that technology has changed our relationship to money: that the credit card has incited an "out of sight, out of mind" mentality, and that ads reach us easier than ever before.

Though it rarely came up in my interviews, clothing is a subject touched on in Shteyngart's book that I think many of the elders would say has changed, sometimes in a shocking way. As Sylvia Gutierrez of Florida says,

> People have changed a lot. At that time, when I moved [to New York], something that impressed me was how polite were people . . . And [no] different looks, because of my color. And here everybody . . . used to be very elegant, very well dressed. That's something that has changed. In Manhattan, you see women going to the office with sneakers, but then when they come to the office, they changed.

Today, a bare midriff is hardly given a second thought, while it would have been shocking 60+ years ago. In his book, Shteyngart invents the onion pant, a nearly see-through garment that trendy ladies wore without an undergarment. Even at 40, Lenny found them a bit risqué for his taste.

Times have changed, and as the elders I interviewed and Shteyngart's book implies, these changes seem to be accelerating. Technology cannot seem to evolve fast enough for our appetites. New digital startups are founded daily, each hoping to disrupt the market enough to win the interest of a Venture Capitalist (VC) with seed money for its growth. VCs want a fast and large return on their investments, so pressure continues to grow for the startup to be even bigger, even better, even more disruptive to the market. Existing tech companies like Facebook must innovate and pivot often in order to keep up with new emerging technology and trends. Medicine is changing, too, with molecular technology allowing for the discovery of DNA, stem cells, and cancer-fighting viruses. Food, too, has changed since the discovery of DNA. Travel, communication, music. Everything is affected, a domino effect with no beginning.

Every innovation changes our society, sometimes with a speed that is dumbfounding. I'm still trying to adopt Snapchat and never did find a use for Vine. My friend is excited about his new Cinder, a 'smart' cooking plate that blows the George Foreman out of the water, while I continue using my grandparent's cast iron. The irony of my life doesn't go unnoticed to my friends.

I first wrote this book by hand on notepaper, then typed it on my olive-green typewriter, and finally typed it onto the Apple laptop I use for hours a day to run my tech and entrepreneur coaching companies. I find it easiest to promote an event on Facebook but still write letters via snail mail. I prefer French press coffee over Keurig but used instant coffee every day I was traveling to conduct these interviews — just a cup of hot water from the gas station and a scoop of mix from my trunk and I was caffeinated for the day. My iPad plays music through my vintage Sony record player, and though I love books, I also enjoy Netflix.

It seems that today's stark contrast between new and old has never been seen in history. Even the Industrial Revolution developed goods that were recognizable to the elders in the society that used them, only stronger, better, and faster. Were I to exit today's society for even a year, would I recognize it when I returned? In 2017, we developed self-driving trucks which will be tested in 2018 by DHL,[72] quantum Internet firewalls,[73] and SpaceX launched its first reused ("Flight Proven") Falcon 9 rocket.[74] Archaeologists and physicists discovered a hidden chamber in the Great Pyramid of Giza by using mores (quantum sensors) to detect cosmic radiation passing through the matter of the stone.[75] The medical industry has only just begun mapping

[72] CNN, *"DHL to test self-driving delivery trucks in 2018,"* http://money.cnn.com/2017/10/11/technology/future/dhl-autonomous-delivery-truck/index.html.

[73] The Telegraph, *"China to launch unhackable quantum messaging service,"* http://www.telegraph.co.uk/technology/2017/07/25/china-launch-unhackable-quantum-messaging-service/.

[74] LA Times, *"SpaceX, in another advance, launches supplies to space in a reused capsule,"* http://www.latimes.com/business/la-fi-spacex-launch-20170601-story.html.

[75] National Geographic, *"Mysterious Void Discovered in Egypt's Great Pyramid,"* https://news.nationalgeographic.com/2017/11/great-pyramid-giza-void-discovered-khufu-archaeology-science/.

the skin biome, and yet can 3D print body parts, one of which was just put into my friend's spine.

As I stated in the introduction to this book, I believe it's the speed of development that causes our discomfort with tech. Intergenerational communication is strained by a lack of commonality. The story of what it is like to grow up in America has changed in only 20 years — I, too, have a hard time understanding the experience of my younger cousins who grew up with smartphones though our childhoods are barely a decade apart.

So, how will we navigate this brave new world? It is the opinion of the author that firm roots in history will provide a steady foundation for this evolution. Only time will tell.

"I'm so happy we experienced all of it. So, happy, because it makes us have a greater appreciation for things."
— Mary Muscatello

INDEX OF PARTICIPANTS

Participants are listed in alphabetical order by last name. I have included their relationships to each other, where they were born, where they lived at the time of the interview, and what year they were born. You can find their comments on the pages listed by their names. I am incredibly thankful to each and every participant, and sincerely wish I had had more time with them. Each elder is pictured on the cover.

John Wilkes Booth — 94-96
Husband of Dagmar Booth.
b. New Orleans, LA   1945
l. St Bernard, LA

Onalee Jean Cable — 83-85, 102, 103, 113, 140-141, 204
Deceased.
b. Mackinac Island, MI   1930
l. Riverview, MI

Lillian Carrara — 88-89, 96-97, 232, 234, 251
b. Pittsburgh, PA   1937
l. Long Island, NY

David Chicoring III — 106, 110-111, 228, 241, 265, 270-271, 275
b. Belding, MI   1937
l. Baraboo, WI

Rhea Wark Currie — 144-145, 194, 221-222, 229, 241
b. Peck, MI   1916
l. Midland, MI

Fr. Jaques DePaul Daley, OSB — 284, 285-286
Deceased.
b. Detroit, MI   1936
l. Latrobe, PA

Margaret "Marge" Darger — 11-12, 69, 138, 151, 220
b. Scranton, PA   1934
l. Midland, MI

Ray Dirks — 120, 171-173
b. Longmont, CO   1932
l. Longmont, CO

David Netterfield — 226, 235, 242
b. Toledo, OH   1938
l. Rantoul, IL

Richard Paquin — 134
b. Fall River, MA   1936
l. Tiverton, RI

Sister Ardeth Plattie, OP — 27, 233, 238
b. Wilmington, NC   1936
l. Baltimore, MD

Gerrie Powell — 123
b. Detroit, MI   1932
l. West Bloomfield, MI

Joan Pryor — 276
b. Chicago, IL   1934
l. Rantoul, IL

Br. Luke Robert Reddington — 6
Deceased.
b. New York, NY   1934
l. New York, NY

Charles William "Bones" Rhodes (& family) — 255
Roddy LeBlanc, 129; **Honey LeBlanc,** 252, 253, 273;
Mark Rhodes, 255
b. Mississippi   1947, 1975, 1972, 1997
l. Pass Christian, MS

Hal Royer — 39, 81, 88, 103, 104, 111, 148, 173, 206
b. Newton, KS   1926
l. Longmont, CO

THANK YOUS

Thank you so much to every one of my Kickstarter backers. This book would have been absolutely impossible without you. Special thanks especially to:

Steven Assarian
Paul Soltysiak
Jeff Lewis
Suzanne Elasivich
Gillian Henker
Traci Marcero
Rob Macy
Dot Hornsby
Paul Kirin
Anton Angelich
Lee Bristol
Michael Kirin
Mike July
Tyler Newkirk
Priscilla Kimboko
Robert Caretto
John Verbrugge
James Mitchell
Kevin Liening

Hayley Freedman
Cindy Hull
Johnny Dudeck
Kim Dudeck
Timothy Elrod
Jack Baty
Nancy Pope
Michael Kurley
Derek Moore
Carol Wilson
Laura Kopp
Sue Segerstrom
Nelson Cooper
Andrea Napierkowski
Jeremy Collins
Catie DiCiuccio
Gregg Hampshire
Zach Tolan

ACKNOWLEDGEMENTS

This book is the culmination of three years of dreaming, planning, hard work, research, and the dedication of so many supporters. There is no possible way for me to name them all, but I will do my best to try.

First, I'd like to say thank you to three special women who believed in this project before I was sure it would become a reality. Katie Kirsch, Carolyn Yarina, and Gillian Henker, thank you for guiding me in developing a project that would be viable on Kickstarter and compelling to our generation.

Thank you to Gregory Diehl at Identity Publications for believing in the book when it was still a draft manuscript. I appreciate your guidance and tolerance for bringing a new author to market. And thank you JC Preston for introducing us.

Thank you to Dan Salas at Vida Video Productions for your patience as we recorded the audiobook, and Tim Sokoloski for keeping us on track. I couldn't have done it without you.

Thank you David Astudillo for reaching out to me early on about creating a documentary using the footage from the interviews. You have created a beautiful legacy for everyone who is featured in this work and their families.

Finally, thank you to every one of you who connected me with an elder, and to every elder who met with this strange young woman driving across America. This book truly belongs to you.

Made in the USA
Lexington, KY
19 July 2019